A SHEARWATER BOOK

THE
HEART
OF
AMERICA

ALSO BY TIM PALMER

America by Rivers
The Columbia
Lifelines: The Case for River Conservation
Yosemite: The Promise of Wildness
The Wild and Scenic Rivers of America
California's Threatened Environment: Restoring the Dream
The Snake River: Window to the West
The Sierra Nevada: A Mountain Journey
Endangered Rivers and the Conservation Movement
Youghiogheny: Appalachian River
Stanislaus: The Struggle for a River
Rivers of Pennsylvania

THE
HEART
OF
AMERICA

OUR LANDSCAPE, OUR FUTURE

TIM
PALMER

ISLAND PRESS / Shearwater Books

Washington, D.C. • *Covelo, California*

A Shearwater Book
published by Island Press

Shearwater Books is a trademark of
The Center for Resource Economics.

All photos and maps are by Tim Palmer.
Cover photo: Mount Whitney and the Sierra Nevada in California.

Palmer, Tim.
The heart of America : our landscape, our future / Tim Palmer.
p.   cm.
Includes bibliographical references and index.
ISBN 1-55963-436-7 (cloth : alk. paper)
1. United States—Description and travel. 2. Landscape—United
States. 3. Land use—United States. 4. United States—Environ-
mental conditions. 5. Environmental protection—United States.
6. United States—Environmental conditions—Forecasting.
I. Title.
E169.04.P32   1999
917.3—dc21   99-33646
                                                      CIP

Printed on recycled, acid-free paper

Manufactured in the United States of America

10   9   8   7   6   5   4   3   2   1

To Ernest Callenbach

friend, author, and editor,
whose imagination and eloquence
have enriched our lives

CONTENTS

THE
PLACE
WE CALL
HOME

E VER SINCE the first hunters arrived during the last ice age, America has attracted people to its mountains and forests, its grasslands and deserts, its riverfronts, lakesides, and seashores. Irresistibly drawn by the lure of open space, the fruit of the land, and the desire to live in a good place, people have settled the country and consumed its natural gifts.

While there's still time, think about what remains of this homeland and what is at stake as the future of America unfolds.

From the cliffs at Big Sur to the dunes at Cape Hatteras, from the bogs of the Boundary Waters to the deserts of the Rio Grande, the landscape has helped to shape us into the people we are. At the same time, we've changed the land in untold ways. We stand spellbound at natural scenes still brilliant on the horizon, yet in many places the intrinsic wealth our ancestors knew has been lost.

How we use what remains will determine much about the health of our country for our children. Knowing the real value of land is essential if the generations to come are to share the privileges of the earth that people so far have enjoyed.

Now is a good time to celebrate this fabulous creation, to think about what will surely disappear if the forces of change roll on the way they have for the past three centuries, and to search for a better path.

THE
HEART
OF
AMERICA

THE HEART THAT GIVES LIFE TO IT ALL

WHEN I WAS a child, I thought of my family home as paradise. Life there was just the way it ought to be. On that five-acre tract in the Appalachian foothills, I roamed with delight from meadow to woods. I worked the family garden and reveled in the wonder of seeds, germination, and harvest. I lay in beds of grass and stared timelessly up at clouds as they sped by in endless patterns that stirred my fertile and carefree imagination. Thinking about it today, I can still feel the warmth of that ground soaking into my skin as I lay in the grass. I can smell the drying tassels of goldenrod in August and hear the crickets at night.

During the icy depths of winter, I dug into snowdrifts and pretended I had to survive there until the storm blew over. In summer, I climbed high in the leafy canopies of maples that swayed at the whim of a balmy breeze. Nothing could have felt more free.

At a spring along the edge of the woods, water seeped out of the ground, and like magic to me, it flowed constantly, even during droughts. It formed the beginning of a rivulet that soon became a stream. Along the stream and in the woods and fields, I learned the names of the birds and tried to talk to the animals. At times, they seemed to sit and listen, a great joy to me. That landscape mothered me and grounded me in the endless enchantment of the earth.

But all the time, big changes were closing in on our family property in the country, remote when my great-uncle bought the place but destined to become suburbia. Neighbors built homes up and down Tuscarawas Road. Then a subdivision of tract houses by the hundreds went up almost overnight on the other side of our property line. Increasing the scale of intrusion on our world substantially, the Duquesne Light Company built a nuclear reactor six miles away, at Shippingport, with smokestacks that outclimbed the hills and even pierced low-lying clouds. Civil defense workers wired alarms that looked like ugly yellow trumpets on the tops of telephone poles to warn us of an impending meltdown. A few miles away, along the Ohio River, trees died in the pall of fumes downwind of a lead smelter. I never understood much about those spooky dead snags with bleached, rotting limbs. Then the county agricultural agent warned us not to eat root vegetables from the garden because of heavy metal residue that had rained down on us since the end of World War II. Only vaguely did I realize the sinking truth—that the sweet world I had known was coming to an end.

After high school, I hired on as a summertime laborer in a steel mill, not realizing at that young age that I could become just another cog in the wheel. I pushed carts of steel bars back and forth across the mill, and during my first week on the job, one of the loads tipped over and buried my legs in unforgiving metal. They took me to the hospital, but I was back on the job the next day. Armed with sweaty rubber hip boots, goggles, and a hard hat, I enthusiastically climbed into black underground vaults called pickle vats, where I scooped up bucket loads of spent acid sludge that had been used to eat the rust off steel bars so they would be clean for grinding. Then it was time to "pull" a furnace. With three-foot-long tongs, I reached inside the fiery red mouth of an annealing furnace and pulled out fifty-pound loads of heat-treated steel rods, which we stacked on a cart to cool, still as orange as the sun. When there was nothing else to do, I cleaned out the oily, milky white residue of grinding machines, laden with suspended metal filings, and then did as I was told: I dumped them out the back window of the plant.

My bleak and traffic-clogged route to the mill crossed the Ohio River—what remained of it after back-to-back dams had been built for barges and the steel industry had stacked piles of slag right up to the water's edge. One day, through the smoky haze of midsummer, I tried to picture what that greatest of all eastern rivers must have once looked like. It was difficult to fathom. My basis for envisioning the river of the past was the grass-lined, tree-shaded rivulet that led from the spring back home. Maybe the Ohio River had looked like that, only much, much larger. The image played in my mind. First, I removed the rainbow swirls of oil and changed the color of the water. Then I added a riffle or two and a cobbled beach. I planted sycamores as fat around as tanker cars. Then the fish began to jump, and deer even came down to the water to drink. The town of Beaver still sat up on the bench, and some kids swinging sticks at thick underbrush were headed down a path to the river to swim.

At first, I regarded my imaginings as odd and nostalgic fantasies, just once removed from the dreamings of a child. But from those scenes, an idea lodged in my brain, and it nagged at me every day as I waited in traffic on the big iron bridge: "If we can do something as difficult as make steel from iron ore, there has got to be a better way of caring for this river and living here." The vision of blue water and green shores buoyed me toward another future and a worldview that included hope for less damaged places.

Sickened to my heart at what had become of my homeland, I moved away and for some years returned only to visit my family. Later, with the anger of youth subsiding, I knew again that I deeply loved that small tract of land so wisely bought by my great-uncle along Tuscarawas Road—the five acres of forest and field and stream that made me what I am.

It is that land, and the loss of it, that set me on the path of searching and learning, a path of determinedly trying to understand the fate that awaits not only my new home but all of America.

Consider for a moment what makes up this country. I don't mean the flag or the Capitol Dome, not the Constitution or even the ideal of liberty, important as those are. I mean the real thing—the land and water be-

neath our feet and all around us. The heart of America lies in this fundament of rock and soil and sweeping roll of landscape. At the most basic
level, that's what our country is.

My thoughts go first to the mountains, the backbone and bedrock, the
cloud-veiled source of water and soil. Then I see the forests, shading a
cradle of life, providing habitat for so many creatures. The woods enrich
not only the soil but also our rivers and streams, and they give us timber
and siding for our homes.

The grasslands follow with an openness that sings of freedom. Here,
the work of sun and soil create the continent's great green carpet, which
gave rise to legendary buffalo herds and then to farms. Farther west, the
deserts house their own array of life adapted to the hot, dry air.

Rivers everywhere express liveliness, dancing and swirling from mountains to sea. The lakes shimmer like gems, and the wetlands serve double
duty, half land, half water. The seashore encloses everything within its
dazzling edge of beach and cliff, literally defining the continent.

In writing these chapters about the American landscape—about the
heart of the country—I felt its natural splendor in my bones and in my
blood. As I tracked the wondrous geography we've inherited from those
who came before, I strived to see what is really happening to this land. I
tried to strip away the window dressing of deception that so often colors
our impressions when we expect to see something as it used to be, as we
would like it to be, or as it's advertised by promoters with something to
sell. Finally, I searched for hope in the presence of rooted people who are
working to sustain the lives of their places and themselves, all as one.

What are the special qualities of this land we call America? What have
we done to this place, and what forces continue to change it from what
our ancestors discovered to what our children will find? What are people
accomplishing in their efforts to protect places where the natural world
thrives? How will we sustain or restore healthy communities in which to
live and work? These are not just environmental questions. They are the
most fundamental issues of life and health, jobs and happiness, legacy and
inheritance.

The land that surrounds us forms the basis of our economy and national pride. It recurs as a theme in the stories that shape and sustain our
culture. It's our *place*. It's our *home*.

Some two hundred years ago, the explorations of Meriwether Lewis and William Clark bridged the two oceans in the national eye. Yet when I look out across the broad sweep of America today, it seems we are a long way from a unified America or one that lives out the principles of its founding, such as a belief in life, liberty, and the pursuit of happiness. America the Beautiful isn't what it once was. How could it be? We've cut 98 percent of the original forest, plowed 99 percent of the tallgrass prairie, polluted a third of the river miles so much that we can't fully use them, and crowded the seashores with the lion's share of our population, which is still growing, with no end in sight. To accommodate population growth and a consumptive way of living, we've made violence on the very thing that can nourish us the most—our home.

Not only our living space but also the material goods of our society—the things we buy—come from forests, canyons, prairies, and mountainsides, and nearly all of those goods sooner or later end up in landfills. By the age of twenty, the average American has seen a million advertisements talking him or her into buying things, most of which are unneeded. Today, the average American consumes two times as much per person as in the 1950s. That fact may be related to the next: 1957 was the year when the most people responding to an ongoing poll said they were happy.[1] While we've doubled our per capita rate of consumption, we've also nearly doubled our population since 1950, and it will likely double again in the 21st century.

We've cut off the tops of mountains, chopped down the trees, killed off the large wild animals, fished out the seas, churned up the soil until the wind blew it away, drilled for oil and spilled it from the Tropics to the Arctic, fouled entire groundwater supplies with toxins, and filled or drained more than half the wetlands. If a foreign nation had done one-tenth the damage to America that we've done to it ourselves, we'd declare war.

Being a good citizen now means taking good care of the land, a responsibility that's proving to be more difficult than going off to war. In the latter regard, we have shown little cowardice. We've lost loved ones and children, whom we kissed good-bye with faith that the wars were worth dying for. If we've been able to sacrifice American lives in the distant countries of Vietnam, Kuwait, Korea, France, Germany, Italy, Morocco, Cuba, and Panama, why can't we protect our own land from the ravages that strike so close to home every day?

Today's war against America is real in the most grounded sense. We are losing our land. In too many ways, we squander its ability to support life, and what else is land for? Here is just one aspect of the loss: nearly 30 percent of our native plant species face the threat of extinction.[2] Degraded and disappearing habitat is the most frequent extinction threat—many of America's plants and animals simply don't have a healthy place to live.[3] If it's wrong or at least illogical to drive life to extinction, then much of what we're doing needs correcting across the 2.3 billion acres that house all the plants, animals, and people in the United States.

America is suffering heavy losses while patriotic people sit and watch. It's happening while lawyers argue about the rights of individuals and corporations to ruin land even when that recklessness usurps the rights of others. It's happening while businessmen opt for a few dollars today and sell out the productive wealth in forests or soil for the generations to come. It's happening while public relations departments say that "more study is needed" of everything from acid rain to extinction-bound salmon and while some rural westerners rant that public agencies have no right to control the use of publicly owned land.

All of the American landscapes have been beleaguered by problems that for years seemed to have little connection to one another. What did it matter that the Deep South was being clear-cut for the fourth time? The groundwater of distant Kansas tainted with nitrates? The snail darter and spotted owl driven toward oblivion at opposite ends of the country? Yet when seen together, these problems are oddly similar, a function of the same attitudes, the same myth of conquest, the same machine of destruction, the same greed, and the same population growth. In each of the following chapters, I will look at those causes and similarities with an eye on what can be changed.

As I've traveled and learned about my country during the past thirty years, I've grown to believe that the damage we do results from a lack of genuine contact with the land. Growing up with a suburban lawn out back and an asphalt street out front is not the same as knowing the shade of an ancient hemlock grove or the changing moods of a stream as it rises and falls. Some people see only pavement day in and day out. When the wildest animals we see are feral cats and European starlings, it's difficult to sense the wonder of wolves that depend on deer that depend on forests growing in rich soil and producing annual crops of acorns. Not knowing about these circles of life, we might even fear them.

As a group, maybe we Americans never have had much meaningful contact with our native land. We never really knew the land, never learned to accept it on its own terms, never felt the power of it or realized how much of its wealth we share with other humans and other creatures. Knowing little of those things, or caring little about them, many people have regarded the land foremost as a machine for producing money, either harvesting what the land could yield or turning the acreage into something else—something it *wasn't*. That worldview, scarcely moderated by principles such as stewardship and respect for other life, has led to problems.

Many of the problems can be fixed. We can readopt our homelands by caring for them and restoring them to health. By assuming some allegiance to the landscape, we can tap into a rich endowment of life, both simple and ornate, every part connected to the vital forces that nourish all creatures, in beat with the essential rhythms of survival, in synchrony with the splendid patterns of nature. When we take care of the land, we weave all these forces into a greater fabric of family, community, and government—a true citizenship giving people what they need. Such a life remains rooted in the past with the strength of good ancestors, and it's directed toward the future with love for our children and respect for the children they too will raise. With that future in mind, one of the great chiefs of our time, Oren Lyons from the Onondaga Nation of the Haudenosaunee (Iroquois), restated a timeless message of his people: "Take care how you place your moccasins upon the earth. Step with care, for the faces of the future generations are looking up from the earth, waiting their turn for life."[4]

The land provides the food, water, and shelter our bodies require. It stirs our emotions with its space and beauty. It broadens our intellect and awareness with its cycles of life and death, rain and runoff, wind and weather. It settles our loneliness by giving us other creatures with which to share our lives. It nourishes our spirit because it is so much greater than we are—we can feel that power in the winds and storms, in the sunsets and waterfalls. The soil is where we came from and where we will go: ashes to ashes and dust to dust. Other aspects of our minds, bodies, and spirits also require nourishment, but without a connection to the land as the source of all life, what are we?

Three-quarters of Americans now live in cities and suburbs.[5] Those who never see anything but pavement may have lost the bond, knowing little outside their cement-and-glass world. And oddly enough, those who grow up in woods, fields, and small towns often take the land and its associated life for granted, valuing it as part of the grinding cogs of production but denying its intrinsic worth. Many of those living closest to the land oppose attempts to use it for anything but short-term gain. But people who know both the world of nature and the built-up world are more likely to see the value remaining as well as the damage we've wrought. Today, a knowledge of both is essential if we are to find the motivation to protect the earth from further loss. In this regard, nothing replaces real experience, but between the covers of this book—in chapters that describe what we still have and what we've lost—I hope to offer some of the awareness necessary for change. From mountaintops to seashores, the chapters are aimed at a better understanding of today's land. And an understanding of the land can't help but call up a sense of love for what we've been given, outrage at what has been done to it, and determination that efforts for a better earth will succeed.

While much has been lost, we will never find as much to work with and protect as we have today. Countless times, as I have looked out on the beauty, if not abundance, that remains of natural America, I've thought that the words of landscape painter Thomas Cole ring as true today as they did in 1835: "We are still in Eden; the wall that shuts us out of the garden is our own ignorance and folly."[6] The land still offers us comfort and security, food and drink, mystery and magic. We enjoy the roar of surf and the utter silence of open space. With undamaged landscapes—the way they were created—we have life, and connections, and hope. People involved in their places take sustenance from that life, comfort from those connections, and zest for tomorrow based on hope that we can live well with good ground under our feet.

This interest is not new. In 1898, John C. Van Dyke wrote *Nature for Its Own Sake,* a survey of the landscapes of our country. He strived "to call attention to that nature around us which only too many people look at every day and yet never see . . . to suggest what pleasure and profit may be derived from the study of that natural beauty which is everyone's untaxed heritage, and which may be had for the lifting of one's eyes."[7] Now, a century later, *The Heart of America* offers another view of the same place, a view that addresses the country Van Dyke saw but also the accumulated investment and error of several ambitious generations.

Today we know far more than we did a hundred years ago or even ten years ago. Now we know that the workings of nature are essential to the health of each landscape, that the connections between forests and fish, microbes and prairies, mountains and seashores are all vital. These relationships mean more than the "pleasure and profit" Van Dyke wrote about. Soil, forests, water, air—these are the elements of survival itself. Though Van Dyke gave us a eulogy to nature and the land, he was unable to foresee even a fraction of the change we would cause to his mountains, woodlands, and prairies. Today, foresight is critical if much of America as we know it is to survive during the next hundred years.

The chapters and stories that follow are about today's America and its future, and they are about all of us because we all live in these seven great landscapes. We all interact in ways that give and take, that both recognize and ignore the life of the world around us. In our actions and lack of action, each of us shapes the future of the land and the fate of our country. How we act depends on our awareness of these landscapes, on our vision for their future, and on our connections with land we have known.

CHAPTER 1

AN
UPLIFT
OF
MOUNTAINS

WITHIN TWO steps, I felt the thrill of the mountains. Underfoot, the earth lay hard and rocky, but the soil around me grew brilliant crops of penstemon, paintbrush, and cinquefoil in blue, red, and yellow. This vivid garden didn't fade away in the distance but ended abruptly where the forest arose in a grove of wind-sculpted subalpine fir, resinous in rarefied air a mile and a half above sea level.

I drew that sweet air deep into my lungs, partly because I had to get an extra quota of oxygen at the high elevation, partly because it smelled so good with its lemony scent, and partly because I felt so free and light-headed that I just wanted more, more. Simply being in that place and breathing made me feel good.

The sun added its rays to my mountain euphoria. It shone bright in that morning meadow, yet its warmth was buffered by a breeze sweeping down from the refrigerator of night-chilled rock. The yellow light reflected off dew and frost, unlike the arid intensity of sun-bake in the desert, unlike the sweaty broil of lowlands in the East. It was a *mountain* sun, and the light it cast was a reflective, glowing light that dazzled my eyes as if everything had been given a new coat of nature's colors just an hour before dawn.

The essential life-giver, water, was everywhere, and I could see it, feel it, hear it, taste it. It lay trapped in soil particles and sponged up in moss and the mattresslike roots of heather. It beaded in prisms on the petals of blue gentians. It trickled from spring seeps in cliff walls. It showered down from tiny waterfalls below lingering drifts of snow, and as it collided with rock rubble blackened by lichens, it sprayed in a billion drops like Fourth of July sparklers arcing out through space and coalescing downward into streams, creeks, and brawling rivers.

Above me, most mountainlike of all, stood the peaks. The Livingston Range saw-bladed the sky to the north, running from Montana into Canada. Gray-and-white ridges etched that skyline in a scale deceiving in the enormity and clarity of it all. Mounds of sifted flour seemed to top the summits, and glaciers had chomped huge bites and left jagged northern slopes.

On this morning along the Highline Trail in Glacier National Park, I didn't hike alone. With wisdom in his dark, shining eyes, a tuft of white beard, and a stoic disposition, a mountain goat stood sentinel on a rock outcrop above me, his coat a creamy white fleece. Adapted with thick insulation for winter storms, hooves outfitted in soft soles and two flexible toes for traction, and a stomach that craves native forbs and grasses, *Oreamnos americanus* ranks as one of the ultimate mountain creatures. I don't know what the goat really saw, but my eyes and his were both set on the panorama as if the scenery were the topic of a conversation.

Upthrust, downwarped, knobbed in resistant rock, and with fearsome canines jutting into the sky, here lay the spine of the continent, and I strolled along its side slope absorbed by all I saw and by the perspective that comes only with elevation. I didn't just look *out* to the rest of the world; I also looked *down* on it, thousands of feet down to whole worlds of forests, streams, rivers, hills, and lakes. And I looked up at crags that often disappeared into clouds.

After a few hours of trail-walking, now and then stopping to laugh at boxing marmots or to snatch up handfuls of huckleberries and then

Brooks Range

Alaska Range

Canadian Rockies

Pacific Coast Ranges

Cascades

Basin and Range

Sierra Nevada

Rocky Mts.

Black Hills

Ozark and Ouachita Mts.

Appalachian Mts.

MOUNTAINS OF NORTH AMERICA

chomp down for that sweet explosion of purple juice, I abandoned the trail and began my scramble upward, toward the very apex of the backbone itself. The ridge above me split the runoff of snow and rain; on my western side, water flowed into McDonald Creek and then to the Flathead River, the Clark Fork, the Columbia River, and the Pacific Ocean. On the eastern side, it trickled down to Swiftcurrent Creek, St. Mary River, the Milk River, the Missouri, the Mississippi, and the Gulf of Mexico.

As steep as a stairway but still grassy with wildflowers, my route led me upward in a heart-thumping, lung-puffing ascent. Then the rocks took over—a talus slope of broken shale—many thousands of sharp-sided rocks, as if the Library of Congress had dumped every one of its books here and they had all turned to stone. The talus rests at its angle of repose, the slope at which tumbling stops, temporarily, on the rocks' eons-long journey to the valley. Above the olive-colored, lichen-coated talus, bigger rocks took over. Carefully now, I stepped from one to another, every fifth rock or so tipping slightly under my weight and clunking into the one below with the gritty crunch of pulverized minerals.

Soon I was climbing over some really large sandstones by gripping the sharp-cut edges with my fingertips and wedging my feet into cracks or toeing them onto ledges. I stepped up only to see more rocks blocking my route, but their handholds and footholds lured me on.

Finally, I approached the high ridge. Only the sky rose above me now. With one more step—the step that motivates people to climb whole mountains—a new world, unknown and unexpected, burst upon me, a view to take my breath away if only I had any breath left. Here, I could see the northern side of the mountain. Colder and heavily glaciated, it fell away from me in a dizzying free fall. I lobbed a small stone from my perch and didn't even hear it land. Maroon cliffs directly beneath me ended at a gaping black moat between mountain and glacier—the opening where the ice, in summer, pulls away from the rock. Farther below, the glacier's snowy surface rumpled across a steep slope and then fell in a chaos of crevasses and crusty dirt to rock fields. These licked like tongues of dark honey down to lakes and forested slopes, then to more drops beyond ancient glacial moraines, and finally to the pinelands that parade eastward for miles until they meld into the shortgrass prairie of the Great Plains.

I ate my lunch at the top of the continent, looking down at the rest of it and thinking about all that lay before me—not just mountains and more mountains in this range and others but also forests on lower slopes, grasslands stretching out beyond, deserts in the rain shadow of the peaks, rivers threading the land, silvery lakes like shining jewelry, and finally the seashore, farther away than I could imagine, out there where the land finally comes to its inevitable end.

The Meaning of Mountains

Encounters with really big mountains such as I enjoyed in Glacier National Park happen only on special days, but mountains of some kind are a part of many people's everyday lives, whether in the farmed valleys of the Appalachians, on weekend escapes to the Catskills, or within view of Mount Baldy on a smog-free day in Los Angeles. Even if we can't see mountains, they have their importance. They touch us all.

While looking out at steep topography, I once wondered what a completely flat America would be like. The Coastal Plain, where Captain John Smith landed his sailboat in Virginia, would continue westward, uninterrupted by the Appalachians. This forever-tabletop would drone across the Midwest and to the Pacific without the Rocky Mountains, without the Sierra Nevada, without the Cascade Range's snow cones, without even the headlands of the California coast. A flat America wouldn't *be* America, but rather, a whole nation of Louisianas and Floridas, or maybe a big Western Hemisphere Bangladesh. Instead, mountainous regions cover about 40 percent of the country.[1] Except for the Atlantic seaboard, the vast Midwest–Great Plains tabletop, and lesser pockets of flatness here and there, mountains or their remnant hills corrugate the continent. Summits edge the skyline virtually everywhere west of the Great Plains. It's the uplift that makes America what it is and that makes possible much of life as we know it.

Along with prevailing winds, which result from the sun's intense heating of equatorial latitudes combined with the earth's rotation, it is mountains that govern our climate. They force the air upward, cooling it three to five degrees for each thousand feet of rise, and this produces rain and snow because the cooler air cannot hold water vapor as well. This action causes deep snowfalls on the high ranges. In the West, rain shadows or dry belts occur on the leeward sides of mountains, where the air coasts down once again to lower elevations. Most western forests grow in mountain country because that is where adequate rain or snow falls.

We can credit the mountains of the West as the source of 90 percent of the water in the region, with virtually every city water supply and irrigation system dependent on snowmelt or its derivative groundwater seeping down from high country.[2] In Colorado, alpine tundra alone produces 20 percent of the state's stream flow, even though that highest terrain accounts for less than 4 percent of the land. Runoff from the Catskill and Adirondack Mountains provides for the sinks and tubs and toilets of New York City. The mountains might be crudely thought of as a water machine for towns and farms that couldn't exist without the high slopes, however distant, that collect the snow and rain that flow into rivers that feed the canals, ditches, pipelines, and spigots.

As basic to life as water, much of our soil also comes from the mountains. While the rocks in the high country impart a comforting feel of permanence and a Gibraltar-like sense of stability, in the test of time they are weaker than water. Grain by grain, stone by stone, they erode under the force of ice, runoff, and wind, which redeposit the pulverized rock as soil in the valleys. The fertile dirt of the eastern Piedmont lowlands didn't just happen; most of it washed off the Appalachians or weathered from chemical decomposition of the foothills. The fertile loess of the Snake River plain, which grows Idaho's famous potatoes, blew in on winds from northwestern mountains and wafted eastward until the wind lost its grip and the dirt drifted into thick, brown piles of soil.

Mountains are mostly water rich, and they offer a splendid succession of habitats; as elevation climbs, the air cools, rain and snowfall increase, and lowland plant life yields to mid-elevation forests and then to alpine forbs, flowers, and lichens. Adding even more variety, slopes shift in aspect from south-facing warmth to cool northern exposures, all these features creating ecological niches for distinctive forms of life. The mountain goat I admired at the Continental Divide is only one of many species adapted to gradient, rock, and snow. Like that white-coated ungulate, other species respond with the savvy to linger year-round; in winter, the tiny pika whiles away the hours in dark rock piles, eating grass it harvested all summer and stacked in underground cavities. Some species sleep through the tough months. The groundhoglike marmot is the largest true hibernator (bears wake up now and then in winter). Deer and elk winter at low elevations and migrate into higher country with the advancing springtime, which progresses an average of a hundred vertical feet per day. Even at lower elevations, many populations of cold-water fish, including trout, steelhead, and salmon, need mountains for the cold waters that flow from up above.

With their hard-to-tame terrain, mountains have been developed less than flatter land. Far less. Though ranchers run cattle in many mountain regions, farming is scarcely seen there at all. Cities in mountain country are rare, and towns tend to be small and tucked into the valleys between steep slopes. Rural development does occur, especially in the Appalachians, but it doesn't compare with the amount of home building down below.

Because there is less development in mountain country, more of nature survives there. Elk once grazed heartily on the Great Plains, but they eventually retreated to the safety of mountain enclaves. Grizzly bears once ruled the lowlands, pawing at salmon along the shores of San Francisco Bay and at prairie dog tunnels in Kansas, but their habitat has dwindled to include little but the remotest mountain sanctuaries in 1 percent of the country. In 1995, when biologists reintroduced gray wolves to places the animals had once ranged, they selected the mountains of Yellowstone National Park and central Idaho to give the howling wild canines the opportunity to reinstate an ancient balance in the food chain, weeding out the weakest among grazing animals that can otherwise overrun the range. The irony is that many of the areas originally richest in species diversity lay in lower country, where winters are milder, soils richer, rivers larger, and life easier. But because settlers claimed those areas for private ownership and then logged, farmed, and developed them, the mountains by default have become the refuge.

While people still live mostly on the flatter land down below, it's to the mountains that so many now turn for recreation and escape. Recognizing this trend a century ago, mountain protector John Muir wrote, "Mountain peaks and reservations are useful, not only as fountains of timber and irrigating rivers, but as Fountains of Life."[3] The crowds and forces of change, like rising floodwaters, now push people higher in search of undeveloped open space.

By hiking on scenic trails and paddling on white-water rivers, people enjoy the beauty of mountain landscapes. Skiing—our most popular form of winter recreation—usually requires mountains or at least hills. Downhill skiing and snowboarding alone account for more than 55 million visits per year to U.S. resorts, and uncounted numbers of cross-country skiers tour and telemark in the backcountry.[4] Wildlife-based tourism—much of it in the mountains—generates $60 billion per year in the economy.[5] And many of our icons of outdoor recreation, the national parks, share one thing in common: mountains. Destinations as varied as a lake nestled beneath snowy peaks, a footpath through rugged forested country, and a cabin in the Appalachian highlands all serve as popular mountain retreats.

Beyond all these uses, people come to the mountains for peace, tranquility, and even a spiritual bonding with the earth or their God. Mountains are holy places in virtually every religion and culture that has had mountains available. The Greek gods lived on Mount Olympus and Mount Parnassus. The Bible says that Moses received the Ten Commandments on Mount Sinai. Jesus imparted one of his best-known lessons during the Sermon on the Mount. American Indians hold as sacred the San Francisco Peaks, Mount Rainier, and scores of other summits. The Lakota Sioux described the Black Hills as "the figure of a recumbent woman from whose breasts flowed life itself and to whom both humans and animals went as children to a mother's arms."[6]

Clouds swirl at mountaintops as if they were a land belonging more to the sky than to us, and there is something superordinary about them, something celestial. The summits fading in purple light or in gauzy cloud masses have infinity about them and express a beauty of enormous reach and scale. Something in mountains and their durability speaks of forever.

Touring the Mountains

Ever since I saw my first mountain—the long brow of Chestnut Ridge in Pennsylvania—I've wanted to know them all. It doesn't matter whether they're straight up like the Palisades of the Sierra Nevada or melted-wax profiles like the glacial drumlins of Connecticut. America has eleven mountain regions, each with its own world of wonders.

Elder among them all, the Appalachians had become a worn-down, ancient range long before the western peaks even began to exist. These summits of the East were once like a Himalayan massif, possibly reaching

15,000 feet at their height 300 million years ago. Now softened to rolling green mounds with the occasional rocky crown or bald knob, this great complex of sometimes folded, always upraised topography runs for more than 1,550 miles in the United States and 2,150 miles altogether from Alabama to Belle Isle, fifteen miles off the northern coast of Newfoundland in Canada.[7] High profiles are capped by hard, weather-resistant sandstone, as are wide plateaus on the western side of the range. Granite accounts for many skylines in the north, and in midlatitudes, shale and coal appear as cake layers of sedimentary deposit. Calcium-rich limestone underlies many fertile valleys tucked between long paralleling ridges from Pennsylvania through Tennessee.

Subranges along the way include the bulky, wrinkled grandeur of the Great Smoky Mountains. These southern Appalachians house a greater diversity of plant life than does any other place in America, and Mount Mitchell, at 6,684 feet, rises higher than any other mountain in the East. In neighboring Kentucky, the Cumberland Plateau supports a rich forest with rivers and streams plunging over waterfalls. The impressive Blue Ridge in Virginia rises suddenly from Piedmont farmland. In the Allegheny Mountains of Pennsylvania, scenic rivers incise a high plateau, and the ruler-straight backbones of the Ridge and Valley Province are upraised as if somebody had pushed on one end of a carpet, causing multiple buckles in its middle. The picturesque Catskills in New York gave rise to a culture of early American literature and painting. To the north, the Adirondacks rose up separately as part of the ancient rock of the Canadian Shield but adjoin the Appalachians in a nearly continuous mountain mass. In Massachusetts, the Berkshire Hills introduce us to the shapely mountains of New England. The Green Mountains of Vermont rise higher, with ridgelines cast out to the horizon, topped in red spruce, accented by windy peaks. To their east, the White Mountains of New Hampshire soar even higher and express the rugged character of northern forests, with tumbling rills and meadows perched breathlessly above timberline. Here, Mount Washington tops off the Northeast with its road-accessible summit of 6,288 feet. The Longfellow Mountains of Maine are crowned by the lonely monolith Mount Katahdin, matching the bedrock grandeur of an ice-carved landmark in the Rockies.

The Appalachians surround the quintessential New England of dairy farms and quaint villages tucked into lower slopes, the broad valleys of

limestone so fruitfully harrowed by Amish farmers in central Pennsylvania, and the tortuous amalgam of hills and hollows that give West
Virginia its raw edge and remote charm. Hazy blue skylines like overlap-
ping cutouts cross Virginia, and the forested plateaus of the western
foothills drop with increasing industrialization into Ohio, Kentucky,
Tennessee, and Alabama.

West of the Appalachians, it's a long way before much more than a
knoll bumps up on the horizon. But in southern Missouri and northern
Arkansas, the Ozark Plateau and adjoining Ouachita Mountains make a
miniature Appalachia of rolling hills. Species from all directions intermingle here with whole catalogs of creatures; the Current River region,
for example, houses twenty-six kinds of snake. Most mountains in
America run north–south, but the Ouachita Mountains and neighboring
Boston Mountains of Arkansas lie on an east–west axis.

Also small in stature but well known for the granite carvings at Mount
Rushmore, the Black Hills rise in South Dakota. A welcome, cool relief
amid the heat of summer sun on the prairie, this outlier of the Rocky
Mountains domes up out of the flats like a mirage come true, a prelude to
the big western uplift to come.

The Rockies, North America's largest range in area, sprawl 1,000 miles
from New Mexico to the Canadian border and then another 1,500 miles
northward. With the same complex arcing across Alaska as the Brooks
Range and southward through Mexico as the Sierra Madre Occidental,
the greater Rockies cover more area than any other mountain range on
earth.[8] Up to 450 miles wide, the American Rockies combine sixty
major subranges and many minor ones, often separated by wide valleys.

A part of what geologists call the Laramide Revolution, which began
70 million years ago with seismic uplifts and downwarps, the Rockies are
a fault-block topography with sudden, dramatic relief, such as the Front
Range climbing from the Great Plains in north-central Colorado. Subranges include the red-tinted Sangre de Cristo Mountains in northern
New Mexico and the massive San Juan Mountains of southwestern
Colorado. The Sawatch Range and Elk Mountains lord over central
Colorado. The Uinta Mountains of Utah are our highest range aligned
east–west outside Alaska. The Wasatch Range at Salt Lake City forms one
of the most spectacular urban backdrops in America. The Wind River
Range of Wyoming displays some monumental peaks and sizable glaciers

quite far south for year-round ice. Poster child of Wyoming, the mountains of the Teton Range rank as our most dramatic for their high and sudden lurch skyward, young peaks pushed up and then sculpted by glaciers to their bony core. To their north, notable ranges ring the Yellowstone plateau, including the long expanse of the wild Absaroka and the hulking granite plateau of the Beartooth. The Sawtooth Range of central Idaho reaches up as an escarpment of ragged peaks yawning over a scenic valley floor.

Montana's very name boasts of its ranges, and from Helena northward, the unfractured spine of the Rockies runs with scarcely a break to the Canadian border and beyond. Beginning in Montana's Glacier National Park, these are the famed Canadian Rockies, postcard classic in vertical relief, with horizontal layers of colorful sedimentary rocks, thick evergreen forests, and glaciers adhering to chilled northern aspects of the higher peaks.

The Rockies are best known for the aspen-ringed meadows and rocky ridgelines that scribe almost any horizon line across a huge swath of the West, but much of the region's acreage lies in forests, foothills, and valleys between the ranges. These mountains also encompass some of the greatest expanses of wildland in the lower forty-eight states, with the largest blocks in the Yellowstone region, central Idaho, and western Montana. Most of the large valleys are checkered with ranches, their cottonwood riverfronts irrigated with stream diversions. Towns sprawl in the valleys as well, and at higher elevations, mining settlements have evolved into posh ski resorts.

Often overlooked as a mountain mass because it's also a desert, the Basin and Range Province stretches across a wide expanse, with alluvial fans coasting down from the slopes and landlocked valleys between ridges. This harsh region extends from eastern Oregon to Texas and from western Utah to California. The likeness of these 150 distinct subranges on a map was described by an early geologist as "an army of caterpillars crawling northward out of Mexico."[9] The White Mountains of eastern California soar to 14,246 feet. The mountains of the Basin and Range are the most bone-dry in America, some a moonscape of rock and rubble, especially in the blistering hot south. High country, such as in the Ruby and Independence Mountains of Nevada, receives enough snow to support an artful mix of dryland, meadow, and forest. Though the mountains of the Basin and Range remain some of the least populated, they've been heavily bladed by mining roads, and ranchers graze cattle wherever the slightest lick of water trickles out or can be pumped from underground.

Farther west, preservationist John Muir adopted the Sierra Nevada as his favorite mountains. His "Range of Light" extends 400 miles north–south and offers our finest example of a granite batholith—a molten mass that hardened to a coarse crystalline structure underground. Seismic action then heaved this beluga of rock to the heights we know today. In the southern Sierra, 14,494-foot Mount Whitney reigns as the highest American peak outside Alaska. Five hundred Sierra summits top 12,000 feet.

Unlike the other ranges of the lower forty-eight, the Sierra Nevada runs long and high as a continuous massif, with passes but no low breaks in the skyline from the Tehachapi Mountains in the south to Lake Almanor in the north. The range's western side slants down a forested incline to foothills, but the eastern side drops precipitously by fault block—the most dramatic long front of steep terrain in America.

John Muir was right: no other range dazzles with such a display of mountain magic. The light of the Sierra, even tainted by the tailpipes of urban and agricultural California, can only be called exquisite—warm and gold as it shines and reflects from gray-white granite, girthy golden trunks of cedar, and the transparent lakes and streams that dot and thread the high country. Where spared from logging, enormous conifers populate parklike settings amid clusters of azalea, all of it elegantly composed against a backdrop of granite cliff, misty waterfall, or drifted snowbank.

The snowfalls here pile up as some of the deepest on record. An aggregate of eighty-six feet fell on Donner Pass in the winter of 1982–1983. Medium and upper elevations of the western slope typically see twelve feet of consolidated snowpack by springtime—a reservoir of water for the arteries of rivers and a compact base of snow offering the best springtime skiing anywhere. Winter dumps can humble the heartiest snow shoveler, but the weather is typically sunny between storms.

Public land accounts for two-thirds of the Sierra, and national park and wilderness designations protect a greater percentage of mountain country there than in any other range outside Alaska. Our longest swath of designated wilderness extends for 145 miles along a roadless Sierra crest.[10] Adjoining it lie four of only sixteen wild areas in the contiguous

Mount Katahdin, Maine. This peak is a highlight of the northern Appalachians, protected in Baxter State Park.

Mountain farm in northern Pennsylvania. Home to many thousands of people, the Appalachians extend from Alabama to Newfoundland.

Old Rag Mountain, Shenandoah National Park, Virginia. Among our most popular mountains for recreation, the Blue Ridge rise from gently rolling hills of the Piedmont.

The Continental Divide in Glacier National Park, Montana. The northern Rockies include our wildest remaining acreage outside Alaska.

The Grand Teton in stormy weather. These mountains in Wyoming create some of the most spectacular vertical relief in America.

Yosemite Valley of the Sierra Nevada, California. Like much of our mountain scenery, this valley beneath high granite walls was carved by glaciers.

The Sierra Nevada crest near Carson Pass. Heavy snowfalls but mild temperatures make the Sierra a paradise for backcountry skiers.

Cascade Range, Oregon. Typical of this snowcapped, volcanic chain, the Three Sisters rise above forested terrain of the Northwest.

St. Elias Range and glaciers near the Alsek River. Part of the Coast Ranges, these peaks in Alaska and British Columbia are the highest continuous mountain mass on the continent.

Brooks Range, Alaska. Beyond the Arctic Circle and above timberline, this extension of the greater Rockies arcs across northern Alaska.

Suburbia in the Rockies. Vail, Colorado, shows the intensive development that is occurring in ski towns of the West and illustrates the need for good planning.

Strip mine in southwestern Pennsylvania. Coal mining in the central Appalachians poses the most extreme threat to the mountain landscapes of America.

states enjoying a ten-mile or greater distance from any road. But problems still abound. Because the foothills on the western slope are mostly in private hands, new homes are trussed up at breakneck rates as Californians flee crowded cities.[11] Most pervasive of the problems, air pollution from the urban and agricultural maw fans upslope like a bomb of tear gas.

Interlocking with the Sierra in a north–south mountain band, the stately Cascade Range extends northward into British Columbia. A dozen stratovolcanoes highlight the northwestern landscape as America's most distinctive mountains, topped by snowcaps as symmetrical as if drawn by a second-grader. A few of the major Cascade peaks include the towering cone of Mount Shasta in northern California and the white visage of Mount Hood lording over Portland. Just north of there, a pyroclastic explosion blew Mount St. Helens sky-high in 1980, reducing its perfect snow-cone profile to a scooped-out hulk of pumice above a scorched forest. The event awoke the nation to the fact that the earth is still in the process of being reformed in truly astonishing ways. Mount Rainier reigns as queen of the Cascade Range and its highest peak, at 14,410 feet. In the North Cascades, volcanic cones intermingle with granite summits and ripsaw ridgelines, forming a mountain mass whose combined steepness, size, and wildness are challenged in the lower forty-eight states only by the southern Sierra Nevada and the Wind River Range of Wyoming.

The Coast Ranges, our longest and youngest mountain range, run on and on with stunning variety. This thin mountain belt continues, with only a few interruptions, for more than 5,000 miles from the Baja Peninsula in Mexico to Kodiak Island in Alaska. Typical peaks top out at 1,000 to 3,000 feet from California to Washington but soar much higher in the north. A jumble of volcanic, metamorphic, and sedimentary rocks results from the unfathomable tectonic forces of the Pacific Plate being overridden by the North American Plate, a collision that grinds rocks together, pushes summits up, and creates a fabulous chaos of ridges and valleys undergoing constant change, threatening to anything we build in the way.

Dozens of coastal subranges link like spliced ropes, end to end. In southern California, the Palomar Range, east of San Diego, leads to the Santa Ana Mountains, veering up out of Los Angeles suburbs. They in turn tie into the transverse ranges that track an east–west axis and include the Tehachapi, San Bernardino, San Gabriel, and Santa Monica subranges. The Sierra Madre then bends to the northwest, merging into the Santa

Lucia Range of Big Sur fame. North of San Francisco Bay, ridgelines proceed as a strip of grassy or forested topography facing the ocean. Adjoining this part of the Pacific Rim in northern California, a 230-mile-long agglomeration called the Klamath Mountains defies order in a topographic mass as indecipherable as any in America.

The Coast Ranges of Oregon, a breathtaking edge of surf and cliff, slant up without hesitation to rolling summits trapping abundant rainfall. Then the sea-level topographic dip at the Columbia River serves only as the quiet before a magnificent storm; the Olympic Mountains of Washington rise to 7,965 feet at the glacial summit of Mount Olympus. Not ending but just picking up steam, the Coast Ranges continue in Canada on Vancouver Island and on the mainland, followed by the mountain-and-forest archipelago of southeastern Alaska, where hundreds of forested islands reveal only the tops of mountains, whose bases sit undersea.

The crescendo increases beyond mountaineers' wildest dreams in the St. Elias Range of Canada with 19,850-foot Mount Logan, and then no less dramatically in the Wrangell and Chugach Mountains of southern Alaska. This belt of ice-age grandeur forms the highest continuous mass of mountains in North America. Still in the process of being built, the Coast Ranges finally arc out into the northern Pacific to Kodiak Island, which has impressive peaks of its own.

The Coast Ranges defy generalization except to say that the whole piece defines the western edge of North America. The range rumbles with earthquake faults, including the San Andreas Fault of California and the mountain-making fractures of southern Alaska. The California coast boasts a Mediterranean climate, with dry weather much of the year but wet winters, while the Lost Coast of northern California, the Olympic Peninsula, and the coast of Alaska get more precipitation than any other area in the United States outside Hawaii. (There, on 5,170-foot Mount Waialeale on Kauai, all records are dwarfed by 600 inches of rain per year—a curtainlike downpour nearly all the time.)

Lying north of Alaska's portion of the Coast Ranges and roughly paralleling it, the Alaska Range swings from the center of the state to the southwest, including Denali, or Mount McKinley. The highest peak in the Northern Hemisphere, Denali is 20,320 feet above sea level and 18,000 feet from base to summit—a higher rise above surrounding country than any other mountain on earth.[12] The range then dips to the smoking

craters of the Alaska Peninsula and continues across the Pacific as the
1,600-mile-long Aleutian Islands chain, a volcanic world of rock and
grass where trees have not yet taken hold.

In northern Alaska, the Brooks Range can be considered an extension
of the Rockies, wild country running 600 miles from Canada to the
Bering Sea, almost lacking woody vegetation in the Arctic climate. The
Brooks Range, Alaska Range, and Coast Ranges of the north stand as the
least developed mountains in America and among the least touched in
the world.

Finally, the Hawaiian Islands are not just a collection of eighteen tropical isles, farther from mainland than any other islands on earth. They are
also mountains of volcanic severity. The islands vary in age from 700,000
to 16 million years, and they vary from the weathered green of Kauai to
the continuing lava buildup on Hawaii—the Big Island—where volcanoes spit fiery rock that bubbles down to sea. Here, Mauna Kea, 13,796
feet above sea level, is the world's tallest mountain if measured from its
base, below sea level; the cone-shaped giant rises 33,465 feet from the
floor of the ocean.

Gridding Off the Mountains

The mountains of America are undergoing a shift from remote cultural
backwaters and strongholds of nature to a landscape on the front line of
change. Some of that change has been happening for a long time—we
had logged off the Appalachians by 1910, and the rapacious era of coal
digging there began in the 1800s.

In most regions, the heyday of the extractive industries has faded, but
today's economy fuels a new boom, bringing more and more people to
once isolated mountain settings. From the pastoral hills of North Carolina to the wildflower meadows of the Rockies and mossy slopes of the
Cascades, people now flock to the mountains for living space. In contrast
to earlier booms based on the extraction of resources, this one is driven
by the search for quality of life. Many people now regard the mountains
as a good place to live, but that doesn't mean their effects on the land are
benign. Highway engineers punch new roads through foothills and into
unsettled valleys. Streets zigzag up steep slopes once immune to the developer's trade. Bulldozers scrape off wildlife habitat for homesites, water

suppliers tap and divert the streams, commercial strips light up the high-ways even in tight hollows, and housecats belonging to the new residents roam loose and exterminate small animals and birds by the thousands in rural neighborhoods.[13]

Throughout many mountain regions, expansion of ski resorts has led to real estate booms and the construction of shopping centers and air-ports. More than anything, these amenities transform quiet mountain en-claves into year-round magnets for business. Erasing remoteness and the rigors of winter travel, airports cause the demise of places once distinct and captivating. After a critical mass of development occurs, business flourishes with a life of its own beyond the recreational pull. Jackson, Wyoming, is a telling example. There, an airport within Grand Teton National Park was approved only temporarily but then scored a fifty-year lease under Secretary of the Interior James Watt, who regularly flew in and out from his retirement home, only a short drive from the runway.[14]

The growth boom in mountain states has led to what *High Country News* editor Ed Marston called the "second conquest of the American West." In the first half of the 1990s, 2 million people moved to the Rockies. Thirty-nine counties in the interior West grew by 20 to 65 per-cent. In the Yellowstone region, more than 3,000 square miles have been carved into plots of 200 acres or less. Much of the development takes the form of typical suburban sprawl, which alters local character and causes other problems. One study showed sediment loads in streams to be 300 percent greater with suburban-style development than with the denser development typical of older towns.[15] Roads, water pipes, sewer lines, and other services cost 40 to 400 percent more for suburban sprawl than for compact housing.[16] With these costs as well as mortgage deductions for single-family but not multifamily housing, and with federal incentives to build new homes but not to repair existing ones, suburbs everywhere in America reflect subsidies for sprawl.[17]

Where communities have the will to grapple with their future—all too rare in rural regions—zoning remains the bread-and-butter tool for steering growth to the least damaging, most cost-effective areas. Tra-ditional approaches to saving open space called for large lot sizes, any-thing from two to forty acres per home. But these regulations cut two ways; while the big-lot approach limited the total number of houses in a given area, it extended sprawl farther and faster, fragmenting wildlife habitat and resulting in endless repetition of homesites surrounded by acres of noxious weeds. Planners have long maintained that zoning works best when acreage minimums are teamed with incentives to cluster at high densities within established communities and thus to consume less open space in total.[18] Reflecting this approach in the 1990s, Jackson, Wyoming, enacted a plan to encourage cluster development, keep ridgelines open, and protect wildlife habitat and scenic views.[19] It's far from a complete fix, but Jackson and a few other mountain communities are proving that thoughtful zoning can help control sprawl.

It makes sense to phase in the construction of roads, streets, water lines, and sewer pipes according to a community investment plan. This can prevent the worst drains on tax money needed to accommodate new growth. For example, Summit County, Utah, including the ski town of Park City, requires owners of outlying land to wait until proper services are available before constructing new homes. But this is uncommon in rural areas, and while such "growth management" techniques encourage orderly and economic development, they may do little to save open space or preserve mountain character in the long run.

One impressive approach can be found in Oregon, where the legislature passed a statewide land-use planning law in 1973. Under this model, municipalities must draw up plans that meet state standards. Towns establish urban growth boundaries—lines within which development is encouraged and beyond which rural character prevails. Nationwide, this is the most successful among nine state-level land-use laws, and it helps keep the mountains of Oregon somewhat free of subdivisions and commercial strips. Vermont has adopted similar statewide standards.[20]

Most state governments have declined to enter the hostile battleground of land-use regulation. But empowered under state planning codes, municipalities have a whole box of legal tools to do the job of planning for development. Though some people attack planning as uneconomic, unconstitutional, or even un-American because it can regulate the use of private property, those claims have no basis when regulations are carried out in well-reasoned ways. The U.S. Supreme Court has been clear on this point since 1922.[21] But under pressure from bankers, realtors, building contractors, chambers of commerce, and private-rights zealots, local decisions are eminently subject to the whims of politics, influence, and money. Even where officials enact good ordinances, they routinely water down restrictions to satisfy developers' or landowners' wishes. The plan for Jackson, for example, accommodated a generous population increase, from 17,000 to 40,000, but even then the county commissioners over-rode planning decisions six times in 1997 to allow further development.

A case study of pitfalls awaiting the best intentions in land-use planning can be found at the border of Glacier National Park, where Flathead County swirls in the vortex of change. In the decade 1985–1995, population in this Montana county grew by 14 percent, a rate ten times the state average. Local people became concerned about everything from air pollution and traffic jams to crowds at fishing holes, jam-packed schools, and productive forestland bulldozed for homes. A 1992 survey revealed that 90 percent of the residents supported control of development.

After a lot of public participation, county planners drew up a master plan to address runaway growth through zoning and moderate growth-management strategies. Realtor and planning board chairman Bill Dakin explained, "We realized our prosperity was based on quality of life, and that that quality was threatened by a total vacuum of planning and zoning."[22]

But during the next two years, reactionary groups staged what journalist Florence Williams called a "right-wing hijack" of the plan. Amid inflammatory rhetoric, an anti-plan candidate won election as a county commissioner. Agitating against the plan, Chris Brown of Montanans for Property Rights summed up her case: "People came here to get away from zoning. Who has the right to tell somebody who pays taxes what they can and can't do with their lands?" According to *High Country News,* anti-planning ringleader John Stokes said, "I came here to escape government regulation. Planning is pure socialism."[23]

As the flames of this cultural conflict were fanned, planners and zoning supporters received death threats by telephone in the middle of the night. Facing an alarming deterioration of democratic process and order, officials felt obligated to pass an ordinance banning weapons in public meetings. With individual liberty as their rallying call, opponents of planning intimidated anyone who disagreed with them. Supporters of the plan didn't even turn out at hearings, and consequently the pro-plan view was not heard. County planner Steve Herbaly commented, "What's breaking down is civilized, functional debate."[24] The county dropped the carefully executed and publicly supported plan.

Many people saw great irony in the Flathead fiasco of 1994. Those who said they supported the status quo in fact guaranteed the rapid transformation of the county to something almost unrecognizable. The triumph of shrill opposition to planning meant that changes delivered by unrestricted development would continue to degrade the land and communities other people cared for. Under the rhetoric of individual freedom, supporters of uncontrolled growth continue to convert parts of Montana into California-style suburbs. The grid of new lots displaces wildlife, eliminates hunting, encroaches on floodplains, trashes trout streams, causes property taxes to soar, and multiplies problems of untold kinds while new development and more people create increasing demands for services from sewer lines to drug rehab. Those who support planning make a convincing case: people touting private rights the loudest cause the loss of traditional rights and even their own way of life. But in the process, the anti-planning element makes money selling land for condominiums and shopping centers.

One mountain community getting a better grip on its growth problems is Steamboat Springs, a Colorado ski town. Investors proposed an additional resort at nearby Catamount, and though it faced opposition by people who wanted to protect the area, the proposal steamed ahead until its supporters backed out for financial reasons. Commissioners meanwhile zoned Routt County in an effort to concentrate new development nearer the town and the existing ski area. Addressing the Catamount problem, a group of conservation investors bought the contested land and planned to recoup their costs by the sale of only fifty homes, with open-space easements preventing further development. Also complementing the county's zoning efforts, a local land trust solicited donated easements from ranchers in order to keep meadows and range as open space. Meanwhile, The Nature Conservancy acquired several preserves along the Yampa River. And these efforts marked just the beginning.

Jamie Williams, northern Colorado director of The Nature Conservancy in 1997, described a wave of local advances in protection of mountain land along the Yampa. "Success came in four steps," he explained in a 1998 interview.

First, the Land Trust and Nature Conservancy formed coalitions with the ranchers who own most of the open land. We bought the first conservation easement from the president of the Cattlemen's Association, which went a long way toward building trust in that community. Second, the county hired a consultant to engage landowners, create a dialogue, and draw up an open lands plan. Third, the voters of Colorado passed an initiative to set up the Great Outdoors Fund to buy open space. With projects having community support, the fund aims at larger landscape systems, not just parcels here and there. Finally, we built a coalition of seventeen groups, called it the Yampa Legacy Project, and helped the community pass a county-wide initiative for a 1 mil property tax to buy development rights. This generated $360,000 in 1997—money used to leverage a $6 million grant from the statewide program, all of it earmarked to keep the most scenic and biologically important land undeveloped.

As of 1998, 12,000 acres of conservation easements had been donated or acquired.[25]

Routt County's success could be a model for mountain communities elsewhere. "The lasting value of what we did was the coalition building," Williams concluded, "because now, the efforts to protect the landscape will continue far beyond the work of any single group or funding source."[26] More and more towns and counties are engaging in this kind of community-based conservation, meaning actions that local individuals and groups take to address their own environmental concerns.[27] People have formed land trusts in many regions of the country. These are buying important mountain acreage, and some are building the kinds of coalitions that Williams described. The Foothills Conservancy in Tennessee, for example, acquired 4,000 acres adjoining Great Smoky Mountains National Park after a community fund-raising drive. Some municipalities have approved bond initiatives, and Boulder, Colorado, has used a local sales tax to raise $90 million and buy 25,000 acres.[28]

These local efforts mark a new era in protection of mountain land, and some states are taking a strong role as well. Colorado voters earmarked state lottery funds to be spent on parks, wildlife, recreation, and open space. California, Michigan, Pennsylvania, New Jersey, New York, and Vermont also freed up funds through taxes or bonds to buy development rights and protect open land. Maryland and Florida enacted real estate transfer taxes that generate $10 million and $100 million per year, respectively, for open space.

This beehive of local and state action to save open space is in contrast to the past, when the federal government often played the only land protection role in the mountains through the Forest Service and the National Park Service. In the 1990s, those agencies' already limited acquisition efforts were crippled by budget cuts and anti-government sentiment.

But none of this means that a federal role in safeguarding the most important open tracts in America should be ignored. In fact, Congress intended to take the lead in this role when it set up the Land and Water Conservation Fund in 1964. A deal was cut between oil development and conservation forces, and the settlement called for proceeds from depletion of federal offshore oil and gas holdings to be used for acquisition of "land of natural beauty and unique recreational value." The fund saved an impressive 7 million acres at places such as Olympic and Acadia National Parks, Green Mountain National Forest, and Lake Tahoe. Some of the funds were channeled to states and local communities for parks and recreation. But Congress and administrations since 1980 have diverted the money to deflate the federal deficit. In 1996, Congress spent only $139 million of $900 million intended for open space. In an aberration of this record, Congress in 1998 allocated $699 million for land acquisition and park maintenance, but with no indication that the money won't be usurped again. Funds from the offshore oil program are expected to grow from $4.7 billion in 1997 to $10 billion by 2002, but unless a political constituency forces Congress to abide by its original intent, little of the money will be used for land.[29]

The raid on the Land and Water Conservation Fund is just one illustration that the struggle to save open space is endless. While regulatory processes face a buzz saw of opposition in rural areas such as Flathead County, funding sources run a gauntlet of raiders siphoning money for other purposes or for tax breaks. All the time, the forces for change on the landscape are growing, and the push behind those forces is an increasing population everywhere.

In an odd twist of fate, the new demographics often result in stronger planning programs within the more altered mountain communities, such as Jackson and Steamboat Springs. This is because the newcomers—now outnumbering old-time residents—often accept planning for at least a modicum of quality control. They've seen firsthand the deterioration of their communities of origin, and they're more accustomed to regulations aimed at protecting public values. Yet many of those new residents are just as reluctant to take progressive action as the old guard. Wealthy, retired, and politically conservative, they emigrate to the mountains to escape the problems of urban America. Many associate liberal politics, which may seek to address everything from air pollution to crime, not as a response to those problems but as a cause of them. In their minds, progressive government is guilty—simply by association—of the problems it seeks to solve. These people might enjoy their newly acquired amenities but fail to see the need to protect the land from the very changes they have so recently fled. Counteracting that influence, other pilgrims come because they love the mountains, and they're committed to protecting what they can. Thus, a complex new social battlefield has been drawn on the landscapes of America.

How the demographic shift will wash out politically is anyone's guess; incidents such as the hijacked plan in Flathead County show the potential for land-use reform when new residents seek to protect the best of mountain places, and also the anti-government leverage of the far right—incendiary when wedded with private-rights rhetoric. The success of land stewardship efforts in mountain communities may depend on local conservation groups reaching out to new residents with the message that their adopted homeland is vulnerable and that protection of the land is a fundamentally conservative goal of keeping something the way it is. The bottom line, in mountain towns and all across America, is that people in the coming years will have to grapple with the conflict of either changing the land and erasing what was there or changing the libertarian ideal of unlimited private rights.

With the population boom occurring in many areas, one thing for sure is that most of today's mountain states and towns depend less on the old powerhouse industries of resource extraction. Take mining, for example.

Excavating the Mountains

Mining once formed the bedrock of mountain economies, and while the profits from those operations left the area as fast as the minerals did, the residue of rusty old equipment and polluted streams is still evident from Pike County, Kentucky, to Butte, Montana. Nationwide, 400,000 mines have been abandoned without adequate cleanup.[30] Though mining now comprises only a tiny sector of economic activity in most mountain states, the political power structure that has served mining companies for decades still persists.[31]

In the Appalachians, old tunnel, or "deep," mines have long honeycombed the coal country of green forests and undulant landscapes. But since World War II, mining companies have increasingly turned to strip-mining. First they cut the forest; then they dig up the overburden of soil and rock, storing it nearby or dumping it in adjacent valleys, until they finally reach the black seams of bituminous coal. The whole process causes creeping mudflows and heavy siltation of streams. When excavation of shale overlying the coal exposes it to air and water, intensively polluted runoff containing acid, sulfur, and iron spills into streams, sterilizes them, and leaves a residue of Day-Glo orange that lasts for generations. In this way, 12,000 miles of waterways in Kentucky, Tennessee, Ohio, West Virginia, and Pennsylvania have been ruined.

Wanton abuses have caused polluted runoff to kill all the fish in rivers as large as the West Branch of the Susquehanna. Though new mines are at least cosmetically reclaimed, Pennsylvanians alone have inherited 1,700 miles of mine-polluted streams and 200,000 acres of abandoned, unreclaimed land—the most in the country. One estimate of reclamation costs throughout Appalachia totaled $15 billion.[32]

To understand the strip-mining process better, imagine the mountains as layers of rock lying flat, like thick cards stacked in a deck. One of those layers is coal, but it's never on top. In Pennsylvania and northern reaches of the Appalachian Coal Province, relatively shallow seams are reached by peeling off the entire overburden of rock and soil from mountaintop plateaus. To the south, on the Cumberland Plateau of Kentucky, deeper seams lie in horizontal beds that cause black outcrops to appear at a uniform elevation around the mountainside. "Contour stripping" scoops out the rock above these seams, digging out an enormous notch encircling the hills. This overburden is pushed into valleys, and then draglines operating truck-sized buckets scoop up the exposed seams of coal. The steep headwall is abandoned to erode through the ages to come. In his classic *Night Comes to the Cumberlands,* Harry Caudill described the ultimate effect: "A relatively stable mountain, whose soil and water were to a high degree protected by grass and trees, has been reduced to a colossal rubble heap. The long-range impact of such wrecking on the economy of an already poor and backward state is incalculable."[33]

With elected state officials controlled by the industry, laws regulating mining were long a joke in many Appalachian states, a sorry situation that finally led to the federal Surface Mining Control and Reclamation Act of 1977. The rationale of this legislation was that reasonably regulated mining offers the chance to have coal for electrical power generation and also undamaged communities and mountains—to have both jobs and a decent place to raise a family, with maybe even a stream to go fishing in. But with an anti-regulatory agenda, federal administrations following that of President Jimmy Carter cut staff, weakened enforcement by neglect, and cast a blind eye to state infractions.[34]

While strip mining spread poxlike across the mountains, new technology in deep mining has now given us long-wall mines. Much larger than the tunnels of the past, these mines cause subsidence on the land above after the substrata has been gutted out. Damage to homes, farms, and water supplies often results. Laws in Pennsylvania don't forbid mining companies to ruin property but only require compensation after the fact. "Water buffaloes"—holding tanks that replace ruined well or spring supplies— proliferate like unsightly lawn ornaments across the front yards of Appalachia. Near the town of Washington, Pennsylvania, the local water company had to replace a water line damaged by mine subsidence, a $3 million expense leading to a 16 percent rate hike request in 1997. Wyona Coleman of the Citizens Mining Network asked, "What other industry has the right to deliberately destroy or damage people's homes or to destroy or pollute their natural water supplies?"[35]

Meanwhile, the old curses of strip-mining were dwarfed in the 1990s by an even more ravaging technique: mountaintop removal. With earth-moving equipment taller than a twenty-story building, mining corporations simply decapitate entire mountains to skim off a seam of coal. The overburden fills adjacent hollows, and in the process, the mountains and valleys both face utter ruin. Waterways silt up when rainfall eats at the dirt-filled landscape and flushes rubble into rivers, wreaking havoc on people downstream.

The most extreme type of destruction occurring on any mountains in America, mountaintop removal in a matter of days converts the green hills and skyline ridges of the Appalachians to a gray-brown moonscape of scalped terraces, poisoned spoil piles, towering heaps of rock rubble, and knifed-in haul roads, all of it cut and filled as if in some cubist's schematic of an earth restructured by a crazed God. A single mining permit in West Virginia can cover 4,500 acres and allow 500 or more vertical feet of mountain to be removed.[36]

Cindy Rank of the West Virginia Highlands Conservancy said, "This has gone far beyond the old idea of strip mining. And it's not just a question of mountains, either. The entire culture of communities is being destroyed. The problems are so severe that some people have to move away. More than 150 miles of streams have been obliterated in southern West Virginia by mountaintop removal, and another 500 more will soon be gone, all for seams of coal just a few feet thick." People's homes are bombarded by rocks, and dust near some of the mine facilities requires the use of headlights during the day.[37] A bitter duplicity in what chambers of commerce call the Mountain State, mining companies are eliminating the mountains.

It is no isolated phenomenon; 15 percent of the summits of south-central West Virginia have been decapitated, and the state dealt out permits for another 13,000 acres of mountaintop removal in 1997 alone. At the current rate, half of the region's hills will be reduced to flat-topped, acid-bleeding rubble in two decades.[38]

The federal mining law states that strip mines are to be backfilled to the "approximate original contour," but under the influence of payoffs such as the $500,000 given by coal companies to West Virginia governor Cecil Underwood for his 1996 campaign, the regulations are simply ignored.[39] In 1998, the governor appointed a recently retired coal company executive to run the state's mine-regulating agency, an action that sparked lawsuits claiming conflict of interest.

The industry justifies the highest mining rates in West Virginia history because, unlike Pennsylvania coal, the more southerly deposits are low in sulfur and therefore are cleaner burning. Coal company spokesmen also tout the industry's creation of jobs, but the highly mechanized mountaintop removal offers far less employment than do other mining methods. For a bit of economic perspective, mining in the 1940s employed 130,000 West Virginians; by 1996, the number had been cut to 22,000, even though production was up.[40] Besides regarding this loss of jobs as a gain,

Governor Underwood claimed that elimination of mountains was good for its own sake: "My view of mountaintop removal is it creates a lot of artificially flat land in places we don't have flat land."[41]

Grassroots efforts to enforce the federal mining law and enact reasonable controls at the state level have been thwarted by the industry. In response to landowners' accusations of harm, the president of Arch Coal Company said, "With few exceptions, this mining is conducted in a careful, safe and responsible manner."[42] Fighting back, Cindy Rank said, "Unfortunately, high-extraction mining has made the lives of residents—and the mountains they love—a mere engineering problem."[43]

In response to the mammoth threats associated with mountaintop removal, citizens and organizations across the mining region built new coalitions and fought in 1998 with publicity, lawsuits, and political lobbying. Following two decades of minimal federal enforcement, Kathy Karpan, director of the federal Office of Surface Mining Reclamation and Enforcement said she would add staff to the troubled West Virginia office.

Enough reserves remain in the 10,500-square-mile Appalachian Coal Province to last until the 24th century at current rates of consumption, but if that much coal were used, little would remain of the west-central Appalachians or the region's streams, let alone the great swaths of high plains in Wyoming, Montana, and New Mexico where coal is also strip-mined. And more immediately, concern over acid rain and global warming tempers enthusiasm for this dirty-burning fuel. Though coal still generates half of America's electrical production, atmospheric scientists insist that its use must be restricted if international global warming accords are to be taken seriously. Coal has forever engendered a boom-and-bust economy in mining towns, and its failing profitability under Clean Air Act and global warming requirements may signal a long-term downslide for this troublesome fuel.

With a depressed market for high-sulfur coal and with increased mechanization in strip-mining, Pennsylvania's production fell from a peak of 177 million tons in 1918 to 66 million in 1992, and the number of miners plummeted from 181,000 to 12,000. "King coal" is now a pauper. In an unexpected development, bankrupt operations present an opportunity to protect the mountain recesses of Appalachia in coalfield after coalfield. The Northcentral Pennsylvania Conservancy plans to acquire from coal companies thousands of acres bordering the upper West Branch of the Susquehanna River. Some of the mined-over watersheds have escaped the modern clutter of subdivision because acid drainage has rendered the streams so unattractive. But today, even in a tortured landscape such as the mined-out Moshannon Creek basin of Pennsylvania, wildness is slowly being reclaimed, and if these canyonlike corridors can be bought by forward-thinking land trusts today, the water might be cleaned up sometime in the future. This type of restoration has already occurred on the Youghiogheny River of southwestern Pennsylvania, which now serves millions of people each year at Ohiopyle State Park.[44]

As for the mountain battleground of West Virginia, Cindy Rank and a growing army of local residents and civic organizations need the help of more people from both inside and outside the region if they're to halt the mining-and-money juggernaut that controls the once sweet hills of Appalachia and regards them as little but a warehouse of commodities to be used up and abandoned as fast as possible.

The mountains of the West have their own set of mining problems, deeply rooted in the frontier abandon of yesterday. Mines have been dug out with minimal restrictions wherever marketable minerals have been found. On much of the land managed by the federal government, congressionally granted incentives to mine are irresistible and lead to some of the most irksome threats to mountains anywhere.[45] As in the Appalachians, past mining has branded the landscape. Here, another 12,000 miles of streams have been blitzed by hard-rock digging—a problem that could cost $3 billion to repair.[46] And new problems surface all the time.

Three miles from Yellowstone National Park, a Canadian corporation planned to tunnel into the earth and excavate a mountain of sulfide-bearing rock in order to extract and export gold valued at $600 million. The company would have dumped acid, poisonous metals, and chemical leachate into a reservoir the size of seventy-two football fields for "containment." At the epicenter of some of the most earthquake-prone real estate in America, this repository would have remained a threat for thousands of years. But in a matter of hours, seismic ruptures in the dam could have made an acid sewer out of the famed Lamar River of Yellowstone, the Stillwater River of Montanans' pride, or the Clarks Fork of the Yellowstone River—Wyoming's only national wild and scenic river.

The threat to Yellowstone pointed out a quiet, unnoticed collision of values taking place in America. To extract the gold needed for a single 3-gram, 14-karat gold ring, miners would have had to unearth 2.8 tons of ore.[47] The crown jewel of the National Park System would have been endangered for the production of jewelry. Some of the minerals being mined in our country are central to our culture and technology; others are not. In all cases, lower levels of consumption and population growth would mean less demand for the products of mining. But recognizing that at least some mining will be done, the question remained, should it be at Yellowstone?

The mine would have employed 175 workers for twelve to twenty years, but the Greater Yellowstone Coalition pointed out that the operation could have eliminated the jobs of many more people who depend on fishing and hunting—a big business. Mine opponents argued that economic health depends on good living conditions, clean water, and safe, stable communities—not on Appalachia-style mines that would turn the mountains bordering our first national park into a raw-resource colony for foreign corporations.

Conservation groups "nationalized" the issue with relentless press coverage until President Bill Clinton announced a settlement in 1996. The mining company agreed to abandon the location if it received $65 million worth of land or assets elsewhere, and in 1997 the land was bought.

The Yellowstone case marked a success for opponents of destructive mining in the West, but many people believed that taxpayers should not have to *pay* to keep a corporation from turning public land upside down and risking everyone's water quality. As Philip Hocker of the Mineral Policy Center put it, "The nation has paid a high price to ransom Yellowstone National Park."[48]

At the root of the problem, the narrowly averted disaster threatened Yellowstone because the antiquated Mining Law of 1872 encouraged it. Under this statute, mining companies can buy public land for $2.50 per acre simply by claiming its minerals, for which they pay nothing. In this way, 3.2 million acres of public domain have been transferred to private ownership.[49] For a 310-acre tract appraised at $1.2 million near booming Las Vegas, the government was paid $775.[50] Nothing can prevent the claimants from later selling the land and pocketing a windfall profit. In the Yellowstone case, the Canadian syndicate that proposed the mine would have paid the American government a token $135 for 27 essential acres of public land. Then they'd have shipped the profits abroad without giving a dime to the American public in royalties. With economic absurdity that can only astonish, the 1872 law dictated that the mining company had to pay the government $135 to mine on the public's land but the government had to pay the mining company $65 million to keep it from doing so. One might argue that the law made some sense in a 19th-century era of abundance but makes no sense today. Yet the outlook of frontier lawmakers still prevails in Congress, which gives away the minerals.

For decades, reform-minded people have fought to update the Mining Law by seeking to compensate the public for extracted minerals, to halt the private takeover of public land, and to regulate pollution and damage at the mines. Resisting reform, the industry says it's already regulated. But the Summitville Mine in Colorado shows a different reality. In 1992, another Canadian corporation walked away from that site and left taxpayers with a tab of $40,000 per day simply to contain toxic wastes. Cleanup, if it can be done, will cost $150 million—taxpayer money because the Summitville company disappeared into bankruptcy.[51] In Idaho, the federal mining law forced the government to sign over 110 acres of public land to a Danish mining company in 1995. Though the claim was valued at $1 billion, we were paid $275. This kind of giveaway is not unusual; in 1993, foreign companies owned twenty-three of the forty largest gold mines in America.

Those in the mining industry say that new requirements will drive them out of business. But Dr. Thomas Power, chairman of the Department of Economics at the University of Montana, Missoula, maintains that the collection of a modest royalty would have virtually no effect on the market. Hard-rock mining is no longer a central activity of the West, accounting for only 1 job in 1,000. And only 1 in 2,500 jobs in the western states depends on federal land subject to the federal mining law. In fact, Power has predicted an increase in jobs with the reclamation work that would accompany mining law reform.[52]

When confronted with these arguments, National Mining Association representatives maintain that "mining literally takes a part of nature that has little or no economic value and creates something of value from it."[53] The industry states that "it is now necessary to produce more than 40,000 pounds of new minerals each year for each American and to use about

7,700 pounds of coal per American for generation of electricity."[54] The association supports a 5 percent hard-rock royalty, but the small print reveals this to be only on net proceeds. The association says it's willing to pay fair market value for federal land instead of $2.50 per acre and that land not used for mining should revert to government ownership.[55] But behind this public relations front, the industry's caretakers in Congress continue to stonewall reform.

The same political payoffs that have permitted destruction of the Appalachians are at play in the West. Taking the gold and escaping scot-free when something goes wrong, the mining companies pay western politicians to vote against modernizing the 1872 law. Idaho's senator Larry Craig, who led the industry-backed fight, received $51,400 from mining-related political action committees for the 1990 election, not counting contributions by individuals in the industry.[56]

Though conservationists defeated the most egregious new mining proposal near Yellowstone, and though the growing forces for mountain protection will likely curb future projects of that magnitude, for now the Mining Law of 1872 remains intact—one of the most subsidized, damaging, anachronistic forces of destruction in the mountains of the West.

Stewards of the Mountains

Fighting for mining reform, Philip Hocker moved from his home in the Rocky Mountains of Wyoming to Washington, D.C., and founded the Mineral Policy Center. "Proposals against destructive mines were being fought one-by-one," he explained. "But each of those efforts was aimed at a single piece of the minerals problem—one mine, one lawsuit, one wilderness. We needed a new group to take a comprehensive view."[57] His organization, pushing hard with the help of former secretary of the interior Stewart Udall, is just one among hundreds of groups dedicated to better protecting the mountains of America.

Starting the first major mountain conservation group, easterners formed the Appalachian Mountain Club in 1876. Based in Boston, it continues as a voice for protection and responsible use. In the same era, the Sierra Club, founded by John Muir and others in 1892, battled first to preserve the Range of Light and then to maintain the health of mountain landscapes across the country. Today, every range has its champions.

For decades, the West Virginia Highlands Conservancy has been the voice of the mountains in that embattled state where awesome beauty still survives beyond the scars of strip mines. In Seattle, The Mountaineers played a key role in establishing Olympic and North Cascades National Parks and in designating northwestern wilderness areas. The Greater Yellowstone Coalition pushes for better management of one of the least disturbed ecosystems in the Temperate Zone—a region where two great national parks cover 2.2 million acres but where 17 million additional acres in national forests and private ownership are critical to the survival of wildlife such as the threatened grizzly bear, the whistling swan, free-ranging bison, and large herds of elk. The Sierra Nevada Alliance works to halt federal subsidies that encourage the cutting of forests and to protect remaining roadless areas and lower-elevation habitat vital to wintering wildlife such as California's dwindling deer herds. Each of these groups attracts citizen activists dedicated to the health of mountain regions—people who adopt these lands with a sense of stewardship, working to preserve them for the future.

Among all the strategies for protecting mountains, wilderness designa-tion has been one of the most successful. It offers us the best and last chance to see America as it existed before we had highways, mowed lawns, power lines, trail bikes, snowmobiles, and jet skis. Applying only to congressionally approved land already owned by the federal government, wilderness designation means that no logging, road building, or develop-ment will occur. One hundred million acres, or 4 percent, of America has been named wilderness, most of it in mountain areas. Much of this land lies in Alaska; only 1.5 percent of the land area of the lower forty-eight states is designated. Nationwide, another 50 to 80 million acres of federal land remains roadless but unprotected and up for grabs in the resource conflicts to come.[58]

Because early conservationists were so taken with the spectacular beauty of the high mountains, and because lawmakers have often regarded the most rugged land as economically worthless, the high country of the West is the only sizable ecosystem in America where a large share of the land is safe from human-caused change. In California, for example, alpine and subalpine zones are 90 percent protected, while only 1 percent of wildlife-rich riparian zones are safeguarded.[59] The high country repre-sents only one piece of the stewardship puzzle, and people have increasingly come to recognize the intrinsic value of all mountain land and of the lower elevations as well.

Here is evidence of the change: At Lewis and Clark National Forest in Montana, south and east of Glacier National Park, a soaring mountain front swells up from the grassland sea. With a 4-million-acre stronghold of wilderness and parkland as a backdrop, this eastern slope of the Rockies is where grizzly bears roam down from the heights and the largest herd of bighorn sheep in forty-eight states thrives on unspoiled land.

In this "overthrust belt" of folded rock strata, some unknown quantity of natural gas lies underground, and oil companies want to build roads and drilling sites to get it out. Because oil company representatives were not seeking high country wilderness or parklands, they expected their permits to be approved in 1997. Weighing the choices was Forest Supervisor Gloria Flora, who had risen through the ranks of the Forest Service after starting as a landscape architect. Almost anyone aware of the agency's past would have predicted a compromise, but Flora banned drilling for fifteen years or more. "When you have a place this special," she said, "it requires special attention." She wrote that "social and emotional values have figured prominently into my decision not to lease." Though Flora recognized that other forest supervisors have been transferred or pushed out of their jobs for taking a stand to protect the mountains, she said, "How could you live with yourself if you made a decision just so you could be employed in the same way?"[60] Whole batteries of lawyers working for Chevron Corporation and other oil companies appealed Flora's decision, and the Helena National Forest supervisor and the Bureau of Land Management negotiated to allow drilling nearby.[61] But Flora stood firm and was flooded with citizen support for her stance to protect the mountains.

On the eastern slope of the Rockies and throughout America, people such as Gloria Flora, Philip Hocker, and Cindy Rank are blazing a new path in caring for the land, and their force of insight and dedication gains strength by the day. The people on this path recognize the value of the land itself, the life it supports, the beauty it reflects on us, and the inspiration it conveys.

Perhaps land development throughout the mountains will someday follow the logic of sound planning, Congress will reform the Mining Law of 1872, and mountaintop removal in the green home of the Appalachians will be allowed no more. Beginning with the high refuges and working our way down to protect the other realms of landscape would honor the mountains as the heartland, the source of water and soil, and the fundament of so much life.

CHAPTER 2

THE
FOREST
FABRIC
OF LIFE

THE WOODS were my refuge, my training ground, my whole private world. As a child, I went there often, and the trees enveloped me in their leafy green canopy. They screened out the houses and the roads as a closed curtain would do onstage, hiding an entire ongoing drama from everybody on the outside. Sunshine filtered softly through the branches—beams of light that I'd later call "God rays." They served as a reminder of who was in charge of my woods, and they illuminated something fundamentally right that I felt in my bones and only later had a word for: nature.

Like many other people whose first exposure to the natural world lay behind the house, at the local park, or just beyond the grid of town, I grew up in a woods. For me, it became the baseline landscape, the standard against which all other places would be measured. For years, everything else was exotically dry or wet, high or low, urban or wild. The

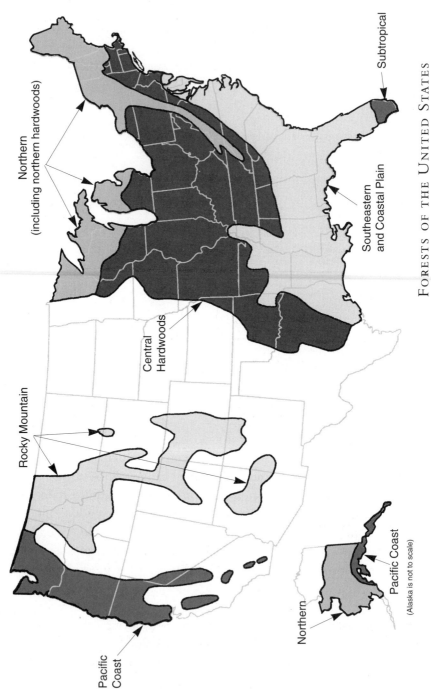

Northern
(including northern hardwoods)

Subtropical

Southeastern
and Coastal Plain

Central
Hardwoods

Rocky Mountain

Pacific
Coast

Northern

Pacific Coast

(Alaska is not to scale)

FORESTS OF THE UNITED STATES

woods where I grew up and the comfort I felt in them became the standard for other things as well.

My early motives were to find risky adventure and escape from the protective borders of home. In the woods, I stretched my legs and spirit. Then I "moved in," claiming tiny glades where the sun rays reached the ground or where an old, leaning cherry tree created a sheltered space where I could sit or hide, the way kids do in small places. Next, I flexed my young muscles and challenged myself to climb the highest trees and to jump from limbs eight feet off the ground. I built tree houses and knotted ropes to high branches so I could swing from one perch to another. I turned twelve that year.

All the time, wild animals breathed a certain magic into the place, a presence of otherness, yet oneness. My childhood fascination with the woods grew into an avid interest in hunting, a steadfast family tradition going back at least several generations and perhaps the whole way back. Each fall, I stalked rabbits, squirrels, and grouse with my beloved grandfather, who lived next door, just up a path from our house. I rarely missed a single day of hunting during October and November. Make no mistake: killing and eating wild animals was the goal, but I accommodated—as many hunters do with little sense of conflict—a feeling of love for the animals. During the ten months when I couldn't legally hunt, I stalked, waited, watched, and recorded in pocket notebooks all that I saw, from deer to groundhogs, crows to vireos. Then I returned home to pore over my Golden guides of birds and mammals. When I finished with them, I began to study the trees because it somehow made sense that almost everything alive depended on the forest.

I learned that it was wild black cherries and sugar maples that shaded my favorite haunts and that honey locusts towered at the edge of sun-swept fields, but going barefoot under them was risky because of their thorns. I learned that serviceberries made great summer snacks. Sumacs pioneered the fields already overgrown with goldenrod, milkweed, and thick tangles of blackberries. This brushy land had been farmed some years before my grandfather's brother, John Gremer, bought our five acres after the Great Depression. Almost until the day he died, at eighty-nine, Uncle John gardened and raised chickens, but mainly he was happy just letting the blackberries grow. While I grew up and changed, the brier patches yielded as well to a forest of sapling trees.

Going beyond our family plot, I discovered that the woods ran non-stop for miles through a deep hollow. Lured by the unknown, I explored farther and farther. Each new forest revelation fueled my wanderlust to higher levels. In a towering grove, I spotted the twig-woven nests of gray squirrels, which preferred red oaks to white oaks. In a thick trove of timber, I came eye to eye with a fox—quick, red, and silent. At the base of a cool northern slope, I wandered into a grove of hemlocks and beeches that looked like pictures I had seen of Canada, and it stirred my fantasies of going north.

With memories rooted in those childhood wanderings, I still regard the hemlock as my favorite tree. Having needles so short that they give a lacy appearance to the whole evergreen, hemlocks grow tall and thick on the sandy, cobbled soil of floodplains. They shade the ground so well that a parkland of open space often lies under the branches, though riddled with mossy fallen logs melting slowly into the soil. The lustrous rhododendron sometimes grows nearby, with broad, leathery leaves that curl down on subzero days—a shrubby thermometer. The American beech stands among the tall hemlock as a perfect complement, its pale gray bark popping out in a somber forest as if sketched with white chalk, its twigs branching like fine articulated pencil lines honed to Andrew Wyeth precision, its buds pinpoint sharp, then pregnantly swollen when ready to burst in springtime. Beech leaves of yellow-green shine translucently in early summer. Creamy yellow in fall, the same leaves adhere to their twigs like rustling flags in the skeleton forest of winter.

On a family outing once, two hours from home, my father introduced me to the old growth of Cook Forest State Park, a small but splendid grove of primordial white pines and hemlocks that left me wonder-struck. I stared up at the sky-bound crowns. I spread my arms against a giant's superior girth. I felt the sponginess of the organic soil underfoot. Learning of the ancient trees' scarcity, and that virtually everything else from the East Coast to the Rocky Mountains had been cut, I thought about what I might have seen if the early landowners had exercised more foresight. The loss of the old forest in Pennsylvania—a state whose name means literally "Penn's woods"—led me to consider how foolish it had been to cut everything. Of course, I reasoned, people would not do that again. Now we know better. We need wood, yes, of course; but the cathedral-like forest was so wonderful, surely we'd leave at least one or two acres out of each ten if we had the chance again.

When I prepared to launch longer journeys in my teenage years, unknown forests were among the sights I most wanted to see. I longed to stroll through sunny aspen groves in Colorado, among fogbound redwoods in California, across windy ridges of spruce in New England, and into the swampy netherland of baldcypress in the Deep South.

Forest Wealth

Among America's major biomes (forest, grassland, desert, chaparral, and tundra), the forest is the second largest, covering 32 percent of the country, or 731 million acres.[1] Only grasslands—including those converted to crops—occupy more area. Worldwide, trees likewise cover 30 percent of the landmass, though the proportion is far less in arid and Arctic regions and countries where deforestation has been heavy.[2] In the once wooded Great Britain, for example, only 4 percent of the land remains forested after intensive cutting centuries ago.[3]

For twelve millennia and probably much longer, Indians lived within the original forests of North America. They often burned brush and trees to encourage the growth of grasses, berries, and forbs that, along with deep woods, are needed by deer, elk, and other staple species of the hunter-gatherer cultures. Lightning also ignited fires, especially in the drier West. These fires played a critical role in the forests' ecology because they reduced the deadfall and undergrowth to fertile ash, returning nutrients to the soil. They also groomed wide expanses of big trees, which survived with thick, fireproof bark and long trunks of clear, limbless wood that elevated the more flammable branches beyond the fires' reach.

To arriving Europeans, the forests were the defining feature of the New World. Approaching the eastern seashore, those anxious, alien people saw nothing beyond the sandy lap of waves but an unbroken canopy of trees. For more than 200 years, the forests of the East and Midwest were all settlers knew of America, and they regarded the woods as the enemy of civilization. William Bradford, the Pilgrims' journalist, wrote of a "hideous and desolate wilderness" beyond the white man's stockades. Yet it was trees that made survival possible. The pioneers needed wood for building materials and for fuel, and the life of the forest made up an important part of early American meals.

Irrespective of the settlers' desire to cut the endless forest if for nothing more than sunlight, a love of trees may be culturally or even genetically imbued in people whose ancestors hail from northern Europe. In *Landscape and Memory,* historian Simon Schama reports that the northern European forests—rich in myth and human associations—overpowered the other landscape features.[4] Those ancestors of many Americans lived unequivocally as people of the forests. And so, in a sense, do we.

Many of us grow up with trees outside our windows and yearn all our lives for the comforting sanctum of the forest. When we go for walks, we go to the woods. For rest, we sit or lie beneath domes of starry leaves. If trees don't exist, we plant them in our lawns and along our streets, even if we have to water them and rake the leaves five times each fall. The shade relieves us in summer's heat, from Philadelphia to Phoenix. Columns of trunks dissipate roaring winds from the headlands of Maine to the Great Plains. We breathe the oxygen that trees produce. Now, with the howling wilderness gone, forests may be the most beloved landscape of all, more livable than mountains or deserts, more sheltered than grasslands or seashores, rooted in the past and associated intimately with shelter, home, and warmth.

Not only do we love the presence of trees in our lives, but we depend on what is made from them. The products include far more than the wood we harvest to make paper, cardboard, fiber products, and lumber. Medicines originally derived from plant, microbe, and animal species in the forests account for 40 percent of all commercial drugs.[5] We reshape tree trunks to make the finest tools, toys, and musical instruments. Old-growth wood is so coveted for its beauty, clear grain, and wide boards that giant timbers salvaged from an abandoned factory in Connecticut in 1998 were bought and shipped to Tunisia for use in remodeling a palace. We prize good wood fashioned into furniture, sleek and smooth to the touch, yet to truly appreciate it, we have to appreciate the living trees that grow the wood. If we want to continue to have good wood available, we need to know what those trees require. We read the newspaper every day and live in homes hewn from trees, and in doing so we need to appreciate where the paper came from and what the wood in the wall once was. What role did the tree fulfill before it was cut for our home?

Fulfilling Their Role on Earth

While other landscapes provide for life, the forests produce the rich, thick biomass that accounts for so *much* of life. The forest zone houses thousands of creatures, from microbes to moose. This biome is the richest in life and greatest in mass, its web of pulsing organic extravagance extending from billions of microorganisms under each square foot of earth through the root masses and ground covers and shrubs and saplings and tree trunks, all the way up to the towering crowns of leaves and needles—the skyscrapers of the natural world.

In healthy forests, warblers and dozens of other songbird species occupy the tops of deciduous trees. They sing their hearts out in springtime in an orchestra of exquisite music, at times chaotic and shrill, bursting with proud announcements of life. Lower down on those trees, dark cavities aren't just holes in rotten old trunks but are homes to chickadees, nuthatches, woodpeckers, barred owls, mergansers, and raccoons. Underneath, deer find shelter during the harshest of storms and wild turkeys scratch for food in the lean months of winter, well protected by the umbrella of hemlocks or other evergreens that intercept snowfall.

But the connections between trees and other forest life are not always so evident to the human ear and eye. A hundred species of lichen live in the canopies of northwestern forests and can make up four times the weight of the leaves on a bigleaf maple. Serving vital purposes, these basic building blocks of forest life trap moisture, which drips down onto the tree and feeds its roots. In woodlands throughout the northern and middle latitudes, lichens fall to the ground during heavy snowfalls and serve as emergency forage for deer and other animals converging under the big canopy. The endangered woodland caribou in northern Idaho depends on lichens for food. If we look carefully, we can see the riot of forest life from the ground up in squirrels, slugs, and snails; mice, mites, and millipedes; dozens of species of salamander; and insects by the millions. Yet half the biomass of many trees lies hidden underground, and the root masses live in association with staggering quantities of other life.

The trees *depend* on other life. Mycorrhizal fungi, for example, are not just musty parasites in the soil but beneficial organisms that wrap themselves around tree roots and help them collect water and take up phosphorus, nutrients, and minerals.[6] Firs, cedars, spruces, and all the choice trees used for lumber depend on these hitchhiking fungi making their livelihood on tiny root hairs, as do the deciduous beeches, oaks, walnuts, and others. The aid of fungi can bolster the growth rate of pines by 20 percent. Even less celebrated than the lowly fungi, bacteria in the soil exhale carbon dioxide, essential to tree roots. Researchers working in one beech grove found 6,000 species of bacteria in a single gram of soil. The same serving can also contain 136,000 cells of algae—simple plants that contribute carbon, nitrogen, sulfur, and proteins for other forms of life.[7] One square foot of soil in an old northwestern forest can house 250 species of invertebrates, all of which have a role to play in the health of the woods. They're all needed for the forest ecosystem to work. The fungi, bacteria, and algae help the trees to grow. In turn, the trees and related vegetation, including forbs, berries, mushrooms, nuts, seeds, twigs, buds, bark, and leaves, feed a menagerie of wildlife, which leads us on up the food chain to people.

The workings of the forest ecosystem are critical not only to the plants and animals that live there but to the health of the whole earth. We know how important heating and cooling systems are to our homes. Well, it's the forests that help regulate the temperature of the Big Home—the earth—cooling it with shade in summer and warming and sheltering it in winter. The effects extend to suburban neighborhoods; air-conditioning costs in Atlanta can eventually be decreased by 40 percent if a home owner plants just three trees.

Hidden values of forests include such unexpected phenomena as the accumulation of woody debris in streams, whose aquatic health depends on large logs and the buildup of dead trees over hundreds of years. Fallen logs trap gravel, where fish spawn. The logs create pools, where the fish feed and rear their young. Studies of streams in Alaska showed that waterways with natural woody debris supported five to fifty times the number of salmon as did logged watersheds with no large, woody debris.[8] Decomposing wood and its breakdown products supply vital nourishment to streams and also to aquatic systems as distant as ocean water hundreds of miles from where the trees fall.

In many ways, the forests are intimately connected to the vital fluid of water; the woods are a backstage operative in the hydrologic cycle. The canopy of an old coniferous forest can hold 264,000 gallons of water per acre—a life-affirming shield of moisture, shade, and windbreak. The root masses and accumulated duff absorb rainfall and snowmelt, holding and then releasing it to spring flows later on, decreasing flood levels and serving as a natural reservoir that dwarfs by far all the dammed-up reservoirs ever built on rivers. An undisturbed forest floor in the Pacific Northwest can soak up twelve inches of rainfall in an hour—a fact that would make floods quite rare if the forest floors had not been disturbed.[9] The forest canopies do their part as well; the trees suck up water from the soil and expel it via their leaves into the atmosphere. Through this transpiration and through water storage in the root zones, mature woodlands in the East can reduce flood levels by 75 percent.[10] During summer, overhanging trees keep creeks and rivers cool and hospitable to aquatic life; it's the trees as much as the water that make trout fishing possible in many streams. Water quality is just as important, and runoff from a healthy forest is generally clean, unlike the silt-laden flows from cutover land crisscrossed with roads.

The forests' role in sustaining water quality serves people's needs directly, and for this reason, protection of forests is an economic issue of top importance. Because most of the nation's drinking water is runoff from forests, forest protection is essential to public health. Facing the prospect of paying $8 billion or more for treatment plants to make water drinkable, New York City in the 1990s opted to spend $1 billion to protect the forested watersheds surrounding its reservoirs by acquiring development rights.[11] Understanding the tight tie between watershed health and drinking water is nothing new: in 1947, the Forest Service documented that cities in North Carolina with watersheds half denuded spent $27 per million gallons to treat drinking water, while Asheville, with an intact watershed, spent $8.50.[12]

Beyond their roles as habitat of myriad creatures, temperature regulators, controllers of floods, and keepers of clean water, forests literally hold the earth together. Their masses of roots and associated humus not only build soil from an inorganic smorgasbord of minerals into a spicy recipe ripe for life; they also bind the soil in place. They stabilize stream banks and prevent hills and mountainsides from turning to jelly when wetted.[13] Thus, trees are the greatest guardians of private and public property.

And now we find that forests are even critical to the atmosphere we breathe, the air enveloping all of life, and the climate sustaining our world. Principally composed of carbon, trees occupy the front line of defense against the catastrophe of global warming. This is caused by burning of the earth's fossil fuel reserves—coal, oil, and gas—which converts solid carbon to gaseous carbon dioxide. Accumulating in the atmosphere, the gas traps heat by allowing sunlight in but preventing the heat's escape— the greenhouse effect. Since the industrial revolution in the early 19th century, atmospheric carbon dioxide has increased by 30 percent owing to our burning of coal, oil, gas, and wood.[14] While just the existing carbon dioxide concentration causes grave concern, scientists predict another 40 percent increase in the next sixty years. An eventual sixfold increase in carbon dioxide, along with increases in the other greenhouse gases, methane and nitrous oxide, is quite possible.[15]

In 1996, the United Nations Environment Programme—the most comprehensive panel of scientists ever assembled to deal with the topic— confirmed that global warming has already begun and will accelerate. The scientists expect an average warming of 5.4 degrees Fahrenheit by the year 2055, a change that promises monumental disruptions to life as we know it.[16]

For starters, melting at the polar ice caps will cause the oceans to rise. A group of top climatologists assembled by the United Nations—the Intergovernmental Panel on Climate Change—predicts a sea-level rise of four inches to four feet during the 21st century, which will flood large coastal areas, including many cities. Warming will render entire agricultural and forest regions unusable because of heat and associated changes in precipitation. The new climate will displace trees and other plant species from their home ranges faster than they can naturally migrate northward—ten times faster than any known rate of adjustment. Forest fires will become more common and regrowth less complete with drier conditions at mid-continent latitudes. Extreme effects await not just forests but every type of landscape: grasslands will become more dominated by brush, and prairie potholes, where 80 percent of America's ducks are hatched, will dry up.[17] Warm-climate diseases, such as malaria, may become more common, along with severe tropical storms caused by superwarmed ocean water.

According to this global warming scenario, which is widely agreed on by scientists, the climate will change more in the next 100 years than it ever has in a 10,000-year span of time. The earth's average temperature is already up 1 degree Fahrenheit from the past century.

While the media often report on disagreement over this subject, most of the disagreement involves only the extent of expected change. The perceived doubt about global warming's importance is a result of what biologists Paul Ehrlich and Anne Ehrlich call the "brownlash" of industries resisting the changes that must be forged to address the problem.[18] In spite of heavy lobbying by industries, including the oil industry, and the resulting foot-dragging by American officials, an international treaty signed at Kyoto, Japan, began to set a course of correction in 1997. Though the Intergovernmental Panel on Climate Change projected that an immediate 60 percent reduction in fossil fuel burning was necessary simply to stabilize the climate, the United States agreed to shave only a few percentage points off carbon emissions by 2010. Even this modest goal will require substantial change: at the current rate of growth, U.S. carbon emissions were expected to increase by 15 percent between 1990 and 2000 alone.[19] The Clinton administration signed the treaty in 1998, though it will not be enforceable in the United States without Senate ratification, which at the time of signing had no chance. Though the effort to combat global warming could scarcely get off the ground on the eve of the year 2000, author Bill McKibben predicted that this struggle is "likely to define the next century."

In the face of atmospheric catastrophe, it is forests that offer some hope. By sequestering carbon, trees tie up some of the excess carbon dioxide produced by burning fuel. In this way, forests can correct part of the imbalance that will worsen as long as we consume large amounts of coal, gas, and oil in our cars, power plants, and homes—consumption that most people are not ready to reduce very much, very soon. One tree can absorb twenty-six to forty-eight pounds of carbon per year; an acre of forest can absorb ten tons.[20] This good grace of the forest cannot begin to solve the problem of global warming, but it does provide amelioration while we decide whether or not to tackle the essentials of improving energy efficiency, switching to solar and wind power, and curbing population growth.[21]

While living forests are part of the answer to reversing the trend in human-caused climate change, the same altered climate quietly kills the forests that we increasingly depend on. But before we look further at that and other conundrums of this much-loved landscape, let's consider the makeup of the forests themselves and the estate of trees that deliver all this wealth, from one side of America to the other.

The Tapestry of Forests

Enlivening the geography of our country, 865 tree species fill every conceivable niche of suitable habitat, which includes most land with even a sprinkling of soil and about twenty inches of precipitation per year.[22] The community of trees, whether scrub oaks in Texas or the great conifers of the Northwest, not only determines the type of wildlife that will live underneath the spreading branches but also defines much of the essence of regional character—why a place looks the way it does.

Ancient on the scale of life in the Western Hemisphere, the Appalachian Mountains house the country's greatest diversity of tree species and largest expanse of forest. Regional biographer Maurice Brooks called these "the most extensive broad-leaved deciduous forests in the world."[23] Though they're commonplace to Americans, the only similar forests lie in China. From New England to Alabama, several hundred tree species blanket the green mountains and Piedmont hills in a cover that's nearly complete except for farmed fields, pavement, and lawns.

Part of an even larger deciduous region known as the Central Hardwoods, the Appalachian forests blend seamlessly with those of the Coastal Plain, Deep South, and Midwest, as well as the Northern Forest of conifers. These woodlands thrive not only on year-round moisture delivered by prevailing winds from the west but also on moisture from the Atlantic Ocean, the Gulf of Mexico, and the Great Lakes.

Ridge after Appalachian ridge fades into the hazy eastern skyline, each landmass a lighter shade of gray-green than the one before it and each covered with broadleaf forest, like a woolly green blanket shaken out and dropped gently over the aged hills. More than in any other region, species here are mixed; dozens of varieties might bud and bloom on a single acre. Oaks, the largest genus of trees in the East, predominate across much of the region, especially on drier hillsides. Hickories, walnuts, white pines, dogwoods, and many others share the Appalachian mountainsides. Floodplains are richly endowed with silver maples, yellow and black birches, black willows, and magnificent, fat-trunked sycamores. In the central and southern forests, tulip poplars can reach immense girths. Green and white ash trees with hard, resilient wood grow to impressive heights. In the north and on high, shady slopes, the dark needles of conifers enrich the scene, adding color in winter and variety all year long to the dominant broadleaf greenery.

In the Great Smoky Mountains of the southern Appalachians, some fantastically large trees can be found: black cherries six feet in diameter and red oaks 170 feet tall.[24] This Cove Hardwoods community of the southern and central Appalachians ranks as the continent's exemplar of forest diversity, with 130 tree species, 1,400 flowering herbs, and 2,000 species of fungi.[25]

The central Appalachians' Mixed Mesophytic Forest includes many different kinds of trees growing in moderately wet conditions. One location might have forty species sharing the high canopy. Uninterrupted by glaciation, this is among our oldest of forest associations, considered the seedbed of other hardwood forests by naturalist Lucy Braun.[26]

The Northern Hardwoods, made up of beeches, hemlocks, white pines, and yellow birches, cover much of New England, an area also graced by the sugar maple of syrup-making fame. Though mostly woodland at the time of the Pilgrims, 80 percent of this region had been cleared for farmland by the time of the Civil War, but today, 80 percent is woodland again. Second- and third-growth trees now sprout up even in the middle of toppling stone fencerows, and New Englanders now claim the most forested region in America. Though the woods have recovered, the intervening axmanship took a toll on native flora; from Maryland to Maine, the Northeast has lost more than 8 percent of its native plant species, the worst record of any region.[27]

At the upper tier of the United States, the somber, green Northern Forest is dominated by red, white, and black spruces, balsam firs, and larches, with alders along streams. The paper birch, a quintessential signpost here, stands out with its white bark against a dusky green backdrop. Continuous with the boreal forests of Canada, the 400- to 800-mile-wide greater Northern Forest spanning the continent constitutes one of the world's largest coniferous belts.

At the opposite latitudes of the country, forests of the South and the Coastal Plain thrive in the spongy world of wetlands. Here, the charismatic baldcypress buttresses out at its base like a Gothic column rooted in black swamp water. The oldest tree in the East, a 1,650-year-old cypress grows in North Carolina. Draped in moss, girthy oaks preside over drier sites, and pines cover much of the sandy expanse of southern land. Symbolic of the Deep South, magnolia trees photosynthesize year-round through broad evergreen leaves. Yet industrial forests here are more common than natural ones. Loblolly and slash pines now line up like corn in endless rows on commercial tree plantations; the South produces three times as much wood fiber as do all eight Rocky Mountain states put together. Logging has eliminated 98 percent of the elegant longleaf pine, with its remarkable eighteen-inch needles, a tree that once covered 92 million acres from Virginia through Texas.[28]

While the eastern forests have been drastically changed, most midwestern woods are altogether gone. The original magnificence of the seventy midwestern tree species of the Central Hardwoods has almost been forgotten. Since the 1930s, some forests have grown back, but agriculture prevails, with only 29 percent of the land now wooded.[29] Along green threads of riverfront, sycamores, eastern cottonwoods, silver maples, and green ashes constitute one of few forest types still common in the Midwest, though dense hardwood islands remain on the Ozark Plateau and in the Ouachita Mountains of Missouri and Arkansas. Stands of stately bur oaks finger out into the prairie until the climate is too dry even for this stalwart of the eastern plains, and to the south, low canopies of oaks cover the hills of Texas and Oklahoma—the forest's last stand, abutting windswept grasslands to the west. There and beyond, the riparian, or riverfront, forest is thin and discontinuous but nonetheless is a mainstay of life in the drylands.

Rugged high country accounts for the allure of the Rocky Mountains, but much of the range's deeper character derives from its forests—wide slopes of evergreens sweeping down both its eastern and western flanks. The tree species change rapidly from mountaintop to valley; a hundred-foot drop causes a climate change equivalent to that of zooming sixty miles southward.[30] Up near timberline, alpine krummholz consists of miniature wind-sculpted trees. Just below them, subalpine firs dominate, along with whitebark pines or limber pines, yielding to Douglas-firs at lower elevations. At middle and upper elevations, vast monocultures of lodgepole pines sprout in the wake of fire; the intense heat opens the cones, allowing seedlings to pop up like ground cover. Stately ponderosa pines tower above dry slopes. Aspens brighten sunny slopes and ridges,

Giant tulip trees reach for the sky in the Appalachians of Virginia. Old-growth forests nationwide have been reduced to only about 2 percent of their original extent.

Appalachian wildness in Pennsylvania. This second-growth woods shows the recuperative powers of the temperate forest, given adequate time and protection.

Aspen forest in the Rocky Mountains of Wyoming. Aspens regrow quickly after fire and serve many species of wildlife.

Blue oak. Oaks are keystones of ecosystems in the East and West alike. Their acreage here along the West Coast is dramatically decreasing owing to land development.

Giant sequoia, California. The largest trees on earth, the sequoia are protected in several dozen groves, but threats persist due to air pollution and logging in surrounding areas.

Clear-cuts south of Mount Rainier, Washington. Clear-cutting, which causes erosion, increased flood runoff, water pollution, and fragmentation of habitat, has scarred many forests.

Clear-cut on North Carolina's Coastal Plain. More than half of America's logging now occurs in the South, where vast areas are owned by industrial timber companies.

especially in the southern Rockies. Narrowleaf, black, and Fremont cottonwoods preside over Rocky Mountain riverfronts.

Seventy percent of the West is mostly unforested, with drylands stretching between the Rockies and the Pacific ranges, but scattered pinyons and junipers still dot many mountain slopes. Even in the dry state of Arizona, trees cover 26 percent of the land.[31] Farther west, shrinelike groves of bristlecone pine highlight a few forests in Nevada and eastern California. The longest-living trees in the world, these high-elevation specialists can survive for 4,600 years, easily outlasting entire civilizations.

The Sierra Nevada of California hosts a stellar collection of great conifers, with eighteen species mixing at middle elevations. Fantastic in their towering presence, humbling in their cathedral groves, the Sierra conifers reach enormous size even when restricted to small pockets of soil amid granite-block terrain. Giant sequoias grow as much as 300 feet tall and thirty-six feet in diameter—the largest trees on earth.

The Northwest kingdom of conifers rises abruptly from the Pacific Ocean and stretches eastward across the Cascades crest. This land of great forests accommodates the largest variety of giant cone-bearing trees in the world.[32] In height, the elegant coast redwoods of northern California exceed every other species, topping out at 368 feet. Western hemlocks dominate in the shaded climax forest.

Along with twenty-nine species of conifers, the madrone, with its polished red bark, indicates rich diversity in the Klamath Mountains of northern California.[33] Like the woodlands of the central Appalachians, the forest here never disappeared under the continental glaciers; the Klamath might be considered a Great Smoky Mountains equivalent in the West. Along the Oregon coast, the Port Orford cedar is the most threatened of all coastal trees, plagued by an exotic fungus spread in part by mud from the tires of logging trucks that pound up and down a haul road network of thousands of miles.[34] Farther north, Washington's Olympic Peninsula stands out as one of the premier temperate rain forests on the continent.

Halfway across the Pacific, the country's largest tropical forest is the Wao Kele O Puna, on the island of Hawaii. Also in the Tropics, Puerto Rico has been ravaged by tree cutters, but the 10,000-acre El Yunque River Forest remains, with 105 species of trees—a natural arboretum of diversity.

Finally, in the far north, the 200-foot-tall Sitka spruce of coastal Alaska typifies the largest temperate rain forest in the world, a dripping, chlorophyll wonderland of giant trees furred in moss. Rainfall averages 50 to 200 inches per year and can reach a thoroughly soaking 350 inches. Giant 800-year-old conifers are common, and some Alaska cedars have lived for 3,500 years. Even farther north, black and white spruces predominate in a type of low forest called taiga, where stunted trees look like bottle brushes and black cottonwoods, willows, and alders crowd the stream fronts. Eventually, even stunted spruces give way to the barrens of the Arctic, so cold, with sap-freezing winters, and so armored with permafrost that trees cannot take root or survive. Here in the Arctic—as on the broad horizons of deserts and prairies—one stands face to face with the raw, windy world of treelessness and can easily realize just how extraordinary and valuable the forests of America really are.

Cutting the Forest Down

To understand the modern landscape of America, it's important to know that nearly all the original forest has been cut down. As historian Michael Williams wrote, "Possibly the greatest single activity in the evolution of the rural landscape of the United States has been the clearing of the forest."[35]

In New England and Virginia, pioneers cut and girdled all the trees they could to clear farmland—a pattern repeated almost everywhere settlers went. On founding Pennsylvania in 1681, William Penn ordered that for every five acres cut, one acre of forest should remain. But non-Quaker settlers soon overran the colony, and logging went unrestrained.

The Euro-American settlers' clearing of forests was in stark contrast to the Indians' treatment of the woods. Though they burned forests in many areas to clear underbrush, native people cut trees only sparingly and for specific purposes, such as for carving out canoes in the Northwest. Some tribes that relied on acorns and nuts eschewed tree cutting entirely. Stephen Barton recorded the following incident in frontier California: "Intelligent Indians tell of a company of two or three white men who came through here, perhaps as early as 1845. In each of [their camps] they cut down a tree. The cutting of these trees filled the Indians with more consternation and horror than any phenomena they have been privileged to witness before or since. The word was sent from tribe to tribe that a large coyote, with white eyes and long, red hair covering its face, had destroyed two trees by force—a work thought to be impossible with man."[36] Wholesale leveling of California's forests began when the loggers' axes reached the West Coast during the gold rush, only four years after the incident Barton described.

Clearing of farmland and failure to reforest logged tracts have reduced the area of forest in the United States by about a third since European settlement.[37] The reduction lies principally in the East and Midwest, where 279 million acres are now cultivated in crops.[38] Forests have also been replaced by sprawling cities such as New York, Atlanta, and Seattle, all once as densely wooded as the Cook Forest I knew in Pennsylvania, the Joyce Kilmer Memorial Forest in North Carolina, or the Opal Creek Wilderness in Oregon.

In the lower forty-eight states, only about 2 percent of the forest remains as old growth, defined as virgin forest that has been growing for a long time without interruption by cutting, usually with a variety of species and trees of all ages, including dying and fallen timber.[39] Loggers left only token stands of old growth, and not many of those, as they sawed their way westward. In the East, the original woodlands included 200-foot-tall white pines and hemlocks nine feet across. Now, only 1 million to 2 million acres of eastern old growth remain, most of it in tracts of a few acres to a few hundred acres.[40] Virtually no old growth survives in some states. In Wisconsin, only a mistake in boundary descriptions left eighty acres uncut. Even in the famed Great Smoky Mountains, now protected as our most visited national park, five-sixths of the forest was logged.

Nationwide, most of the old growth that remains can be found in the National Forest System, where perhaps 10 percent of 191 million federally owned acres has escaped the saw. Much of this occurs at high elevations, representing forest types less productive, diverse, and commercially valuable than those at lower levels. Designated wilderness areas and parks ban logging in only about half of America's remaining old-growth forests.[41] Elsewhere, timber companies have gone on to cut many of the forests a second, third, and fourth time, often cutting too many trees too fast for sustainable logging in the future. Frequent results include soil loss, watershed damage, nutrient depletion, herbicide pollution, decreased species diversity, and monocultures of "cash crop" trees susceptible to pests and disease.

While the forest's timeless mission of photosynthesis, growth, death, and decay creates life and constantly recycles energy and nutrients into the soil and then back into new generations of plants, and on and on in a system that links microscopic bacteria to the tallest trees, the process of unsustainable cutting takes the energy *out* of that system, leaving it impoverished and scarred. The real texture and character of old-growth forests takes a lot of time to develop — 175 years, for example, to grow a large Douglas-fir on the West Coast, followed by many more years for associated plants and animals to weave together their intricate ecological relations. Drier forests need even longer. But low-elevation conifers of the West are now harvested every 60 years. Appalachian forests are cut every 40–100 years, and pulpwood-mowing machines crunch through large sections of the Northern Forest and the South on a 30-year cycle. The timber may bring a good enough price to continue this process for a while, but the circle of life that the old forest served is gone.

Heavily impinged on by logging and development, the forest regions coincide with hot spots of endangered species. The woodlands of the Appalachians and the Southeast are the largest block of undeveloped land having great numbers of imperiled species, with the forest of the Sierra Nevada and northern California also ranking high on this lamentable list.[42] The ivory-billed woodpecker, which disappeared with the loss of the last big oak and gum forests in the 1940s, depended on southern old growth. In turn, it eradicated insect pests in the bark of the trees. Suffering a similar fate today, the red-cockaded woodpecker — once thriving in longleaf pine forests — barely survives in the remnant pine and grass woods of the South and Midwest.[43] Logging threatens the northern spotted owl in the Northwest; other species requiring old growth include sleek furbearers called the fisher and marten; the northern goshawk; and the northern red-legged frog. The western salamander must have ponds in shady woodlands for breeding. The marbled murrelet feeds at sea but nests in old forests far inland, if such a homesite can be found. The loss of old forests means loss of life for these creatures and others all the way through the food chain.

Many second-growth forests look green and healthy and may in fact be growing fast. But the middle-aged forest, 20 to 100 years old, is usually the least valuable for wildlife and species diversity. Surprisingly, logging's worst effects on wildlife come *after* the unpopular scars of clear-cutting have greened up.[44]

Their canopies closed to sunlight, regrowing forests become mono-cultures of adolescent trees with little understory, without the openings that result when individual old trees topple over and without the large downed logs and old standing snags that make homes and food supplies for a host of forest species. To make way for its commercial crop, the forest industry routinely poisons the hardwoods most valuable to wildlife, such as hickories, papaws, and persimmons in the South. In these market-driven tracts, all the trees look about the same, and being monocultures, tree plantations fall victim to disease far more than diverse forests do.[45]

Excessive logging destroys not only habitat for wildlife but also the very life systems that serve the trees themselves. As early as 1864, George Perkins Marsh, in *Man and Nature,* warned of what happened when earlier civilizations denuded their forests in the Mediterranean and Middle East regions: the soil washed away, and the trees, including the famed cedars of Lebanon, never grew back. Warnings of forest collapse have continued ever since Marsh's day, and in a growing chorus in recent years as we've come to understand more about forest ecology.

With poorly executed logging, soil—the very basis of the forest—is lost, sometimes in wholesale slabs. In Siuslaw National Forest in Oregon, all but 27 of 245 landslides following a heavy storm were traced to logging and road building.[46] Loss of soil and its symbiotic systems of microbes accounts for the failure of many new conifer plantings attempted on logged-over sites. Ninety-five percent of the fungi may disappear when a forest is clear-cut, some of them not reappearing for a hundred years.[47] The soil washed off sites of reckless logging ends up in streams, where it plays havoc on freshwater life. And without shade after logging, stream temperatures often climb to levels fatal for fish.

Whether poorly or carefully undertaken, the logging is done because we have plenty of uses for the lumber. Thousands of products depend on the harvesting of trees. Forty-four percent of the wood now cut in the United States is for construction, 27 percent is for paper, and 22 percent is for fuelwood.[48] While forest issues are often portrayed as a choice between wood products and healthy forest ecosystems, scientists and foresters today recognize that if the industry is to continue logging, it also needs healthy forest ecosystems. Ample evidence shows that the two can coexist.[49] But logging by the old model—harvesting to the exclusion of other values—continues to extract a high toll.

Logging Everywhere

Logging occurs almost everywhere trees grow—certainly on the 15 percent of forestland that's owned by the timber industry and also on the 28 percent that's in public ownership and the remaining 57 percent owned by individuals.[50]

In the Southeast, the magnificent mixed hardwood forest wasn't just clear-cut; it was also burned and replaced with fields of rice or cotton and then, after those industries exhausted the soil and died out, with mile after mile of loblolly or slash pine—perhaps the most intensively managed forests anywhere. Owning nearly one in five acres of southern forest, large timber companies typically clear-cut all vegetation in the harvest area, disk the ground as though preparing for a crop of corn, plant seedlings in rows, douse it all with herbicides, and then recut the trees on a rapid rotation, eliminating the mix of species and rich habitat that have made the South a biological hothouse since before the ice ages.

The rate of cutting in the Southeast increased in the 1990s. A hundred new chip mills were built, and more than a million acres per year were clear-cut to feed an industry that exports nearly half its wood chips to Japan. State regulations on use of southern forestland scarcely exist; if anything, they are limited to voluntary "best management practices."[51] Yet 55 percent of all the timber harvested in the United States comes from this region.[52]

On the dry ranges of the Southwest, 98 percent of the girthy ponderosa pines have been cut.[53] There and in the Blue Mountains of eastern Oregon and elsewhere, the survivors and second growth are now threatened by additional high grading, which plucks out the "pumpkins" of superior genetic quality and leaves a forest of tangled scrub, incapable of withstanding the droughts, fires, and insect pests that the old ponderosa pines had endured so well.[54]

Even in the Sierra Nevada of California, a relatively safeguarded region, 85 percent of the original forest has been logged. In northern California, 95 percent of the tallest trees in the redwood forests have been sawed up for decks and siding.[55] The public owns more than half the remaining old-growth coastal redwoods. But the largest unprotected grove, the Headwaters Forest, was slated for cutting after a Texas financier gained controlling interest in the Pacific Lumber Company, which until his takeover had excelled in sustainable management. The battle that resulted, with court cases, legislative bills, and sit-in protests by thousands of demonstrators, may have been the most intense struggle ever to protect an old-growth forest.[56]

With the state of California failing to take adequate action to curb the unsustainable rate of redwood logging, the federal government finally earmarked money from the Land and Water Conservation Fund to buy 7,500 acres, including 84 percent of the remaining old-growth redwoods of the Headwaters forest. Preservation groups persisted in efforts to protect a larger area.

Aside from logging for lumber, forests in all regions are also cut for land development, with no likelihood of reforestation. At lower elevations, where monumental oaks once dotted the California grasslands in a strikingly beautiful savanna, urban sprawl gobbles hardwood forests at the rate of 20,000 acres per year. Cattle graze on 75 percent of the oak woodlands that remain, preventing new germination.[57] In Washington, new housing construction in the 1990s consumed more wooded acreage than was cut in national forests of that state. Nationwide, about 500,000 acres of forest are converted to urban and agricultural use each year.[58]

In Alaska, a temperate rain forest of giant Sitka spruce and cedar remains unequaled for combined extent, age, and untouched splendor. Yet the scope of abuse in this region reached a whole new level. Volunteering the American taxpayers for a gift of extraordinary largess, Alaska politicians muscled legislation through Congress guaranteeing that at least $40 million of government money be spent annually to serve up 450 million board feet per year of public timber at two sawmills, one in Japanese ownership. With this sweetheart deal, our government allowed multinational companies to export each ancient giant tree for less than the price of a cheeseburger, and nearly all the logs went to Asia.[59] By 1994, the industry had stripped more than 450,000 publicly owned acres of old growth from Tongass National Forest and perhaps that much again on land owned by native corporations. Plans called for the cutting of another three times that amount and the bulldozing of 12,200 more miles of road, which promised erosion and silted spawning beds for the state's salmon. The Alaska delegation engineered this lucratively subsidized scheme while seeming to care little for the home-based, age-old industry of fishing, which was devastated by the stream destruction and loss of habitat involved.

The Southeast Alaska Conservation Council battled for years to eliminate this taxpayer giveaway, and in 1990 the Tongass Timber Reform Act finally protected 1 million acres of forest as wilderness and rescinded the guaranteed subsidy. Without the exceptional infusion of tax dollars, the pulp mills in Ketchikan and Sitka folded, and an important corner may have been turned for the forests of Alaska. A new national forest plan in 1997 called for timber cutting to be halved, conservation areas to be set aside for critical wildlife and stream fronts, and harvesting to be set back 1,000 feet from estuaries. The state's politicians strived to undo the reforms but failed. Without their interference, and with obligations to the land and to the taxpayers, the Forest Service is now free to better manage the greatest of all temperate rain forests, if only the agency can change quickly enough to do the job.

Reform Efforts in the Northwest and Northeast

Controversies about overcutting of forests have raged in many parts of the country, with the conflict hitting an especially high pitch in the Northwest and Northeast. In the Pacific Northwest, the greatest of all forests were cut until only 10 percent of the original old growth west of the Cascades' crest remained in the 1990s. Six percent of the original ancient forests were protected.[60] This left a small remainder to be fought over in a war of the woods that dominated regional discussions of forestry at the end of the 20th century.

Conservationists before 1980 had waged efforts to save old-growth stands, but their successes were limited as the cutting advanced systematically through the giant forests. Private land at lower elevations—the richest in tree growth, species diversity, and wildlife habitat—had been cut over by the 1960s, and timber companies moved with hefty momentum into the higher-elevation property of the national forests.

Going beyond the traditional appeals for recreation, scenery, and heritage, ecologists and forest enthusiasts in the 1980s recognized the biological values of old growth and identified many kinds of wildlife that need the old forests. The rare northern spotted owl of old-growth haunts became the symbol of the northwestern movement to save forests for the wealth of life they support. In 1990, after years of study, the owl became the lightning rod of forest protection when the U.S. Fish and Wildlife Service declared it a threatened species.[61] Court injunctions by environmental groups briefly brought the cutting of old growth to a halt, and a cultural battle for the soul of the Pacific Northwest ensued. Mill owners and timber workers battled the "tree huggers" in a conflict of public opinion, lawsuits, and occasional violence. The effort to save some share of the residual forest heated up when thousands of protesters staged rallies, blocked roads, and sat a hundred feet off the ground in trees to prevent logging.[62]

Seeking to solve the conflict through compromise by both sides, President Bill Clinton convened a "Forest Summit" in 1993, and his administration later adopted a Northwest Forest Plan in an effort to protect 70 percent of the remaining old growth and to allow logging on the rest— a substantial 1.4 million acres.[63] Both sides in the contentious debate appealed in court, but the plan was upheld.

Adjusting to the realities of the times, both parties were finally learning to live with the new agreement when western congressmen undermined the compromise with the "Salvage Rider"—legislative language attached to a 1995 budget bill that forced the Forest Service to sell additional timber. Ostensibly directed at burned or diseased forests, the rider included healthy trees and even ones that had recently been safeguarded under the Northwest Forest Plan.[64] The rider kicked off a whole new round of antagonism and activism to save the pieces of old growth that remained. Some stands were lost under the specious name of salvage and others through the compromises in the Northwest Forest Plan, which in 1997 alone allowed clear-cutting of 7,032 acres of ancient forest.[65] Conservationists held fiercely to the hard-earned protections that remained in effect.

At the opposite end of the country, in the Northern Forest of New England, another epic battle over the woodlands of America heated up in the 1990s. Here, the issue was not one of cutting public forests but rather of private forest management and the effects of industrial logging on an entire landscape.

An anachronism in the settled East, the Northern Forest stretches from the Atlantic Ocean to central New York. In Maine—the most forested state in America—almost every woodland is available for harvest. The timber industry owns 13 million acres—half the entire Northern Forest belt—and has harvested and reharvested on a pulpwood rotation, clearing wide swaths of spruce every thirty years by clear-cutting—cutting everything at once.[66] While the rate of harvest used to be slower and left large expanses of unroaded land, industrial-scale logging with behemoth road-building and tree-cutting equipment as efficient as wheat combines expanded in the 1980s. In 1991 alone, timber companies mowed through 2.5 percent of Maine's loggable forest. Though new trees would continue to grow on the stripped land, the 1990s rate of cutting would engulf the whole state in half a lifetime.[67] Selectively cut "beauty strips" several hundred feet wide may border public roads and major rivers but do little to mute widespread ecological damage, and they deceive none who see the shaven, disabled forest from an airplane. Responding to widespread complaints and growing citizen pressure, the Maine legislature passed a Forest Practices Act in 1991, limiting clear-cuts to 250 acres—still enormous swaths as large as several farms—separated by strips of scarcely functional forest.[68] For comparison, the limit on such cuts in national forests was forty acres.

While clear-cuts can be devastating to habitat and watersheds, they are only one part of the problem. Poorly planned roads and indiscriminate use of heavy equipment can cause just as many difficulties in selectively cut areas, where trees are individually picked for harvest. And while large clear-cuts devouring hundreds of acres have become synonymous with heavy-handed forest management, several small cuts can be just as destructive because they fragment the forest even more, with edges and ever smaller blocks of forest between denuded plots. Such cuts have been devastating to threatened species that need larger expanses of forest, including the Blackburnian warbler, ovenbird, and American redstart. In northern New England, populations of more than three-quarters of the songbird species that depend on woodlands dropped significantly during the clear-cutting spree of the 1980s.[69] Similar declines plagued the Appalachian forests as well, owing primarily to fragmentation of habitat.[70] Unsung species such as the pine marten and fisher—large members of the weasel family—may be just as endangered in the Northeast as is the northern spotted owl in the Northwest, but they haven't yet received attention because of a mostly hands-off approach to protecting wildlife and endangered species on private land.

To continue harvesting but protect important values, Malcolm Hunter and Robert Seymour of the University of Maine recommended a "triad" approach that incorporates high-yield harvests where appropriate, eco-logical preserves, and "new forestry" techniques intended to combine sustainable logging and ecosystem health on large acreages. The industry, however, stifled any wide-ranging reform during policy debates with the Maine government. Nonetheless, the issues of habitat, aquatic health, new roads opening up remote woods, herbicide spraying, and soil erosion drew increasing concern from New Englanders. Efforts to reinstate Atlantic salmon further exposed how logging practices caused silted streams and destroyed spawning habitat.

Conservationists in the forest debate took the audacious step of put-ting a referendum against clear-cutting on the Maine ballot in 1996. Timber companies argued that thousands of jobs were at stake, though it was mechanization of the mills, not a lack of available trees, that had shrunk jobs in Maine by 40 percent in a decade; while the amount of timber being cut had increased, employment had decreased. Running scared, the industry tentatively agreed to clear-cut only 1 percent of its holdings per year. Then, with a paycheck-grip on the political views of its employees, past employees, and adherents of the status quo, the industry outspent its opponents four to one and squashed the referendum.[71]

On top of the overcutting problem, the prospect of even greater upset in Northern Forest ecosystems surfaced when multinational timber cor-porations began selling off cutover acreage in northern New England for vacation housing. The potential for quick profits seduced investors who thought they recognized a ripe market; 70 million people live within a day's drive of the North Woods, including the populations of Montreal, Boston, and New York. In an unexpected fall of dominoes, 970,000 acres of timberland owned by the giant Diamond International Corporation were sold and eventually subdivided into 40- to 40,000-acre parcels.[72] The industry's subdivision boom hit hardest at prime wildlife habitat along streams and lakes. Alarmed that so much forest was going the way of subdivisions, residents of the region pushed their states to establish the

Northern Forest Lands Council to consider the fate of an ever more fragmented forest.

In 1994, the council cautiously recommended reform to encourage
investment in responsible forestry, increased research, and modest public
acquisition of natural and recreation areas. Though the council called for
attention at the state level, its reform proposals lay moribund because the
industry and private-rights groups organized well, made themselves heard,
and shocked the general public into fear of big government.[73]

Undeterred, the Northern Forest Alliance, consisting of thirty-five
state, regional, and national groups, worked with the legislature, the
courts, and the general public for better management, planning, and protection. A separate group called Restore the North Woods advocated
widespread public acquisition of industrial forestland to establish a
national park. Other conservationists worked with landowners and promoted greater awareness of the changes and risks at hand. Believing that
neither large-scale public acquisition nor tough regulations on logging
were likely, authors David Dobbs and Richard Ober wrote, "The challenge becomes not how to 'save the Northern Forest,' but how to protect
those woods by using them well."

Some timber operators are doing just that—using the forest well. The
Baskahegan Company has led the way in forest management reform, striving to increase the long-term value of its stands and to avoid reckless use.
Owner Roger Milliken Jr. wrote that his business "has learned that its
best interests lie with the best interests of the forest." Baskahegan cuts
lightly and in small, variable tracts, depending on forest conditions, aim-
ing for a diversity of tree sizes and species and minimum disturbance of
the soil. The company's chief forester Chuck Gadzik said, "What pulp and
paper outfits look for is to grow fiber. What we look for is to grow value.
It just happens that fulfilling our mission is a less grossly manipulative
kind of management."[74]

While larger companies that clear-cut depend on herbicides and costly
replanting, Baskahegan leaves trees of various age groups—a more economic way to allow natural regermination. Gadzik said, "The key is diversity. Without healthy forests, there's no reason to hold onto forestland.
That's when land will get sold out of the industry." Rather than sell for
development, Baskahegan has sold conservation easements to the state to

ban subdivision and development in a 500-foot buffer along waterways. The Hancock Timber Resource Group likewise committed itself to long-term, quality forest management when it bought large holdings in Maine in 1993. Three years later, with help from The Conservation Fund, an easement preventing development on 31,000 acres of the company's land in Vermont was signed over to the state. Progressive work by landowners such as these offers some hope for the Northern Forest of the future.

The Need for Reform

Confronted with a firestorm of protest over clear-cutting and poor forest practices on federal land a quarter century ago, Congress passed the National Forest Management Act of 1976. For all the national forests, the law bars cutting where irreversible damage will result, prohibits logging where trees cannot be restocked in five years, limits clear-cutting, and mandates protection of species diversity. With a sense of order and due process, this farsighted law directed that implementation be governed by forest management plans, to be drawn up for each national forest. But with a change of administration, reform fizzled. Heavily influenced by production-oriented politics of the Ronald Reagan era and congressmen representing the timber industry, the plans called for more cutting than ever.[75] The Forest Service's system of official and unauthorized roads, which already totaled 440,000 miles—eight times the length of the Interstate Highway System—was slated to grow by another 262,000 miles with few questions asked about damages, costs, and an onerous backlog of needed maintenance.[76] In short, goals of the 1976 law remained elusive targets.

Striking an even deeper note of public outrage, most Forest Service timber sales lost the taxpayers money. The General Accounting Office showed that below-cost timber sales cost the Forest Service and the taxpayers $1 billion in 1992–1994.[77] The timber program cost taxpayers $24,000 per year for each logging job in the Southwest.[78] Escaping the budget ax that Congress wielded for other programs from school lunches to aircraft carriers, the timber subsidy continued through the 1990s.

Even where the Forest Service indicated economic timber sales, such as in the Pacific Northwest, the numbers were skewed by the fact that the public value of a standing tree is considered zero. On the accounting ledger, a tree is worth nothing as wildlife habitat, as a sequesterer of carbon, or as a contributor to recreational value and natural beauty. Half the water of eleven western states originates on national forest land, but the forests' value in protecting that water supply is rated as worthless.[79] A sale is considered economic if the receipts simply pay for the costs of administering the sale and building the required roads. But rather than assets, the roads prove to be deadly liabilities, causing landslides, erosion, loss of fisheries, destruction of property, and even loss of life.[80]

Furthermore, some Forest Service officials routinely twisted accounting measures to justify the cut. They amortized roads over a period of 240 years and in one case 1,800 years, when in fact the roads' life spans average 25 years.[81] Using money doled out with corporate-socialist vigor at the behest of western politicians who talk a lot about free enterprise and rugged individualism, some of the wildest reaches of the northern Rockies were chainsawed for the first time, including part of the hotly contested Cove-Mallard tract adjoining the nation's largest protected wilderness in Idaho.

With a graph of red ink on display, taxpayer and environmental groups gained ground in 1997 when Republican congressman John Porter of Illinois and Democrat Joe Kennedy of Massachusetts passed legislation to stop the timber subsidy. But a subsequent bill overturned the action by two votes. Government giveaways for logging continued, but in an era of budget cuts, the purse strings were tightening.

Hard-pressed to defend their case, supporters of the subsidies linked them to the economic health of logging communities. But in a rigorous analysis, economist Thomas Power of the University of Montana showed that logging towns in the West are among the least stable economically and that a lack of logs is not the cause of financial woes. Even in timber-cutting regions, the industry accounts for 5 percent or less of the income. Powers concluded, "The timber industry does not represent a way of life that needs public subsidization. Rather, it is a mature primary industry that is in relative decline. . . . There is nothing special or central about the timber industry that should cause the government to give it privileged access to public resources."[82]

Suffering under the subsidy accusations and frustrated with legal challenges that made it more and more difficult to cut in national forests, the timber lobby changed its tune in the 1990s. With the industry employing fewer workers to mill more and more logs and choosing to export its private-land timber to Asia while forfeiting the associated labor, the logging industry's pitch about needing trees for "jobs" was no longer working.[83] So spokesmen pushed a new message they called "forest health." Pointing to burned areas and tracts overrun with low-grade timber resulting from earlier logging, they argued that the best thing for the forest was to cut it down. The industry's congressmen ludicrously defined salvage material to include any live trees "associated" with dead ones. Failing to expose this tree-grab of public woodlands, the Forest Service itself abetted cutting under the salvage stratagem. A memo from an agency employee leaked to the Associated Press confessed, "We were told that virtually every sale should include 'salvage' in the name."[84] Even where the woods had in fact burned, new logging added destruction by alternately churning up and compacting charred and fragile soils, by requiring bulldozing of new roads, and by encroaching on wild areas and habitat of endangered species.

Apparently unworried about the transparency of forest health as a pretext for logging, Senator Larry Craig of Idaho pushed a bill in 1997 written by the timber industry (Craig's Resources Committee staff leader had been hired away from his previous job as executive director of the American Forest and Paper Association). The resulting bill would have mandated high levels of cutting, made it possible to fine citizens $10,000 for appealing timber sales, banned court hearings over decisions to log, and rescinded requirements that wildlife agencies review plans for public land.[85] But the senator did not count on the amplitude of opposition, on the general public's outrage at subsidized forest destruction, or on a fundamental shift within the agency itself.

The fate of the national forests reflects much about the way we treat our entire forest landscape. Reforms now on the horizon may spare the small remaining amount of old growth, an issue that has preoccupied forest protection efforts since their start in the late 1800s. Once the old-growth debate is behind us, questions involving management of the replacement forest will receive needed attention. Fortunately, improvement in the care of our public forests is an issue with tremendous popular support, but before we consider the new directions national forest management is taking, we need to consider the final problem of the woods, one large enough to unite all people who love or depend in any way on the forests of America.

The Habitat's Habitat

For the past three centuries, logging has transformed the face of America's woodlands, but the big changes might only begin with the harvest of trees for lumber and pulp. To understand the disturbing context of the greater forest problem, think for a moment about wildlife, a subject in which a striking parallel can be seen. The first efforts at wildlife management addressed hunting regulations and the direct harvest of animals; people were killing too many, so hunting had to be brought under control. Only later did we realize that habitat was the key to continued viability and, rapacious as unregulated sport and market hunting had been, the biggest continuing problems were unlimited development, logging, grazing, and mining that destroyed the *places* where wildlife lived. Today, we know that the main challenge in protecting wildlife is to protect wildlife habitat.

Just as deer and owls depend on the forest, so is the forest dependent on good soil and air. But as a result of unregulated logging, the soil and nutrient base that the trees need has been diminished. Meanwhile, air pollution, including acid rain and ozone, has destroyed forest health and attacked the ability of trees to grow and resist disease.[86] With the trees' immune systems crippled, invasions of exotic plants, fungi, and insects now strike down one tree species after another, with no end in sight.

The vulnerability of our woodlands to these impoverishments and vectors is what really defines the term *forest health*. This understanding recognizes forest health not just as a prerequisite for production of lumber and pulp but as a condition that supports a full complement of native plant and animal species and offers productive habitat to nurture them. Forest health requires plant life that builds soil and protects it from erosion; that moderates the effects of floods, droughts, and the weather; and that provides for people's needs without a loss of ability to provide for those needs in the future.

In *The Dying of the Trees,* which may be the most important book ever written about the forests of America, Charles Little reports on the current forest pandemic—an epidemic occurring everywhere. The problem is not just that we've cut the original forest down, and not just that the replacement forest is commercially managed as sterile tree farms. The new problem is that our trees are dying on a massive scale without ever seeing the logger's saw.

From the time of the first white settlement until the 20th century, the only tree known to become extinct in the wild was the white-blossomed franklinia, in 1803.[87] Curiously, the next passing was not until an Asian fungus struck the American chestnut in the early 1900s, killing all adults of the species. But now insects, fungi, and blights are diminishing many key species, including hemlocks, white pines, beeches, dogwoods, and sugar maples. Hickories, ashes, and oaks of the central Appalachians unexplainably topple over in the prime of their lives. The beautiful butternut that my father pointed out to me as a child in the Allegheny Mountains of Pennsylvania may become extinct—it is the first tree to be named a candidate for the endangered species list. The problems stem from acid rain, air pollution, and weakened ecosystems in the wake of logging that leveled the original forest and tampered in unfathomed ways with its soil.

Acid rain invades the Northeast, where clouds with the pH of vinegar can be found for a hundred days a year in some places. Unpolluted rain has a pH of 5.6, but the forests subject to the greatest acid outfall, in a broad belt from New York to Tennessee, test at 4.2—dramatically lower on the scale of tolerance. Half of the red spruces of Camels Hump in Vermont's Green Mountains show dead or diseased foliage from acid rain.[88] In Allegheny National Forest in Pennsylvania, 28 percent of the sugar maples were dead in 1994.[89] Fish and amphibians succumb to poisoning as the pH of streams and lakes plummets. Primary sources of the acid are coal-burning power plants, which are fueled by the strip mines, long-tunnel mines, and mountaintop removals of Appalachia.

Excessive ozone in the lower atmosphere, caused by our burning of oil, gas, and coal, destroys trees in other ways, damaging leaves and fatally restricting photosynthesis. Even seedlings of the giant sequoia show ozone damage. Fifty-five percent of the trees in national forests of the southern Sierra Nevada have been ozone poisoned by smog wafting up to the mountains from the suburban and agribusiness maw of California.[90] Ninety different plant species in the Great Smoky Mountains suffer from excessive ozone.[91] Even the Forest Service, an agency that long resisted such warnings, released a study indicating that timber mortality nationwide had increased by 24 percent between 1986 and 1991. Worst hit were the hardwoods, whose mortality jumped by 37 percent.[92] In 1998, the Lucy Braun Association reported Appalachian trees dying at two to four times the expected rate; the areas of greatest mortality coincided with the worst acid rain and ozone pollution.[93]

Biologists maintain that damage from acid rain and air pollution makes the trees more susceptible to invasion by pathogens that can normally be resisted. Acid destroys the waxy surface of leaves; open wounds are then vulnerable to fungi and bacteria. The woolly adelgid, which is killing off hemlocks wholesale in the East, thrives on excess nitrogen in the polluted atmosphere of the Appalachians.[94] Moreover, in an effect that is longer lasting, the pollution affects the forest floor. Acid rain dissolves aluminum, nickel, zinc, and lead in the soil, enabling trees to take up these toxic elements.[95] The leaching of calcium from soils, probably caused by frequent logging and acid rain, could result in a 50 percent reduction of forest biomass in about 120 years.[96]

The first place where scientists noticed ozone damage—the San Bernardino Mountains of southern California—now shows signs of improvement as new ponderosa pines sprout up among old skeletons of ozone-killed trees; emission standards in tightly regulated southern California have cleared the air somewhat.[97] But nationwide, pollution continues to worsen. The Clean Air Act Amendments of 1990 ordered that sulfur dioxide pollution be cut in half in ten years. But under the influence of coal and utility lobbyists, Congress failed to contain nitrogen oxides, a key in the epidemic of dying trees. Reform efforts have led to decreased air pollution per capita, but in many areas they haven't kept up with population growth and the increase in car and energy use. It's difficult to be optimistic until society has the will to launch the next great advance in air quality control.

While soil damage from logging and air pollution from fossil fuels stand as two formidable threats for the habitat of forests, other problems also diminish the wooded elegance of our country. The cottonwoods on floodplains throughout the West and the Great Plains turn into skeletons and are not being replaced along many rivers because the germination of new trees requires flood flows that scour shorelines or deposit silt. Dams have controlled the rivers so much that we seldom have floods, silt, or cottonwood regeneration on waterways as significant as the Missouri and Snake Rivers.

Affecting every region, the invasion of exotic species, from tamarisks on floodplains of the Southwest to scotch broom in the Northwest to kudzu in the Southeast, preempts the space needed by our native trees. In California, the majestic blue and valley oaks of the Central Valley and surrounding hills fail to regenerate and grow, suffering from the invasion of annual grasses that mat the soil and make it inhospitable to acorns and oak seedlings.

Yet another monumental reason for collapse in many types of forest has been our misguided compulsion to suppress all natural forest fires. Before white settlement, lightning-caused fires often walked through the woods, burning fallen limbs and small brush, keeping the understory open and parklike, and encouraging the growth of grasses and wildlife forage. The crowns of large trees such as ponderosa pines were out of reach of flames because the frequent small blazes pruned back the fuel at the trees' bases. But to protect homes and commercial timber, we've replaced natural fire with fire fighting that costs billions of dollars each year. Now, without the thinning action of frequent low-level flames, a tangle of unhealthy forest has taken over—thick monocultures prone to disease and, when they do catch fire, to superheated flames. In spite of firefighters' best efforts, blazes in the unpruned forests today sometimes escape containment and rage out of control, with blast-furnace intensity rather than the low-level kindling typical of the natural regime.

At the turn of the 21st century, members of Congress fumbled with legislative bills that would ostensibly improve forest health. In fact, they offered little but increased logging and failed to address the real forest health crisis. It's a crisis of habitat for the trees themselves, and it involves the quality of our air, invasions of exotic species, loss of soil due to erosion from clear-cuts and road building, and the shackling of natural processes such as floods and natural fires necessary for ecosystems to function.

The Forest of Hope

American attitudes toward forests have changed since the days when pioneers believed with religious fervor that the woods harbored demonic evils. Back then, the only good forest was a cut forest. From this beginning of hostility based on abundance, we've arrived at a sense of value based on scarcity. The shift reflects a similar change in attitude toward mountains and, later, wetlands and deserts. Now we desire a shady forest, and we revere the big trees. Among all the American landscapes, the forests might be the one closest to the homes and hearts of the most people.

Amid discouraging losses, there is still cause for hope, especially in places where forests have grown back. In the unlikely woods of West Virginia, trees had been stripped from all but 28 percent of the state by 1930 but regrew to cover 87 percent by 1990. Much of that forest will be cut again, but without the completely careless abandon of the past. Though the reforested lands in the Appalachians and elsewhere are only an ecological shadow of what they once were, they still signify our desire to treat forests better than in the past. As Jim Caplan of the U.S. Forest Service said, "The reforested lands are a testimonial to our will and conservation spirit. They are proof that even abused lands can heal. Most important, when we participate in that healing, we can also heal our relationship to communities and the earth."[98] Many others have spoken of this healing process as well; stewarding a forest gives individuals a well-earned sense of accomplishment, it requires that people work together, and it leaves a sign of tangible progress to look back on and to offer to the generations that will follow.

In Maine, where industrial forestry reached a zenith, hope stems from people's growing interest in the Northern Forest as a real forest rather than just a tree farm—status that few questioned until recently. Throughout New England, people have started scores of land trusts to protect their woodlands in ravines or on hilltops, at the edges of towns or out in the mountains beyond the sound of cars. And efforts are gaining momentum in all regions. Hundreds of groups work for better forest management, from Protect Our Woods in Indiana to the Native Forest Council in Oregon.

Furthermore, responsible members of the forest industry are using time-tested methods for sustainable logging, and they're engaging new techniques as well. The Collins Pine Company in northern California harvests selectively, removing marketable trees but leaving the forest system intact. In this way, the company has profitably sold logs and stewarded an ecosystem for fifty years. General manager Larry Potts said, "Our measure of success is to have our forest looking very similar in a hundred years to how it does today."[99] Logging companies and the Forest Service are working in experimental efforts to thin invasive firs in the ponderosa pine forests of New Mexico and then reintroduce fire to its timeless task of decomposing woody debris and ushering in grassy glades between trees. Then, the giant ponderosas can prosper along with a wide circle of life beneath them.

In dozens of similar examples nationwide, responsible foresters are showing that new ways of logging are both possible and profitable.[100] Together, they offer a vision of what timber management can be, with practical experience in what works and what doesn't. Meanwhile, new strategies involving tax reform focus on economic incentives to improve forests while helping landowners earn profits.[101] On the forefront of better management, ecologist Jerry Franklin at the University of Washington promotes "new forestry" that allows trees to be cut but maintains ecological harmony by leaving broken snags for wildlife, allowing limbs and debris to rot and fertilize the soil, and avoiding the erosion of roads, bulldozing, and log dragging.

Breaking new ground for reform from within the Forest Service, timber planner Jeff DeBonis formed the Association of Forest Service Employees for Environmental Ethics. Through this group, employees speak out for management of whole ecosystems and push their agency to recognize that the national forests are more than a sawlog fiefdom of the big timber companies. This revolt from within followed a twenty-year barrage of conservationist pressure to recognize non-sawlog values of our public land, to protect wild areas, and to reduce the damage being done by road building.

Finally moved to action at the top, Forest Service chief Dale Robertson in 1992 announced a shift in agency policy from logging to ecosystem management. A few states, such as Pennsylvania, likewise adopted an ecosystem approach to their land. The strategy is intended to address values of the whole forest—not just commercial timber.[102]

The new policies sounded good, but on the ground many of the old methods continued. In the mid-1990s, the Idaho Conservation League counted 105 separate Forest Service timber tracts still being offered for sale in unroaded areas of that state alone. Yet real change was happening as well. At Siuslaw National Forest—once a bastion of logging power in Oregon—Forest Supervisor Jim Furnish in the late 1990s reduced the cut to nearly zero and set out to close two-thirds of the forest roads.[103]

The Forest Service maintained that among the 140 million forested acres it administered, only 50 million remained open to harvest.[104] The cutting rate had dropped to one-third of the overinflated rate of 1984— to roughly its level in 1950, before the industrial-political complex captured the agency.[105] Reduced logging reflected the fact that the finest big trees had nearly all been cut and also that incentives for management had fundamentally changed. For the year 2000, agency economists predicted that 85 percent of the national forests' contributions to the economy would come from recreation, fish, and wildlife, with only 3 percent from timber.[106]

Recognizing the trend, Forest Service chief Mike Dombeck took ecosystem recognition to new heights in 1997 when he told a hostile Senate Committee on Energy and Natural Resources that when logging, "it is simply common sense that we avoid riparian, old-growth, and roadless areas." He announced a goal of closing many of the roads that had caused siltation of streams.

With economics, science, popular opinion, and now the leadership of the Forest Service itself aligned behind new policies to care for the land, the only force defending the exploitive ways of the past were a few western politicians and their constituents. Remarkably, their grip in Congress held, but just barely, when a 1997 bill to eliminate a $30 million annual taxpayer subsidy for logging roads failed by one vote.

In one of the most historic turning points ever for the agency, Chief Dombeck in 1998 called for an eighteen-month moratorium on new road building in most roadless areas. He asked, "Isn't it prudent that before we build any more miles of road, we take care of what we have?" Introducing other reforms, Dombeck added, "This agenda will help us engage in one of the noblest, most important callings of our generation . . . bringing people together and helping them find ways to live within the limits of the land."[107] A barrage of mail ran 70 percent in favor of the road moratorium.

Dombeck pointed out, "The agency is now returning to our roots. The 1891 legislation establishing the Forest Service stated that watershed protection was central to our mission. Now, the health of our watersheds is again going to be first and foremost in our work. Fifty years from now we won't be remembered for the resources we developed, but for what we protected."[108] Biting at the chief's heels, senators and congressional representatives from Alaska and Idaho promised to raid his budget in fiscal retaliation if he didn't continue the subsidized road building. But unlike Forest Service chiefs of the past, Dombeck didn't flinch. Whether or not the reforms will survive the heartless crucible of politics remains to be seen, but it was never so clear that management of the national forests was shifting, with recognition of forests as ecosystems rather than just lumberyards, and that the time for change had come.

Forests and the Future

As we enter the 21st century, Americans are acting to promote better care of forests on five fronts. First, the movement intensifies to protect the remaining old growth. Sizable acreages in the northern Rockies, the Northwest, and southeastern Alaska still lack protection from logging, as do a few remaining eastern tracts.[109]

Second, interest increases to reinstate conditions resembling those of old growth in all forest ecosystems. Ecologists argue that if trees can be allowed to grow, forest conditions can again evolve into complex diversity. Biologist Stephen Trombulak pointed to the recolonization of forests after the ice ages as evidence: "Ecologically speaking, old-growth restoration is not only possible, but easy." Yet it does take time. Plant diversity, even in the fruitful Appalachians, takes as long as a century and a half to recover.[110] Conservation biologists warn that such restoration efforts must be bold to be effective. Small tracts aren't enough because they are disturbed by wind, sunlight, and invasive plants. Linkage is also needed from one forest area to another for migration, feeding, and genetic exchange of wildlife. Ecologist Robert Zahner suggested that eight out of ten acres in eastern national forests be reserved for recovering old growth, an area that would still total only 7 percent of the eastern forest landscape.[111] Already, recovering tracts such as Bristol Cliffs Wilderness in Vermont show evidence that we can return to wooded wildness.

Third, the groups involved in the forest debates recognize that the great majority of our forests will be cut again as home owners' woodlots, industrial tracts, or multiple-use public land, and the way owners manage these forests will determine the most about the health of complete ecosystems. The problems of soil erosion, road-induced landslides, and invasion of exotic species after a forest is cut receive growing attention. Conservation biologists advance important new concepts such as minimizing edge effects. They encourage us to abandon the notion that adolescent forests are good for wildlife. More professionals and citizens now agree that health of the whole forest is more important than logging. As forest specialist Nels Johnson of the World Resources Institute wrote, "It is no longer enough simply to sustain timber yields if it is ultimately the forest that one wants to sustain."[112]

Fourth, people acknowledge that everybody uses wood and that our use needs to be more efficient. While Americans consume only 38 percent of the wood per capita that we did in 1900, the population has tripled. Our use of wood now increases by 1 percent per year—the same as the rate of population growth—and we've become a net importer of lumber.[113] More than a quarter of our wood goes to pulp mills, but waste and failure to recycle are widespread, evident in the fact that 40 percent of our landfill space is consumed by paper. The Worldwatch Institute reports that total wood consumption in the United States could be halved with currently available methods of waste reduction and recycling.[114]

Finally and most important, people increasingly recognize that the forest's larger life-support system requires unprecedented attention. Acid rain, ozone pollution, and global warming all need to be reduced if our forests are to survive as sources of life and regulators of vital hydrologic, climatic, and ecological processes. These goals can lead people far afield from the woods they love. For example, with two of every five barrels of oil powering automobiles, setting higher standards for fuel efficiency is the most important step to curb global warming. Goals set in 1975 were reached in the 1980s, but then progress stalled. A 40 percent improvement in fuel efficiency—considered feasible—would reduce the current exhaust of carbon dioxide by half.[115]

Throughout the history of logging, much has been made of the fact that forests regrow; they are "renewable." But now we know that trees don't simply grow back regardless of how we abuse the soil, the watersheds, and the air. The central issue for the future of forests is not one of loggers battling it out with environmentalists, and it is not one of saving a single species, such as the northern spotted owl. The primary issue is the health of whole forests because only with healthy ecosystems will we have a lasting supply of trees. We'll have that health only after we address the deep-seated causes of the diminishment of our woodlands.

The burdens forced on our forests can be suffocating in their complexity, the solutions seemingly intractable. As historian Paul Hirt wrote, "Because forestry is a long-term affair requiring consistency, and politics is a short-term affair requiring constant compromises, the two make terrible business partners."[116] Yet today, people all across the country are pushing the political system for reform and are taking new responsibility for their forests. They work for change, which is all that anybody can do who values the cool shade of summertime trees and the Eden of life that forests everywhere once gave.

CHAPTER 3

THE WORLD OF GRASSLANDS

As I CLIMBED the grassy hillside, I left the cottonwood-shaded valley and entered the realm of prairie space. This was my first walk in a big, healthy prairie. I didn't know what to expect.

Knee-deep and thick, the grass required that I pick my feet up high. It spread out across the prairie world, far beyond the hill, far beyond what I could see, beyond even the curvature of the earth. Native grasses called big and little bluestem, dropseed, and prairie sand reed covered the 270-by 130-mile expanse of Nebraska's Sand Hills. This landscape amounted to windblown dunes at the end of the last ice age—the largest dune complex on the continent.[1] Now the swells lay furred in green, and they rolled out unblemished to all horizons, the way swollen waves might look in the middle of a stormy sea.

The scale of the scene and the breezy freshness excited me. Though

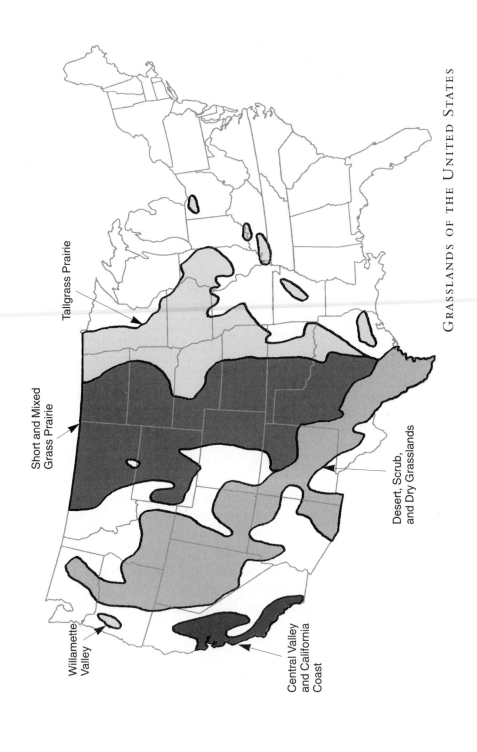

Willamette
Valley

Short and Mixed
Grass Prairie

Tallgrass Prairie

Desert, Scrub,
and Dry Grasslands

Central Valley
and California
Coast

GRASSLANDS OF THE UNITED STATES

what I saw was grass and more grass, I didn't feel bored but spaciously free. I had room to reach out, room to stretch, room to run for whole days across a field that seemed to go forever, one that made me feel as big as the sky-space itself. In it, a red-tailed hawk circled high, screamed a wild, piercing call that must have terrorized any small rodent nearby, and then caught an updraft and lofted away, seeking a place without people.

On a tour of grasslands, Walt Whitman wrote, "The Plains, while less stunning at first sight, last longer, fill the esthetic sense fuller, precede all the rest and make North America's characteristic landscape." I've always thought of mountains or forests as our "characteristic landscape" because they are known, seen, and lived in by more people than are the Great Plains. But why argue with a man like Whitman? Grasslands are indeed central to America and to the American experience.

Later that evening, a storm that had been brewing as a distant threat overtook me. Ominous now, thunderheads piled high and accumulated, sucking in nearby clouds and smoking them up into a crisply edged anvil of soupy, blue-gray vapor. So much for silence; the wind now tuned itself to an orchestral pitch. It swept the land, starched my hair straight back, ventilated my clothing, filled my ears, and penetrated all the prairie world. The entire landscape began to quiver and undulate as the grass blew in waves that glistened when the wind swept like an invisible wand across my view.

Far away, the patterns of turbulence swirled around what seemed to be dark spots on the land. Was something *there?* Were they animals, or rocks? Almost imperceptibly, they moved, and they were large. Were they cows, or possibly—just maybe—could they be buffalo? There *are* buffalo near one part of the Niobrara River. As I strained to see, a shadow overtook me with an almost animate presence, a big, open claw of dark atmosphere. The thunderheads, now directly above, sent me rushing off that lightning rod of a hilltop. Leaving the distant animals a mystery, I hustled back to my tent beside the river. Then, with frightening whooshes, the prairie wind, unhindered by mountains since it swept down off the Rockies 200 miles to the west, buried me in its wet cloud, its buzz of ions, its electricity cutting loose with flashes that could burst into a prairie fire as if exhaled from a dragon's mouth. Thunderclaps jolted me. The soaking downpour, for all the fury, lasted only a few minutes.

The next morning, when I stepped outside my tent, I found the prairie even more lush, freshened and polished by the gift of water. Raindrops clung to the tips of grasses around me, and I imagined the whole expanse of the Sand Hills dotted with the transparent wet jewels. In northern Nebraska, this scene of unbridled abundance in grass did not reflect modern times on the typical prairie. The view served as a window to the past, a green window as if I had awoken early in the 1800s before the grid of barbed wire had made a commodity of the land, before the railroads had served as a pipeline for the liquidation of natural wealth, before the buffalo hunters had blasted away thousands of beasts day after day until nothing remained but rotting flesh in piles as deep as your waist.

The World of Grass

The prairies that covered the midribs of the country, plus sizable outlying areas, once served vital functions in an exquisitely productive ecosystem. Included among grasslands are savannas—the lyrically beautiful transition zones between prairies and forests—nature's lawns, with scattered trees growing alone or in compact groves like islands in a tranquil sea. Anthropologists tell us that these edges of grassland were where humans first excelled, leaving behind the closed-in canopy of jungle and roaming across open space. There, standing high on our hind feet, we could see great distances above the height of the grass. It gave us cover from predators but offered a good view of our own prey. In this habitat, our nomadic ancestors moved freely from place to place and ate well off the bounty of large grazing animals. Anthropologists also credit grasslands on the plains and mountainsides of the Old World as the birthplace of agriculture and civilization.[2] Ecologist Paul Sears wrote, "It is difficult if not impossible to conceive of domestication, either of plants or animals, in the absence of grasses. . . . The taming of large seeded grasses made possible intensive cultivation and great economy of space, leading to the formation of villages and ultimately of cities."[3] Corn, wheat, oats, barley, rice—each of these staples in our modern diet is a domesticated grass.

To understand a wild American grassland, forget any comparison to a suburban lawn. Unlike that monoculture of the chemical age, the native prairies host a botanist's holiday of plants. In an unbroken swath of the Midwest, a hundred species of grasses fill every ecological niche. More than 300 forbs, broadleaf flowering plants, sedges, shrubs, and grasses still grow at the Konza Prairie Research Natural Area in Kansas. Grasslands all over the country house 7,500 plant species.[4] Each, like a useful family member, serves a purpose and has chores to do. Dozens of species employ microbes attached to their roots to fix nitrogen, extracting this essential element from the atmosphere, where it's plentiful, and converting it into plant mass that's recycled into soil, where it's rare but needed by other plants.

On the prairie, scores of wildflowers bloom at different times, April to October. This diversity is good for the land and its community of life; it stabilizes grasslands far more than any strategy of brute force—such as poisoning of insect pests—could ever begin to do. For example, because a variety of species grow intermingled, insects that consume one type of plant can't just eat their way straight across the prairie; the array of different vegetation serves to delay and thwart the insects' progress. Droughts also affect species-rich lands far less than the monocultures that followed our sod-busting forefathers. A study in Minnesota found that during a drought, seven-eighths of the biomass perished on sites lacking species diversity, but only half the biomass was lost on diverse sites.[5] Botanists report that a single plot of prairie might support 250 species of plants; because of that, its health is ensured. With cattle, the number drops to 40. With farming and its attendant pesticides, the number drops to 1 species.[6]

The landscape-sized salad of grasslands provided for the wildlife of the Great Plains. Rich in big mammals like no other place, this region once rated among the greatest wildlife reserves in the world. In their travels across the West in 1805, Lewis and Clark bestowed their most favorable praise on the Great Plains, where they encountered herds of wild animals galore.[7] In his journey across the West a few years later, Francis Parkman wrote, "The prairie teemed with life."

The prairies fed and provided a home for the bison (usually called buffalo) that formed a staple of life in mid-continent. Millions strong during migration, these were the American portrait of wild abundance, an unofficial national animal if ever there was one. By grazing periodically but discontinuously and by trampling seeds into the soil, buffalo encouraged native plant life to thrive. And like the mosaic of greenery underfoot, many kinds of animals made up the community here. Pronghorn—often called antelope—preferred a variety of forbs as well as sagebrush in the drier country. Elk favored sites with shrubs, and the versatile mule deer browsed on combinations of woody shrubs, forbs, and grasses. Smaller grazers included prairie dogs, mice, voles, pocket gophers, ground squirrels, and even the ubiquitous grasshoppers, all interconnected with the lives of others. One hundred thirty-four species of vertebrates associate themselves with prairie dogs, though only a few actually eat them. The others benefit from the mounded dirt piles thrown up by the industrious little rodents, from the plants that pioneer on those freshly cultivated soils, or from the tight shelter of prairie dog tunnels.[8] All these grazers and rodents on the Great Plains set the stage for an impressive cast of predators. Wolves, foxes, and black-footed ferrets hunted here, as well as an owl that, lacking trees, burrowed in the ground. Topping the food chain, the Indians lived exceedingly well on buffalo as a source of food, shelter, tools, and spiritual sustenance.

Animals that people now regard as mountain denizens originally preferred grasslands to all other landscapes. These included elk, wolves, and grizzly bears in great numbers—giants of muscle, fur, and claw but still just half the weight of a buffalo. Only at a Nature Conservancy preserve near Chouteau, Montana, do the bears still wander down from the mountain fortress of the Rockies to forage on the richness of the Great Plains. Today, even buffalo, by default, reside in the mountains; the only sizable free-ranging herd in the United States lives in Yellowstone National Park. But the grasslands once nurtured wildlife of unforgettable vitality.

What we see on the grasslands is not all there is. It's only the frosting on top. Up to 85 percent of a prairie's biomass lies underground. The roots of the tallgrass prairie once grew so thick and knotted—stolidly protective of the soil—that they couldn't be broken until John Deere's iron and steel plows hit the market in 1837.[9] Settlers chopped out bricks of the tough, solid root masses and stacked them up to build houses.

The grass not only provides for animals that graze on it but also produces the very soil that has made the region so rich. It all began with loess—silt, sand, and clay—blown into place during the last ice age. Wind, glacial ice, and streams imported up to 70 percent of the tallgrass prairie's soil.[10] The loess accumulated far faster than does soil that breaks down in place from rock and organic materials—a process typically yielding only one inch of soil every 1,000 to 10,000 years.[11] Once the soil settled to earth, lichens, fungi, and vascular plants colonized the infertile ground, growing, fixing nitrogen, dying, rotting, feeding legions of microbes, and gradually building a rich mulch. Roots of tallgrass can probe twenty feet deep; attached to the finest root hairs, mycorrhizal fungi absorb carbohydrates from the grass and in return boost fivefold the grasses' ability to ingest minerals and water. Microscopic nematodes, along with insect larvae, earthworms, mites, and a diminutive zoo of other soil creatures, constantly enrich the soil with waste and rotting biomass, aerate it through their borings and tunnels, and create pathways for water, roots, and small invertebrates to follow. They are all important, and the total effect transformed the sterile sediment into the rich, blackened, incredibly productive soil that further fed the system of all prairie life, a system that built and built, and finally culminated in a thundering herd of buffalo.

In contrast, today's grasslands are treated as a human food processor, converting sunlight, water, and minerals into crops or beef—and precious few minerals at that, since monocultures have depleted the soil and left farmers dependent on manufactured fertilizers. Modern agriculture might be thought of as a conveyor belt of nutrients, moving from the ground up to the crops, then into the warehouses of middlemen, and finally out through the doors of the grocery store, soon ending up in a landfill or sewage plant along the banks of a river. But in its original form, the prairie landscape described a self-sustaining ecosystem that fed all that depended on it and also fed itself in perpetual balance. Working for free, it constantly built its base for yet more production, no artificial fertilizers needed.

The rich soil originally found in much of the corn belt and wheat belt was a product of solar energy and the grassland ecosystem, and without that system, or some facsimile more accurate than what we have today, the rich soil will vanish. This can happen slowly, over the course of centuries, or it can happen as quickly as a windstorm.

The Grasslands of America

The grassland zone of the United States spans the middle third of America, in a belt from Mexico to Canada. I add the word *zone* here because native grasses themselves are gone from large sections. Today, much of the land is usurped by agricultural crops and pasture, but a view of the grasses that used to grow here, and of what can grow again in some places, can help us understand this big heartland of the country.

Grasslands constitute our largest biome, even larger than the forests. Grasses of many kinds once dominated on 40 percent of the American landscape, not counting all the eastern lawns and farms that would grow up into brush and trees if untended. Worldwide, prairie and steppe landscapes supporting grass cover one-fourth to one-half the terrestrial surface of the globe.[12] Thriving where annual rainfall totals ten to thirty-nine inches, grass grows where it's wet enough to support the juicy-stemmed, thin-leafed, prolifically seeded ground cover but not wet enough to supply trees, with their greater thirst. The grassland zone overlaps and intermingles with deserts in the West and forests in the Midwest.

Beginning to the east, an outlier of the grassland belt infiltrates Illinois, Indiana, and south-central Ohio. Here we find the savanna fringe of the tallgrass prairie, where girthy oaks grew in clusters that gradually thinned to the west until the grasses dominated. Before farmers planted corn, the tallgrass thoroughly blanketed Iowa, northwestern Missouri, and southern Minnesota. With double the rainfall of the western Great Plains, big bluestem, switchgrass, and Indian grass topped out at an amazing twelve feet, capable of hiding a man astride a horse. Among the ecological wonders of the New World, the tallgrass was as extraordinary in its way as the shady old-growth forests of the Appalachians, Coastal Plain, and Pacific Northwest.

Only remnants of tallgrass remain, plots rarer than the buffalo itself. The Midewin National Tallgrass Prairie, forty-five miles from Chicago, survives as the largest grassland ecosystem on the more humid and productive eastern side of the tallgrass zone. Once an army arsenal, this 19,000-acre tract is now stewarded by the Forest Service. In Minnesota, corn farming for cattle feed has reduced the tallgrass to 75,000 acres in small tracts, 60 percent of them protected. In the prairie state of Iowa, 28 million acres of tallgrass have shrunk to a mere 25,000, mostly on privately owned farms and now called "postage stamp prairies." As an expansive museum piece, the largest remnant of tallgrass—the Flint Hills region of eastern Kansas and Oklahoma—borders the drier western country. Cattle graze in the Flint Hills, but because of shallow soil, plows have scarcely touched the ground there, leaving one of the best windows to what the prairie once was.[13]

Farther west, the climate dries up and the thirsty tallgrass cannot pump enough water into its long, windblown leaves and seed stalks. So the shorter, mixed-grass prairie, with little bluestem, sideoats, grama, and wheatgrass, takes over in a north–south swath through the Dakotas, most of Nebraska, Kansas, Oklahoma, and north-central Texas. In its southern reaches, the mixed-grass prairie melds into the oaklands of central Texas and into a scratchy scrubland of juniper and mesquite. Unlike the tallgrass prairie, large reaches of mixed-grass prairie remain intact.

Slightly farther west, beyond the ninety-eighth meridian and especially in the southern reaches of the Great Plains, rainfall drops below twenty inches per year. Here, the shortgrass prairie extends to the Rockies in foot-high grasses. About 45 percent of these have never seen the plow. The blue grama, with 90 percent of its biomass power-packed in roots, has weathered cattle grazing better than most other native grasses; it constantly sprouts back after being cropped off.

These three contiguous prairies—the tallgrass, mixed-grass, and shortgrass—once covered a fifth of the entire forty-eight states and reached northward into Canada for a total domain of 500 million prairie acres, one of the largest grassland complexes on earth.[14] Yet after just a few decades of white settlement, cropland and cattle pasture reigned supreme. The tallgrass prairie became the corn belt. The mixed-grass and shortgrass prairies became the wheat and beef belts, enhanced after 1952 by 100,000 great irrigated circles of hay and a few other crops watered by center-pivot sprinklers.

Other grassland zones, some quite large, lie disconnected from the Great Plains group. Though they all grow grass, the drier western rangelands differ from the Great Plains as much as the Northern Forest differs from the Cove Hardwoods of Appalachia. Even the ownership is different; western grasslands are 75 percent publicly owned, while the Great Plains are 98 percent privately owned. Largest of the western grass provinces, the Basin and Range lies between the Rockies and the Sierra Nevada and Cascades mountain chains. Usually regarded as a desert, this "Intermountain West" grows mostly sagebrush, though hearty, deep-rooted bunchgrasses once thrived in plentiful tufts sprouting up between the shrubs. After ranchers arrived, their cattle quickly snuffed out most of the nutritious and easily targeted grasses, leaving the less palatable plants to dominate. Fire suppression has likewise favored sage, which before white settlement was charcoaled by lightning-induced blazes that benefited grass and grazing ungulates.

Spare desert grasslands also green the plateaus and plains of Arizona, New Mexico, and western Texas during the rainy seasons. The Sonoran and Chihuahuan Deserts support tobosa and black grama grass along with their more characteristic cacti. Like sage, mesquite has expanded its range where cattle have hammered the native grasses; the thorny shrub now dominates on many southwestern plains.

In the Northwest, the gloriously rolling Palouse Prairie region of Washington and Idaho once rippled in native grasses. Nearly all of it has been converted to wheat, the hills tamed with brown striations of the plow, disc, and harrow.

In California, a grassland zone covers the Central Valley and many coastal hills. Here, a Mediterranean climate delivers all its moisture in winter—a seasonality that prevents takeover by forests. Luminous in 19th-century paintings, this remains America's finest exemplar of savanna—a stunningly beautiful landscape of grasslands with well-defined patches of oaks. John Muir, who saw some country in his day, called the Central Valley savanna "a landscape . . . that after my wanderings still appears as the most beautiful I have ever beheld." Though reduced to a small share of what Muir saw, some valley oaks and blue oaks still grow to diameters of six feet amid whole grassy valleys translucently green in winter and spring, golden tan in summer and fall. Savannas depend on fire to period-ically sear the growth of seedlings and sapling trees, thereby maintaining the mix of grass and hard-wooded, fire-resistant oaks. A similar grassland accented with giant oaks graces some remaining tracts in the Willamette Valley of Oregon.

Adjoining some of these areas, chaparral communities constitute a separate but related biome. Here, often on mountainous terrain at lower elevations, grasses can be found but shrubs clearly dominate. Up to forty species branch thickly with leathery evergreen leaves, and they sink roots deep to tap groundwater during scorching dry seasons. The shrubs rarely live more than twenty-five years before crackling up in flames, an ephem-eral demise followed by vigorous new shoots.[15] Chaparral cloaks some of the Rocky Mountain foothills and slopes in the Southwest, and it clearly dominates low elevations of the Sierra Nevada and the Coast Ranges in California.

Also related to grasslands, the tundra of the Alaskan north shows a blend of sedges, mosses, lichens, forbs, grasses, and miniature birches and willows growing on permafrost—frozen ground where only the top few feet ever melt. The moil of freeze and thaw heaves up throngs of tussocks—mounds the size of basketballs—surrounded by troughs sopping with mosses and buggy water, all of it a vivid green in summer. Among other Arctic wildlife, great herds of caribou thrive on the tundra. At the Arctic National Wildlife Refuge, the Porcupine herd alone numbers up to 180,000 animals—an unruined scene of God's plenty.

While large cities, including Chicago, Minneapolis, Des Moines, Omaha, and Denver, have shot up in skyscrapers and sprawled out among freeways on the grasslands, most of the Great Plains is lightly populated. Nearly all the counties west of the ninety-eighth meridian in North Dakota, Nebraska, and Oklahoma have been losing people.[16] This is no short-term trend; North Dakota's numbers peaked in 1930. The rural Great Plains ranks right up with Appalachia as a rare region where population has dwindled in modern times.

This ghost-town trend was evident on a weeklong canoe trip I took down the Niobrara River, when on the third day I couldn't resist checking out a tumbledown barn not far beyond the riverbank. Above the weed-infested ruins of a corral, a two-story ranch house still stood, porch roof sagging, floorboards spotted with rot. The door yielded to a stiff push of my shoulder, and inside, prairie dust lay thick on everything, including an abandoned piano, half its keys mute with the lonely weathering of neglect. The rot will accelerate. The dust will pile up higher. The weeds will grow and die and, perhaps, yield to bluestem grass as nature slowly reclaims this enclave of the prairie.

Though the demographic shift started even before the dust bowl of the 1930s, new forces continue to expunge people from the Great Plains. Now, corporate boards of agribusinesses consolidate the ranches; farmers automate their agriculture, rendering much of the hand labor obsolete; and new generations seek other professions and more temperate places to live. Also prominent in the exodus is the fact that the essential resource of water has simply been used up in some areas. Farmers growing hay in the north and cotton and sorghum in the south have pumped the enormous Ogallala Aquifer so hard that this natural underground supply has been reduced from a 58-foot-thick reservoir to a mere 6-foot-deep pocket of groundwater beneath parts of Kansas.[17] While farmers pump 6 million acre-feet per year out of this resource ostensibly held in common, only

185,000 acre-feet seep back in, a balance that no prudent person would allow in a checking account. At the 1990s pumping rates, irrigation and drinking supplies in a multistate area overlying the Ogallala will expire within thirty years. Facing increased pumping costs, reduced water quality, and dry wells, farmers who established new spreads during the agricultural boom of the 1970s are now abandoning them, especially in the south, where even less rainwater percolates into the aquifer because it's capped by impervious rock. In Texas, dwindling groundwater pressed farmers to idle one of every five irrigated acres in a decade.

Even with a small-town renaissance elsewhere in America, the Great Plains offers no mountain vistas, no source of jobs, and few communities with the amenities modern urbanites seek. The grassland heart of America is considered "flyover country," and that's as close as most people ever get.

Land of Lost Heart

Though open space remains, the original plant life and wildlife that defined the grasslands have been eradicated from much of their range. Natural grasslands are now among the most scarce and threatened landscapes in America. While much of the national estate may still look as if it's covered with native grasses, few acres have escaped major trauma since the time of pioneer settlement. Rarest is the tallgrass. In Illinois, Indiana, and Ohio, 99.9 percent of the original prairie has gone to corn. Nationwide, only 2 to 4 percent of the original tallgrass remains.[18] Within the mixed-grass prairie zone, 31 percent of the northern wheatgrass-bluestem-needlegrass community remains intact.[19] In the shortgrass prairie, 60 percent survives, though nearly all of it is grazed by cattle.[20] In California, native grasses can be found on only 0.1 percent of their historical range.

The National Biological Survey found several grassland types among thirty red-flagged ecosystems that have been reduced to less than 2 percent of their original area. These included the tallgrass prairie of the Midwest, the oak savannas of Oregon's Willamette Valley, the foothills of California's Coast Ranges, the Palouse Prairie of eastern Washington, and the sagebrush steppes west of the Rockies.[21] Even intact grasslands are small and severely fragmented by other land uses. Recognizing the intri-

Buffalo along the Yellowstone River. Here in Wyoming and Montana, our only free-ranging herd of bison serves as a reminder that restoration of this great animal is possible.

Mixed-grass prairie of Nebraska. In the Sand Hills region, native grasses thrive and wetlands provide habitat for waterfowl.

The Great Plains of Montana. Native grasses survive in a lightly grazed bottomland along the Missouri River.

Santa Rita Mountains, Arizona. These healthy bunchgrasses recovered after cattle grazing was reduced on dry mountain slopes.

The Sierra Nevada foothills in California. These introduced grasses have replaced all but one-tenth of one percent of the state's original, deep-rooted, nutritious grasses.

Cow in the Great Basin, Nevada. Overgrazing by cattle has reduced vast areas of the West to sagebrush, weeds, and bare soil where lush bunchgrasses once grew.

cacy of prairie plant and animal relationships and the scarcity of native tracts, ecologists Reed Noss and Allen Cooperrider call grasslands "the most endangered terrestrial ecosystem in the United States."[22]

With the loss of each piece of prairie mosaic, whether through invasion by exotic weeds, soil erosion, displacement by cows, or land development, other pieces of the ecosystem come tumbling down. The prairie dog, for example, has suffered routine poisoning because it eats grass and its tunnels are considered dangerous to cattle. Eradication programs costing $5 to $10 per acre have been subsidized but arguably yield no benefit.[23] Research shows that cattle actually prefer to graze in prairie dog colonies because grass is more nutritious there and that cattle enjoy the same rate of weight gain with or without the rodents.[24] Moreover, the "broken leg" threat that prairie dog holes pose to cattle appears to be a baseless myth.[25] Yet prairie dog numbers have been cut by 98 percent, and with that loss, mountain plovers, ferruginous hawks, and swift foxes—all dependent on the prairie dogs—have been pushed to the edge of extinction.[26] Burrowing owls have disappeared over much of their range—coincident with the eradication of prairie dog towns and ground squirrel colonies. The population of the black-footed ferret, a predator of the prairie dog, was reduced to only twenty-two individuals, making it the rarest mammal in North America. Wildlife agencies have spent $15 million to stave off the ferret's extinction while other millions of dollars are spent to eradicate the ferrets' food source.[27]

The decline of native grasslands has had many far-ranging consequences. In an unexpected twist of fate, the loss of native habitat has meant a loss of wild pollinating insects. Without insects to spread pollen from plant to plant, wildflowers fail to reproduce, leading to a downward spiral for both flowers and insects. And commercial crops also need the wild pollinators. The dwindling variety of insects could impinge on 150 crops nationwide and poses a potential loss of $5.7 billion annually to agriculture, a figure that reflects loss of production and the expense of importing pollinators to replace the once free service of wild insects that depended at least in part on wild plant life.[28]

The loss of so many grasslands to plowed fields, overgrazed range, and exotic plant invasions has also meant the loss of songbirds. In Idaho, scientists discovered a population drop among thirty-seven of thirty-nine species that nest on sagebrush plains. Bird numbers plummeted by nearly a third in the decade following 1985. "We have continual habitat loss and degradation," said ecologist Terry Rich of the Bureau of Land Management (BLM) in 1990. At that time, the agency estimated that 60 percent of Idaho's original 29 million acres of sagebrush steppe had been converted to agriculture. Rich added, "Shrub steppes and grasslands are the habitat most susceptible to being wiped out completely."[29] The grim news repeats itself in other grassland regions. Scientists with the North American Breeding Bird Survey reported in 1998 that 83 percent of grassland bird species throughout America had diminished since 1966.[30] Grassland birds had shown a steeper and more widespread downturn than had any other group.[31]

With the plowing and fencing of the Great Plains, key mammal species or races such as the lobo wolf, the Plains grizzly, Merriam's elk, and the Audubon bighorn sheep faded to extinction, a threat that continues for growing numbers of creatures. As of 1996, the count of threatened or endangered animal and plant species on the Great Plains stood at 55, and a holocaust could be looming on the horizon: 728 species had been nominated for possible listing.[32] The grasslands illustrate the need to take a broad, systemwide conservation approach to avoid the costs and conflicts of repeated, grueling battles over endangered species.

More dramatic than any other loss, the carnage of buffalo appalled people even in the 19th century.[33] Nearly gone after their intentional extermination played an explicit part in genocide during the Great Plains Indian wars, buffalo have again increased in number, but they enjoy almost no free range across the landscape whose fate was so intertwined with that of the herds. In 1902, only two dozen wild buffalo survived, by retreating into the mountain sanctuary of Yellowstone National Park. Even there, where the only sizable and continuously free-ranging herd in the United States still roams, the buffalo are being shot. When the native ungulates that ruled the Great Plains for thousands of years step across the survey line of Yellowstone's boundary, they are killed by agents of the Montana Department of Livestock, acting in concert with the U.S. Department of Agriculture's Animal and Plant Health Inspection Service and cattlemen who fear the spread of brucellosis to their stock. This disease was brought into the country by cattle and can cause abortion of cow fetuses. But records fail to show a single case of buffalo spreading the disease back to cows outside the confines of a corral.[34]

In what became known as the Yellowstone Massacre, 1,084 buffalo in search of their winter range were shot in 1997, even though the nearest cattle stood behind fences forty miles away.[35] Dead buffalo piled up just as they did in the dark ages of the 19th century, when even tourists blasted away at the shaggy, brown animals from railroad trains. Yellowstone National Park's superintendent, Michael Finley, sensibly advocated the purchase of private winter range adjoining federal land, and in 1998 officials planned to acquire a 7,850-acre parcel, though it excluded the most critical valley acreage along the Yellowstone River.

Federal and state agencies prepared an environmental study of the buffalo problem and considered limits on buffalo numbers, open range for the animals on some national forest land now dedicated to cows, vaccination of cattle and buffalo, and continued shooting of animals that try to leave the park. Only one option called for significant acquisition of the private land where the bison are trying to go. In the meantime, dead buffalo continue to provide gruesome proof that existing parks and preserves are too small to accommodate native American life. Biologist William Newmark reported that even in America's largest national parks, wildlife need 1.2 to 9.6 times the amount of land now available within protected areas.[36] Nowhere is this problem more extreme than in grasslands.

The Roots of Decline

Cattle ranching is not just the impetus for shooting Yellowstone bison but also a central cause of the loss of native grasses and their dependent menagerie of wildlife, especially in the more arid grasslands west of the Great Plains. Cows graze on about 70 percent of the acreage of the eleven western states.[37] Nationwide, an area of 841 million acres, or 37 percent of all land, is grazed by livestock.[38] This includes most grasslands and also many forests and cleared fields in the East. Pasture, without a doubt, is the dominant land use in America; the amount of acreage dedicated to beef production dwarfs all other land uses, even though red meat constitutes a shrinking portion of people's diets.

Green pastures with placid, contented cows look as if they belong on the tidy farms in temperate regions of the East and Midwest, and in fact, cattle there underpin a whole cultural landscape of mowed hay fields with fencerows and intervening woods. But the harmful effects of cattle increase dramatically in arid regions west of the Great Plains.

Unlike buffalo, which evolved on the Great Plains, cattle were first bred in the Tropics of Southeast Asia. The Herefords so emblematic of western cowboy country are in fact as British as a Cockney accent; cattlemen bred these bovines in rainy England. Genetically, cows are programmed to stay near water, and so they do. When transplanted to the arid or semiarid West, these Brits of the ungulate world linger in riparian zones, denuding vegetation, compacting soil, and caving in stream banks.[39] They bite off the same shoots of grass repeatedly, leaving the roots to die and rot. And without roots, grassland life is gone. The soil washes or blows away, and massive erosion ensues on steep slopes. With nothing holding stream-bank soil in place, creeks "downcut," or channelize within abrupt banks, causing groundwater stored in the floodplain to bleed into the newly entrenched stream. This dries out the most productive lowland areas. Having lost not only their native vegetation but also their water, the once rich grasslands are invaded by coarse brush and inedible plants.[40]

Fencing the cattle away from watercourses and allowing them access only to drinking water can solve some of the stream-related problems, but ranchers rarely fence stream corridors on the rangelands of the West. Even when free fencing material is provided to farmers, few use it because of the labor involved.

Perhaps the most insidious effect of cattle has been the introduction and spread of exotic plants imported from other hemispheres of the globe. Noxious weeds infiltrate the remotest corners of the country through hay used for cattle feed, through cow droppings that broadcast seeds widely, and by wind and water. These last two mediums are viciously effective when the seeds find a disturbed surface—such as overgrazed range or abandoned crop fields—to land on. And it's easy to find. In the Great Basin, native perennials such as bluebunch wheatgrass once sank their roots deep into the soil to find water. They kept the range green all summer and copiously provided for the wandering herds of pronghorn and other grazers. But when continuously eaten by cattle, bunchgrasses can't store energy or nourish their root systems, and they die out. Where native plants are thus subdued or where they're scraped off by earthmovers along roadsides, alien plants take over. Lacking the checks and balances of predator–prey relationships that had evolved in the Old World, where the exotic plants came from, they spread unopposed in America like viruses for which there are no antibodies.

Though the native plant community has evolved interlocking relationships for widespread mutual benefit, the exotic plants multiply into thorny, barbed, spined, and inedible monocultures of little or no value to wildlife, livestock, or people. As exotic weeds spread, winter range of deer, elk, and bighorn sheep disappears. Small mammals, critical to the food chain, die out for lack of edible plants. Alien species are the second worst threat to endangered species, affecting 46 percent of them nationwide; only the overall loss of habitat plays a greater role.[41] Eventually, even cattle can't graze on many of the areas afflicted by exotic weeds.

Exotic plants have infested 100 million acres nationwide and continue to engulf 5,000 more acres per day, with dry grasslands among the hardest-hit areas.[42] Such loss would provoke alarm if caused by fire, but this epidemic of weeds is far more devastating to wildlife and people's use of the land than fire ever was.

In the northern Great Plains, leafy spurge has taken over 3 million acres, reducing cattle productivity by half.[43] Spotted knapweed in Montana has covered 4 million acres and forces ranchers to throw up their arms and sell out for development. In Glacier National Park, knapweed has caused as many as twenty-one native plants to become rare and is still spreading like wildfire.[44] In California, plush bunchgrasses that covered a third of the state have succumbed to annuals that brown out by mid-May, resulting in an unnutritious fire hazard all summer long. Four hundred exotic species infect that state. The opprobrious star thistle alone spread from 1 million acres to 10 million and counting over the past twenty years.[45] In a span of only a few years, entire mountainsides in northwestern Idaho have faded from a green blanket of grass to an impenetrable hell of star thistle as far as the eye can see; this perverse outcome of poorly managed range makes even walking impossible on the once parklike slopes.

Owing to water requirements, the deep-rooted native sage and bunchgrasses of the West naturally grow with space between them, and because of this, the original plant communities carry fire poorly—a time-tested defense. But invading cheatgrass sprouts in dense, continuous mats and dies after just a few weeks of greening up in spring. Then it serves as a tinderbox for intense fires, which clear the land for yet further invasion by cheatgrass. This scourge of the range has seeds so sharp and barbed that they snag themselves in mucous membranes, infecting the noses and throats of wild animals and livestock alike. Cheatgrass and other exotic species have become *the* landscape that we often see when we travel west of the Great Plains.[46] Farmers and ranchers spend $5 billion per year trying to control exotic weeds; crop damage still tops $7 billion.[47]

According to biologists, much of this plague could have been minimized if cattle had been kept off the most easily damaged ranges or if their numbers had been limited to avoid gross disturbance. Once under way, the spread of the exotics might have been tempered if corrections to overgrazing on public land had been made, but ranchers opposed such limits and still do. In tandem with grazing controls, careful use of herbicides could have helped keep the invaders in check until native plants recovered. But court actions temporarily precluded government use of herbicides. Agency toxicologists now regard the application of 2,4-D and some other herbicides as an acceptable tactic to kill the troublesome weeds, which seem to pose a greater threat than does careful use of some pesticides.[48]

All is not lost; experience shows that many exotic species can be reigned in. Biological pest control offers some promise, though not without scary prospects of its own. To control tumbleweed, a spiny Russian plant that has infected western ranges since 1873, a moth from Pakistan was released in California. So far, the insect has eaten nothing but tumbleweed, and it is hoped that the moth will disappear or establish a stable coexistence with native plants and animals after consuming its host.[49] Limited use of herbicides has also shown good results; at the Snake River Birds of Prey National Conservation Area in Idaho, the herbicide Oust has killed off the cheatgrass.[50] However, hand-pulling is often the best defense; solving the exotics problem may require mobilizing armies of volunteers to take responsibility for certain territories, much as people sign up for litter removal along roads. Jerry Asher, working on weed infestations for the BLM in Idaho, estimated that most outbreaks could be contained if the agencies had as little as 15 percent of the funds now spent for fire fighting on the public lands of the West.[51]

The scale of the exotic species invasion is so massive that a national initiative is needed, supported by science and adequate funding. If even half the subsidies used to encourage logging, grazing, and mining were redirected to eradicate noxious weeds, the health of American land might be restored. In April 1998, Secretary of the Interior Bruce Babbitt called for a national strategy to begin this job.[52]

The causes of grassland loss are many, but because the public owns vast acreage west of the Great Plains, we have the opportunity to reverse this American tragedy. It's a matter of public policy. Cattle are now permitted to graze on 85 percent of the 254 million acres held by the BLM and the Forest Service.[53] One might think that with the advantage of the best available science and management carried out in a public forum at least one step removed from the profit motive, the public-land portfolio would be in good shape, serving cows without ruining ecosystems. But the General Accounting Office in 1988 reported that 60 percent of the public range was in unsatisfactory condition and little was being done to prevent overgrazing.[54] With heavy subsidies and at untold cost to wildlife, recreation, water quality, and range, the agencies allow these publicly owned grasslands to be depleted in spite of the Federal Land Policy and Management Act of 1976, which ordered the BLM to draw up plans "in a manner that will protect the quality of scientific, scenic, historical, ecological, environmental, air and atmospheric, water resource, and archaeological values." Private land of the West may be no better off; in 1987, the Soil Conservation Service (now the Natural Resources Conservation Service) estimated that 64 percent of private rangeland was in unsatisfactory condition.[55]

The cattle industry argued against restrictions, stating that western rangeland has improved since 1936, which happened to be the year when nominal federal controls were first initiated.[56] Perhaps it's not as bad as it was in the dismal era of the early 1900s, but the fact remains that nationwide, half the public range is still considered so severely degraded that even its livestock carrying capacity is reduced by half or more.[57]

Through the 1990s, the BLM came under increasing criticism, not just for the poor condition of its range but even more for administering the taxpayer subsidies that encouraged this situation. For the use of public land, cattlemen paid only $1.35 per month to feed a full-grown cow and a calf—less than it costs to feed a goldfish. Some ranchers simply subleased their federal allotments for up to five times the federal fee and then pocketed the easy profit. While a person paid ten dollars a day to bicycle in Canyonlands National Park or to sleep overnight on public land, ranchers paid five cents a day for all the grass a cow could eat and all the water it could drink, not to mention the damage done to the range and streams.

In 1993, ranchers paid the BLM $22 million in grazing fees, but it cost the agency $78 million just to administer the program. While damage to the grasslands and watercourses goes untended, the nominal fees that are collected go to improve the range for cattle; half the "improvement" funds for public range have been spent on livestock-watering facilities alone.[58]

In its defense, the beef industry contends that the costs of grazing on public land are not too low because the land is often of lesser quality than private property and that the rancher must "comply with multiple use restrictions."[59] Ann Soli, spokeswoman for the National Cattlemen's Beef Association, argued for the low fees in a 1998 interview: "We want to make these lands affordable. We want these family farmers and ranchers to stay in business. We can preserve open space that way. These were the lands no one wanted. And ranchers *improve* the land."

What is accomplished by the subsidized loss? Two percent of the feed consumed by beef cattle comes from federal land in the West.[60] More beef is produced in Florida, Georgia, Kentucky, and Tennessee *each* than in the entire nine states of the interior West.[61] In the Southeast, one cow can be fed on an acre or less, compared with the 50, 100, or 200 acres required for a cow in the arid West.[62]

Even within the West, the 24,000 permittees who graze cattle on public land represent only about 8 percent of the ranchers.[63] And a mere 0.5 percent of all western ranchers use fully half of the public grazing land, according to a General Accounting Office study conducted in 1993.[64] In other words, half of the total subsidized acreage goes to about 1,440 cattlemen. While the cattlemen's groups bring out a few likable, weathered family ranchers to make their pitch for low fees, a select group of agribusinessmen rakes in most of the subsidized prize. It's for this modicum of private gain that the health and wildlife habitat of America's dry grasslands have been traded. All of this could change with a simple act of Congress.

Most reform efforts have focused on simply raising the fees for grazing on public property so that the ranchers can be said to pay their way in a limited economic sense. Yet year after year, politicians acting on behalf of western stockmen and agribusiness block even modest fee hikes.

The federal agencies already have authority to do a better job, and conscientious BLM employees have tried to institute reforms—not attempting to eliminate cattle from public land but simply to manage them for sustainable grazing. But they've met a wall of opposition by a ranching lobby that has the ear of western politicians who, in turn, have their finger on the BLM hierarchy. They usually prevail in having reform-minded government employees transferred to outposts where they can cause no trouble.[65]

"The range specialists could do a good job of managing public land if officials higher up in the bureaucracy weren't catering so much to the requests of ranchers," confirmed Hugh Harper, who should know. Now retired from a lifelong career as a range biologist and supervisor for the BLM, Harper added, "If the provisions of the Federal Land Policy Management Act were followed, our grasslands would be restored to the health and vigor necessary to support a greater variety and abundance of vegetation that in turn would support more wildlife and livestock."[66]

The problems of cattle are not intractable, and the solutions wouldn't affect a large amount of beef or a large number of ranchers. Only about 1 in 2,000 jobs in the West is tied to federal land grazing. Even among those jobs, increased fees for the use of public land would have little negative effect on employment or the cost of beef.[67] Feasible improvements involve periodic movement of cows to allow recovery time for grasses—a pattern called rest-rotation grazing. Many range specialists argue for elimination of cattle altogether from the most arid land, which is not very productive for beef anyway. Seeing no hope where cows are fundamentally incompatible with dry ecosystems, biologists Reed Noss and Allen Cooperrider recommend elimination of cattle from rangeland where less than fifteen inches of rain falls—roughly half the public grassland west of the Rocky Mountains. For the other half, they call for rest-rotation grazing and protection of riverfronts.[68] No revolutionary proposal, the reduction would continue a long-term trend: the number of cattle in the West has fallen from a grossly overstocked 20 million a century ago to fewer than 2 million today.[69]

A 1998 lawsuit succeeded in prompting the Forest Service to remove cattle from streamside habitat in eleven national forests of Arizona and

New Mexico. Seeking to go further with reform, the Southwest Center for Biological Diversity in Tucson proposed that instead of the endless annual subsidies for grazing, the government should simply offer fair market value to ranchers who voluntarily sell their rights to graze cattle on public land. With potential to break a quarrelsome gridlock, the proposal attracted the support of many, including editors of the *Arizona Daily Star*.[70]

A lot of credit should be given to conscientious ranchers who manage their own private land well. Seeing good sense in tending their riverfront areas with care, some cattlemen are instituting excellent reforms. Voluntary programs have led to success in efforts such as The Nature Conservancy's Yampa River project in Colorado, where ranchers have fenced the waterfront and protected streams. Growing numbers of ranchers elsewhere are improving everyday practices to restore the health of riparian areas.[71] A few ranchers even employ beavers to fix their streams and lowlands. When reintroduced in places where there's still enough natural feed for them, these hardworking restoration specialists obsessively build check dams at an appropriate scale. As a result, streams stop downcutting, water tables rise, and riparian lushness returns, benefiting wildlife, water supplies, and cattle.[72]

If political and cultural hurdles can be overcome, better grazing management could go a long way toward restoring grasslands. The importance of this task can hardly be overestimated. After writing this book and after working on scores of land and water dilemmas spanning the past thirty years, I find one point very clear: among all the problems affecting the American landscape, reform of grazing practices would provide the most improvement to the land for the least total cost.

Compared with pastureland, grassland converted to cultivated crops offers far greater value to farmers but presents far greater problems to natural ecosystems. Much of the farmland in America appears as ordered open space that pleases the eye with its good purpose. But large swaths of the Midwest, California, and other regions are scarcely less affected by agriculture than if they were paved. Today's farm industry exports food to the world, but at a dear cost in long-term stability. Erosion eats away at the 10,000-year buildup of soil; a nationwide average of eight tons per cropland acre are washed or blown away each year.[73] Heavy losses of up to fourteen tons typify the corn belt, southeastern uplands, Texas, and the

Southwest.[74] In Iowa, two bushels of topsoil disappear for every bushel of corn produced—most of it cattle feed. And even when deep soil remains, loss of the finest soil on the surface of the land cuts crop yields way down. For example, on the Snake River plain of southern Idaho, still regarded as good irrigated farmland, the U.S. Department of Agriculture found a 25 percent loss of productivity and fertility owing to erosion.[75] Not even counting the loss of fertility and crops, economists estimate the off-site costs of soil erosion—such as silted-up water supplies and harbors—at $17 billion per year in 1992 dollars.[76] Unfortunately, we seem to be following a pattern of soil loss that centuries ago wrecked entire civilizations in the Middle East, Africa, Asia, and Mediterranean regions.[77] Additional problems and projected long-term declines stem from greater and greater dependence on petroleum-based fertilizers and escalating doses of pesticides.

Experience has shown that many of these problems are reversible. Time-tested soil conservation techniques can be reinstated, such as strip cropping, use of organic fertilizers, crop rotation, and restoration of wild grass on steep, erodible, and arid land that never should have been plowed in the first place.

Beyond the problems of agriculture, and with virtually no likelihood of recovery, farmland and ranchland are both being swallowed by urban growth, from the suburban fields ringing Chicago to the oak savannas of California. Land development annually consumes more than 1 million acres nationwide.[78] Statistically, each new person in the population consumes about four-tenths of an acre.[79] Seen mainly as suburban sprawl, new development targets not just farmland but the very best farmland because it's nearly flat and often close to cities that long ago sprang up to serve the original farms. More than 4 million acres classified as "prime" for agriculture were lost in the 1980s. A rare commodity, only 43 million acres nationwide are rated in the prime category. We will need this land; by the year 2050, farmers will have to feed 130 million more Americans but will have an estimated 13 percent fewer prime acres to do it with. Much of the suburbanizing acreage comes from our original grassland estate; the tract houses and strip malls represent the final transition from America's original sea of grass to the increasing ocean of sprawl.

Even in the far north, bordering the Arctic Ocean, the treeless green plains of America face the threat of deep and lasting loss. Alaska's congressional delegation pushes again and again for oil development on the 1.5-million-acre Coastal Plain of the Arctic National Wildlife Refuge, where even the most optimistic plan would supply America with oil for only six months.[80] If Congress compromises the refuge to permit the drilling, new roads, pipelines, leaking oil, and a year-round workforce would overpower one of America's wildest domains—home of tundra wolves, grizzly bears, polar bears, musk oxen, and caribou that still roam as free as the buffalo did two hundred years ago.

The Prairie Path Home

On the Great Plains, unlike the situation on most other landscapes in America, some pressures of modern times have peaked. People have come and gone. Unlike the changes imposed in other places, degradation of unurbanized grasslands need not be permanent. The opportunity exists to reclaim wild prairie wealth, especially where sod-busting hasn't yet converted pasture to plowed fields.

Both the scope of prairie problems and the scale of this grand landscape have prompted reform-minded people to think big. Biological and economic evidence points to a great possibility—one of the grandest of all for restoration of nature in America. We could bring back the buffalo.

Though the Great Plains encompass 20 percent of the land of the contiguous states, only 2 percent of the people live there—nearly all of them in cities. And more rural residents are leaving all the time.[81] Beginning with this reality, Frank and Deborah Popper proposed that a "buffalo commons" be established in drier reaches of the prairie, where the herds could once again provide an abundant source of meat for market, an industry based on buffalo tourism, and a reinvigorated life for the small towns that otherwise face desolate days. This vision of millions of acres turned back to the buffalo drew enthusiastic support from many but harsh criticism from remaining rural residents, who feared they might be relocated against their will, even though nothing in the proposal indicated that they would. Derided for being eastern university professors, the Poppers had to cancel some presentations because of death threats. Frank Popper concluded, "The image of buffalo returning to the plains appears to touch on some primal sense of Edenic rightness, or else some primal apocalyptic terror, depending on the listener."[82] But by the late 1990s, the hostilities had subsided and local groups frequently invited the Poppers to come and speak.

Though the buffalo population was reduced to only a few hundred in 1900, 140,000 buffalo again live in the United States, with another 60,000 in Canada.[83] About 20,000 of these graze on public land; the rest are on private ranches or preserves. Already, to this limited extent, the buffalo stars in a wildlife recovery success story.

Unlike docile cows, the feisty buffalo cannot be told what to do. But beyond that challenge to cowboys, these wild animals offer many advantages. They don't require hay in winter months because, unlike cattle, they push snow aside with their broad heads and live on the nutritious dried grasses of the winter plains. Unlike cattle, buffalo constantly roam, which is exactly what the Great Plains need for healthy regermination of grass and forbs. Buffalo can fight off the rare predator willing to tangle with these formidable beasts; they do not require the brutal programs of wildlife poisoning on which our government spends $35 million per year at the behest of ranchers and sheep herders.[84] Buffalo provide tasty meat, with far less fat and cholesterol and more protein than beef. They do all this without being corn-fed and without the problems of disease, wastewater, and air quality found in the industrial-scale feedlots where virtually all cattle go to be fattened. Buffalo don't need to be shot up with hormones and antibiotics, which have raised health concerns and even the banning of American beef in some European countries. Buffalo require no artificial breeding, no human-made water supplies, and no help in giving birth. And the economics of raising buffalo appear to be as superior for ranchers as the wild animals are superior for the Great Plains. Raising a buffalo might cost half as much as raising a cow, and buffalo fetch as much as twice the price; a buffalo calf commands up to four times the bid on a Hereford calf.[85]

Evidence shows that with good management, the prairie would recover if the buffalo returned. The diversity of native plant life benefits from their presence.[86] This phenomenon can be seen at the Pine Ridge Reservation in South Dakota, home of the Oglala Sioux Tribe. Exotic grasses there had taken over after a century of cattle grazing, but when the Indians reintroduced buffalo, native grasses began to return.[87] With the buffalo, the endangered black-footed ferret and burrowing owl will find the habitat they need to rise again.

The Great Plains once supported 50 million to 60 million buffalo. Some of this land has been converted to wheat fields, but author Richard Manning pointed out an interesting fact in his book *Grassland*. Today, with an impoverished prairie, with costly irrigation and water supplies, with tens of millions of tax dollars wasted every year on killing predators, with the degradation of virtually every watercourse, with hundreds of thousands of miles of wildlife-entangling fence to maintain, with total ranching and farming subsidies topping billions of dollars per year in the prairie states alone, and with dependence on a runaway chemical industry pumping out pesticides, fertilizers, and artificial hormones all destined for our water supplies, only 46 million cattle are now raised on the same Great Plains.[88]

Leading the way to the future through the wisdom of the past, Indian tribes are reintroducing the buffalo. At the Fort Belknap Reservation in Montana, Native Americans have raised a herd of 300. The animals are killed for religious and ceremonial purposes and are eaten, and the herd coincidentally draws 6,000 tourists per year. Nationwide, forty-two tribes keep about 8,000 buffalo. Some, such as the Cheyenne River Sioux Tribe, are adding to their land base by slowly buying back acreage for bison. Pointing out the importance of this task, Butch Denny of the Santee Sioux Tribe said, "Whatever happens to the buffalo happens to us. If the buffalo are well, then so will we be. For years we were dependent on them and now we feel they are dependent upon us to bring them back."

The most ambitious among hundreds of private buffalo ranches, media mogul Ted Turner's 100,000 acres in Montana support 3,350 of the handsome animals, which are raised for profit. By aggressively attacking exotic weeds and by turning the range over to the buffalo, Turner has enabled his grasslands to begin recovering. In addition to the buffalo, the ranch supports a host of other wildlife. Biologists, however, estimate that a million acres are needed to reinstate a wild prairie ecosystem. For the great herds to return, action at a large scale is required.[89]

With a strategy for doing this, University of Oklahoma geographer Bret Wallach has proposed that the federal government make contracts available to interested ranchers and farmers in lightly populated reaches of the Great Plains to reseed their land in prairie grass. In exchange, they would be paid the value of crops or pasture that would otherwise be grown. At the end of fifteen years, the government would buy the ranches, except for a forty-acre homestead on each where the family could stay. Thus, permanent prairie restoration would be possible for a onetime expense and could end the draining off of billions of taxpayer dollars in crop-support subsidies that have been paid year after year for decades.

Retirement of 4 million acres in the wheat belt of Kansas—far higher in value than most of the buffalo prairie—would require a onetime cost of $3.2 billion, according to Wallach, less than the cost of one new aircraft carrier.[90] In comparison, federal subsidies for farmers nationwide peaked in 1986 at $25 billion per year, with half the benefits going to operations making more than $100,000 annually.[91] And in the ten Great Plains states, federal subsidies far exceed the U.S. average.[92] By one estimate, federal expenditures to support grazing in ten western states totaled $1 billion per year.[93]

A buffalo commons program with participation of Great Plains residents and Indian tribes could be a welcome reorientation of federal farm expenditures. Geographer Wallach reflected, "The prairie-restoration project sounds outrageous until it's compared with what we've already got, which is the continuing prospect of an abandoned agricultural landscape, weeds surrounded by fence, largely held by speculators and distant absentee owners. We have an opportunity here as unique as the one facing the founders of the National Forest System in Teddy Roosevelt's time."[94]

A fine precedent for the buyback proposal dates back to the Great Depression, when the National Resources Planning Board recommended buying as much as 75 million acres of dust bowl land and returning it to native grasses. Eleven million acres were actually bought, a New Deal bailout that converted dusty, windblown acreage into today's national grasslands. Cattle grazing remains the dominant use on those prairies.[95]

To move toward a buffalo commons, author Ernest Callenbach proposed that funds for the Conservation Reserve Program (CRP) be reassigned to acquisition of choice buffalo land. The CRP started after a 1981 Department of Agriculture study found that farmers were cultivating 101 million acres of highly erodible land.

To retire cultivation on this acreage, taxpayers were shelling out $1.7 billion per year for temporary rest of land enrolled in the program. The government paid farmers $374 to $814 per acre for a ten-year period to plant grass instead of crops. But to buy the same land outright and protect it permanently would have cost only $138 per acre in the buffalo country of Wyoming and $358 per acre in North Dakota.[96] A diseconomy that no prudent investor would buy into, the CRP has perversely resulted in farmers sod-busting previously unplowed areas in order to collect subsidies when they *stop* plowing them, absurdly destroying good prairie in the process. And in spite of farmers' seeding of grass, many of the idled acres lack the required restoration and grow mostly weeds.

Buying out farmers who are already retiring their land from crop production could save the taxpayers money, protect the land, and provide for a needed transition in the Great Plains economy, where farmers are going out of business anyway but with no alternative except an apartment in town. Voluntary buyout agreements could allow rural residents to remain on their land with their homes intact, but this kind of thinking still ignites a sense of paranoia among landowners who support the subsidy programs the way they are and fear they would be forced from their homes when people start talking about buffalo.

If restoration of buffalo to parts of the shortgrass prairie has merit, it does not imply any failure of the pioneering farmers and their descendants. It simply means that the times, once again, have changed. Under the weight of many forces, the rural population has shrunk. Much of the land was too dry or erodible for long-term farming from the start. Bringing back the bison could present a new opportunity for the people of the Great Plains, a solution to complex problems of the prairie landscape, and a welcome relief from the long-term subsidy bills levied on taxpayers. And beyond all this, the idea of returning buffalo to the Great Plains just seems right. As Ernest Callenbach so eloquently wrote, "Bison fit the western landscape, with its sweeping expanses, its pitiless winters, its austere beauty. In their powerful, shaggy profile, in their ability to forage over limitless areas, find food under the snow, and endure blizzards, bison have always belonged in the West."

Growing Grass Again

While the effort to reestablish a buffalo commons catches the public imagination, people have taken definite strides in protecting and restoring grasslands across America. Prairie conservation had a modest start early in the 1900s, when the government set aside several blocks of grassland. In North and South Dakota, 70,000 acres became Theodore Roosevelt National Park, surrounded by a million acres of the Little Missouri National Grassland. Other tracts administered by the National Park Service include the well-known 244,000-acre Badlands and the 28,000-acre Wind Cave National Park in South Dakota, where a buffalo herd roams on one of the finest restored prairies.

Though these swaths of mixed-grass prairie have long been safeguarded, the tallgrass prairie remains America's only major ecosystem not represented in the National Park System. That's ironic because the first appeal for a national park came from artist George Catlin, who in 1834 called for "a great nation's park," not on the plateau of the Yellowstone or in the groves of giant sequoia trees but on the Great Plains.[97] Picking up the ball a century later, conservationists proposed park status for the Flint Hills of Kansas in the 1970s, but the idea was crushed by ranchers who feared their land might be condemned.

In an era when the federal agencies don't have funds to initiate new programs and when rural people embattle themselves against government (except for the subsidy programs), private action has protected and restored some important grasslands. Without the enmity accompanying the Flint Hills case in Kansas, a rancher in northeastern Oklahoma offered his property for sale as a park. Other landowners followed suit, and in 1987 the Oklahoma congressional delegation introduced a bill to create a tallgrass prairie national preserve in the Osage Hills.[98] The legislation failed, but The Nature Conservancy later established a 36,000-acre preserve in the area and reintroduced buffalo. Working on a larger canvas, the Conservancy's Great Plains project has acquired land and easements and promoted "biodiversity while maintaining the economic viability of local communities."[99] The group uses some of its land for buffalo, but seeking to build alliances with ranchers in order to encourage better range management, it still leases large tracts for cattle.

Also working with rural communities, the Great Plains Partnership of the Western Governors' Association draws together many groups and strives to spur voluntary efforts to mend the grasslands.[100] Chairman E. Benjamin Nelson, governor of Nebraska, said, "The solution starts with intent and commitment. It continues with a full understanding of the rich bioregional history of the Great Plains. It builds on the best available science. . . . Finally, it requires that private landowners get involved." Working for cooperation in this bottom-up process, Jo Clark of the Great Plains Partnership stressed the importance of the proper approach among Great Plains residents. "The concept of stewardship resonates strongly; ecosystem management does not."

Part of prairie management, no matter who the owner, involves fire. Functioning prairies require it as nature's way to battle invading brush, reinvigorate native plants, and process organic nutrients. Without regular fires—common following lightning strikes—some prairie vegetation fails to flower or produce fruit and seeds, especially in the tallgrass zone.[101] As part of the growing movement for grasslands restoration, landowners have started to reinstate fire at sites large and small.

In the 1970s and 1980s, citizens showed interest not only in protecting remaining unspoiled tracts of grassland but also in the challenging job of restoration. When a nuclear power plant proposed outside Des Moines, Iowa, fell victim to the economic collapse of the industry, the U.S. Fish and Wildlife Service acquired the site and set about converting abandoned cornfields to tallgrass. Volunteers enlisted to collect wild seeds and sow the beginnings of a new prairie called the Walnut Creek Preserve. Two years later, the grass grew tall above an understory of forty native plant species.

Expanding on the idea, Dr. Robert Betz of Northeastern Illinois University led efforts to rebuild 1,000 acres of prairie at Batavia. Nearby, Steve Packard was inspired by a slice of original prairie and organized volunteers to eradicate weeds, burn small tracts, collect wild seeds, and reestablish grasslands at a dozen sites along the North Branch of the Chicago River.[102] The program grew into the Chicago Wilderness Partnership, involving hundreds of volunteers and thousands of acres of land owned by various groups and government agencies dedicated to restoring prairie and savanna land.

While saving farmland is not saving grassland, conversion of farms to subdivisions and shopping malls is the terminal step in the process of open space loss—the houses are the last crop. Furthermore, every acre of prime farmland downgraded to suburbia eventually leads to one or more acres of unfarmed grassland being sod-busted in the future. Therefore, saving prime farmland saves grassland in addition to guaranteeing a food supply that most Americans take for granted. The American Farmland Trust, at the forefront of efforts to protect agricultural land, buys easements to curb the loss. More than a million acres have been protected. And other strategies can help as well. Taking the regulatory approach in fighting the force of urbanization, nine California cities in 1997 adopted ballot-box initiatives to contain sprawl and to keep prime soils in agriculture.

Throughout America's grasslands, tens of thousands of residents own smaller plots, from Ohio to Colorado, from North Dakota to Texas, and also in the Great Basin, the Southwest, the Palouse Hills, and the Central Valley of California. Though these landowners cannot bring back a whole ecosystem on their own, they can restore vestiges of prairie, nurturing the native plants for the benefit of birds, wildlife, and people.

Consider the work of author Gene Logsdon, who restored a prairie at his own farm in Ohio, repaired his creek, reintroduced native plants, and revitalized his tired soil. Reflecting on his experience, he wrote about the elusive but essential quality of hope: "If millions of humans join those of us already at this task, we can change the countryside and even most parts of the city into a patchwork of Edenic garden farms supporting a stable, sustainable society in local environments so full of natural and domestic wonder, peace, and plenty that retreats to distant vacationlands would become unnecessary."[103]

Evolution of a Vision

Conservation in America was born at scenic archetypes such as Niagara Falls, Yellowstone, and the giant sequoias of the Sierra Nevada. It also started with efforts to safeguard water supplies, as in the Adirondack Mountains, protected by the New York legislature as "forever wild" in 1894. It grew into a movement to preserve national parks as gemstones of landscape, mostly in mountain terrain, and to protect and steward forests, especially the old-growth remnants, from Heart's Content in the Allegheny National Forest of Pennsylvania to the Headwaters redwoods of California.

The land protection movement expanded to embrace the habitat of fish and wildlife at the Upper Mississippi River National Wildlife and Fish Refuge, at duck reserves along the flyways, at grizzly bear strongholds such as Glacier National Park, and at the spotted owl haunts in the northwestern woods. But little was done for the most outstanding icon of American wildlife—the buffalo.

Because of its less spectacular scenery, along with early and systematic settlement by farmers and ranchers who left few plots unturned, the conservation movement has only peripherally touched the grassland interior of our country. Even deserts—the quintessential "wastelands"—have received more attention, owing to their stark beauty and public ownership. But the time for prairies has now come, with a growing interest in the buffalo, with preserves being established by private and public stewards, and with individuals restoring farms and even fenced-in backyards across the grassland heart of America.

When I stood on the hill above the Niobrara River watching the lush grasslands rippling in waves of green, enjoying that first great prairie experience of my life while a thunderstorm approached, I saw a view of the past. But perhaps I saw the future as well.

CHAPTER 4

THE GREAT, SILENT DESERT

T HE CONTRAST of life in a universe of rock and sand lay before me, and the arid scene commanded a new respect for simple survival. There wasn't *much* life—not compared with that of a forest or a prairie—but it was tenacious and vibrant, adapted to some of the harshest conditions on earth. What it lacked in biomass it made up for in a remarkable success of genetic selection. A claret cup cactus lay close to the ground, spiny and defensive, but it bloomed with scarlet flowers so showy, so bright, so festive that I could see them a quarter mile away. More important, the broad-tailed hummingbirds also spotted the claret cups and wasted no time in feeding on their nectar and pollinating the flowers. The saturated tissues inside the cactus stored water for the intensely hot and rainless season to come. Spines shielded the plant from paws, claws, teeth, and the soles of my boots. Who wants to risk being painfully impaled?

The heat of the desert impressed me next, and with it, my thirst. Though the clear April night had been cool, the rising sun flamed on the horizon like a golden furnace-ball; by mid-morning it had crisped me until I longed for shade. I could find it on the crusty backsides of boulders, some scooped out in a process called cavernous weathering—moisture adheres to the shady underside, where it freezes and thaws, popping tiny grains of rock loose, one at a time. But even that diminutive shelter narrowed to a sliver of almost nothing as the sun—hotter by the minute—arced to midday heights.

I needed to drink water, though its scarcity tempted me to save and save, the way the kangaroo rat does, almost never drinking. But that wouldn't work for me. I would suffer a vicious headache, sweat, turn red, eventually quit sweating, heat up even more, become delirious, succumb to seizures, lapse into a coma, and hike no more. Here in the sun and heat, people need up to a gallon of water a day even if they don't move much. On the hottest days, a person can lose as much as three gallons. So I drank when I felt thirsty. Eventually I would reach Salt Creek, where the water is better than its name would lead you to believe, and where I would refill my bottles after filtering from a pool. But the water was not yet in hand, so traveling in the desert put me on the edge. Fur-trapping explorer Jedediah Smith, who endured plenty of hardships elsewhere, called the American drylands "a country of starvation." Like him, I had little security and felt the power of the place in my belly. Realizing how difficult it is to live in this desert, I was humbled by the life around me.

Not just knowing about my dependence on water but also feeling it on my epidermis and in my throat was fundamental to reckoning with the terms of life in that dry place. The earth lay so exposed in bare-bone rock and soil that it looked undressed. Lacking the furry green shield of trees and shrubs, the bald skin of the planet was revealed, pure and simple. This, I thought, is what underlies the juicy-leafed mantle of the Appalachians where I grew up, the lemon-scented fir forests where I've lived in the Sierra Nevada, the Englemann spruce and sagebrush terrain where I winter in Wyoming. The desert's patterns of fracture and fault line, of mass wasting and wind weathering, of travertine deposit and dune migration—all of it lay bared to see, raw to the wind and sun, exposed to my eyes and feet.

As the afternoon wore on and the sun dipped toward the horizon, the

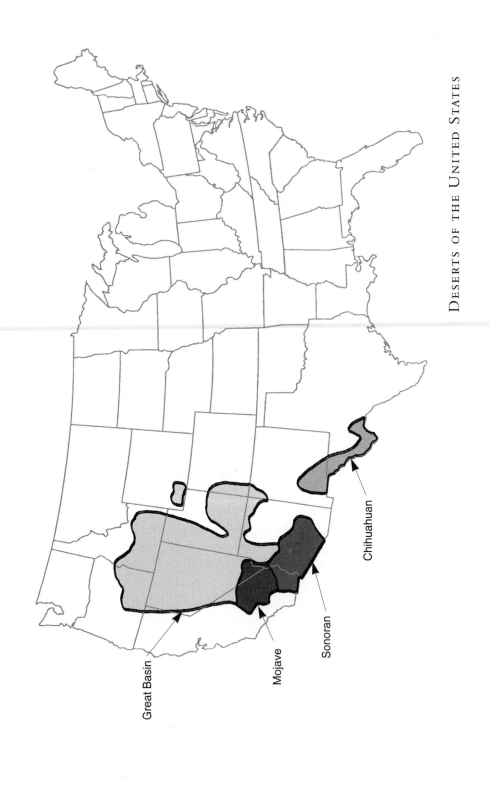

Great Basin

Mojave

Sonoran

Chihuahuan

golden light took over, casting a warm yellow glow on sandstone, throwing long blue shadows across the ground. It spotlighted the green of the junipers with a new vibrancy; it colored distant mountains purple as on calendar photos of the mythic West; it beamed up every grain of roughness. Finally, the light faded and only the silence remained. It had been quiet all day long, but now, at twilight, the silence penetrated so deeply that it seemed as if no other world existed. No wind brushed the rocks, no bird called to its mate, no water gurgled across stone, no saltbush rustled in the breeze, no airplane jetted overhead, no person said a word. The ringing in my ears was the only noise I heard. Because of the bigness of the space—twilight views stretching out across miles of rock, bluff, and plain—the silence seemed so improbable. In all that space there ought to be a noise, but instead everything lay still. Silence at that scale makes me think of forever. Range beyond purple range seemed to go on without end. There in the desert, silence and simplicity describe a terrain found nowhere else.

My seven-day hike took me to some deep recesses of Canyonlands National Park. There, at the midst of the Colorado Plateau, I strolled across slickrock—slabs of sandstone big enough to play baseball on. The hard, clean surface allowed free-form travel. Exquisite scenes delighted me, sometimes in perfectly composed frames of earth and sky, sometimes in abstract swirls of color, in sorted textures of stone, in bizarre twists of rock and life sharing an interwoven existence.

Unlike the case when hiking in thick woodlands, I could go almost anywhere. Yet two rules of travel restricted me. First, I needed to avoid microbiotic crust. This covering of lichens and algae caps much of the desert soil. A rough, blackened, upraised layer as thick as grass on a mowed lawn, but composed of miniature stalagmite-like columns that look like dirt, the microbiotic crust absorbs rainfall and traps it in place, preventing rapid runoff. The crust establishes a suitable home for bacteria that break down organic matter and minerals so they can be absorbed by plants. It also captures nitrogen from the air and incorporates it into the soil for use by plants. It provides microshelter from wind and sun and a hospitable bed for seeds of grasses and forbs. Its presence indicates health of the desert floor. Until recently, few people thought much about microbiotic crust in the desert; they traveled at random and turned cattle loose by the thousands to trample the crust in broad, disabling swaths as wide as cows can roam. But all that was like withdrawing money from the desert's savings account of soil and plant life. A damaged crust requires many years to heal. To avoid destroying it, I stepped from stone to stone, favored rocky outcrops, and hiked in the washes that become choked with rainwater like molten mud during flash floods but offer sandy boulevards when dry, which is almost all the time. While those tiny lichens threw up micro-barriers to travel, my other restriction was the lay of the land, which directed me at the macro scale. Long plateaus of slickrock could terminate in thousand-foot drop-offs or thousand-foot climbs, and I adjusted my route accordingly.

Life, heat, thirst, light, and silence—they all governed my emotions, but desert exploration involves much more than these. The view of wide-open country from the plateaus and mesa tops made me feel exuberant and free. The adventure pulled me along as I strode across rocky table-lands, scrambled up sandstone sliding boards, ascended to headwalls that nearly enclosed me. Spacious terraces of the Colorado Plateau shone so golden at times that it seemed they could melt. Like the prairie, this was big-sky country, and puffballs of white clouds ornamented a dome of blue, floating overhead as silent as weightless rocks.

Rain had fallen recently, and the sandstone collected some of the water in puddles, where evaporation immediately went to work. The rarest of commodities here, water might not be found at all during other months of the year. Yet from some high perches in Canyonlands, you can gaze thousands of feet down to the mother of water sources, the Colorado River. This and all desert rivers, except for ephemeral streams that flash flood once in a while, originate someplace else—in distant mountains, where the peaks accumulate snow and rake off rain to produce waterways with momentum enough to survive the desert journey, almost undiminished until the water is sucked into pipelines and canals for farms and cities. The desert is dramatically shaped by these rivers, which concentrate erosive power at their shorelines and sculpt steep-walled canyons. Wind, rock slides, earthquakes, volcanoes, and lava flows also mold the desert into the land we see.

During my weeks and months of exploring and living in the desert, the sun's low points at dawn and dusk made the two high points of each day—two hours of rapturous beauty. First light offered the slightest softening of the night's blackness, otherwise touched only by the gleam of stars. Pale blue then grew on the eastern horizon, and the silhouettes of giant rocks appeared, egg shaped, square cut, or distended in bulbs and swellings. Then the sky lightened to robin's egg blue, streaked with orange clouds that caught the light smearing up at their undersides. The orange on the horizon intensified in a relentless buildup until the fiery arc of the sun's upper edge seared into the horizon line, announcing the new day.

Twelve hours later, the sunset flared in orange and red on the belly of a big cloud, rays zapping the landscape and throwing long purple shadows with ink-sharp edges out across textured ground. This climax of the day was followed by a shiver of darkness, and the first stars included a few that not only twinkled but also sparkled with blue, orange, and purple explosions of light when seen through binoculars. The earth's heat radiated out into space because there was no cloud cover and little humidity to hold the warmth in, and the rocks cooled quickly in this land of extremes, where a fifty-degree difference between day and night was commonplace.

Fully dark some hours after sunset, the nighttime desert swallowed me into its spacious gut. Even then, this land held me in its thrall of contrast; what had been glaring and hot now lay black and cool. Silent by night as well as by day, it seemed so empty. But cautiously walking across the rock surface, feeling my way along with silhouette statues and starlit mysteries all around, I knew that the desert, like every landscape, was in fact full. If it seemed otherwise, it was only because I lacked the knowing eye and the understanding to appreciate this enigmatic place that at once repels people and draws them to its heart.

The Nature and Use of the Desert

Take away the forests, grasslands, chaparral, tundra, and wetlands, and the deserts are what's left. They miss out on the universal love people express for woodlands, mountains, and rivers. In fact, deserts have taken the brunt of landscape discrimination. Speaking for many people in the mid-1800s, statesman Daniel Webster asked, "What do we want with this vast, worthless area? To what use would we ever put it?"

Mountains once shared similar disdain when genteel passengers aboard stagecoaches in the Alps blindfolded themselves to avoid exposure to the hideous scene.[1] And forests certainly absorbed their share of opprobrium during the early settlement of America, when the dismal, haunted woods were considered a barrier to civilization. Even worse, early settlers equated wetlands with evil. For most people, those biases passed long ago, yet prejudice against deserts is still a real thing.

Even so, a growing core of inspired worshipers now champion this landscape. Deserts appeal to the spiritual, artistic, and mystical sides of many people. Books of essays about most of the other landscapes are uncommon, but a stack of them have been published about the desert, by authors from Mary Austin and Joseph Wood Krutch to Edward Abbey, Terry Tempest Williams, and Bruce Berger. The stark simplicity of this landscape evokes strong expression, and feelings about the desert are as extreme as the conditions of the land itself.

The ambivalence about deserts poses no great mystery. It's difficult to live there. Plant life lacks the soothing depth of green found in forests and grasslands. Wicked thorns await at every turn, and going barefoot even for a step or two is completely out of the question. The tallest trees might be ten-foot acacias or junipers, more often three-foot sagebrushes or creosote bushes. Heat parches membranes and dust clogs airways. But the deserts have a life of their own, extraordinary in its tenacity and its adaptation to dryness, heat, and cold. And who cannot respect the ability of desert life to survive where we—without a supply line all the way back to the factory where plastic water jugs take shape—would fail?

To consider just one marvel of adaptation, look at the Coachella Valley fringe-toed lizard, a creature few people ever see. In the Mojave Desert, this eight-inch, earth-toned, cold-blooded crawler exists entirely in wind-blown sand, where it literally swims underground to escape 180-degree temperatures on the surface and to evade its predators—roadrunners, loggerhead shrikes, burrowing owls; and whip snakes. Its streamlined jaw, clamped shut, cuts a path through the sand. Smooth scales reduce friction. Sharp grippers on its feet propel the lizard along. One-of-a-kind nostrils allow it to breathe from the diminutive pockets of air between grains of sand. Eyelids overlap for obvious reasons, and a "third eye" lies on top of its head, sensitive to light, sound, and vibrations, including those that indicate the presence of insects—the lizard's prey. The third eye also monitors heat and tells the reptile when to burrow deeper underground for its own life's sake. Because urban development has preempted its habitat, this singular animal is classified as threatened under the Endangered Species Act.

Flora and fauna of every landscape adapt wondrously to local conditions, but the desert adaptations seem especially ingenious, perhaps because the desert is so hostile to *us*. Spines and prickles make plants less appetizing to wildlife. Abbreviated leaves, waxy leaves, leathery leaves, or leaves that drop following the briefest of growing seasons cut evaporative losses, whereas broadleaf plants would transpire too much water and then die. We call some plants succulents because they hold water within bladderlike leaves nearly impervious to air, enabling the plant to stockpile fluid when it's available. Perfecting another strategy, saguaro cacti secrete a waxy surface on the side of the trunk that faces the sun; if transplanted, the cacti need to be oriented correctly, just as we rotate a Christmas tree until its ragged side faces the wall. Similarly adapted, Joshua trees store one-fourth of their annual water supply in their trunks; picture a long, lean, contorted, green, spiny living water barrel. Creosote bushes sprout leaves that shrivel and blacken in drought but then reincarnate themselves when it rains. The green woody stems of the paloverde tree carry on 40 percent of the plant's photosynthesis without the help of leaves.

Lying in warmer climes, the southern deserts in particular host an extraordinary diversity of life. Even in the place we call Death Valley, 900 kinds of plants live. Some grow only a few feet high but sink their roots fifty feet underground to mine water. Many desert plants have nine times as much biomass underground as above. They need that much support simply to weather the tribulations of dry air.

While desert life is different because the landscape requires extreme adaptations on the part of anything living there, the isolation of habitat also engenders a highly local brand of endemism. Mountains here are landlocked by arid valleys, and the valleys are conversely isolated from one another by the mountains, resulting in unusual if not unique communities of life. Rivers and lakes, as another example, once watered the lowlands during the ice ages, and now, in the wetlands that remain, creatures such as Nevada's Amargosa toad have evolved into distinct species or races within their own private ponds. Freshwater springs in the desert support rare pupfish remaining from the Pleistocene epoch. The Cottonball Marsh pupfish, hardier than it sounds at 200 feet below sea level, survives in pools of water five times as salty as the ocean.[2]

The deserts are home to an array of native American plants and animals, and now people are also adapting in their technological way. Virtually synonymous with the western Sun Belt, the Southwest has been a hot spot of urban growth since World War II. Mild winters and dependable sunshine draw retirees and newcomers by the hundreds of thousands each year. In the 1980s and 1990s, a population boom likewise occurred in the dryland towns of the interior West—Salt Lake City and Boise, for example. While these cities abut the Rocky Mountains, they sit at the mountains' base and are really desert towns; any unwatered plot passes the litmus test of turning brown in no time. These booming cities grow as nodes of modern Americana, but remote reaches of desert worldwide have also appealed to a wide range of people seeking the back eddies of society, from religious leaders including Jesus and Mohammed to clannish bands of mystics; from saints to outlaws; from artists such as Georgia O'Keeffe extolling the land to hardscrabble miners defacing the same land; from solitary cowboys on horseback to rock climbers jammed into Volkswagen buses and retired sunbirds lined up with designer awnings shading their Winnebago yachts. The desert is a refuge for them all, and with its outlaw heritage, whether in the genial reputation of Butch Cassidy or the twisted horror of Charles Manson, it attracts more than its share of adherents to the idea that individuals have a right to do anything they want. People can get away with doing almost anything, legal or illegal, because they don't get caught in this remote land. It's still a frontier in the worst sense of the word.

The desert has its uses, admirable and otherwise. But most of all, with an appeal that reaches out to people from all walks of life, the space and silence offer relief from the hum of cities. Urban complications stand in sharp contrast to the elegant simplicity and broad sweep of a silent sunset in places such as the Owyhee Canyonlands, the Kaiparowits Plateau, and Cabeza Prieta National Wildlife Refuge, each a part of the great American desert even though each is a creation of different climate, geography, and natural circumstance.

The Geography of Dryness

Creations of the mountains, the deserts of America lie mostly in rain shadows of the high peaks. To picture what this means, one must start in the ocean, where prevailing westerly winds whisk up a lot of moisture and carry it from the Pacific to the West Coast and inexorably eastward.

Mountain slopes of the Coast Ranges, the Sierra Nevada, and the Cascade Range force the air upward, cooling and condensing it, which causes it to fall as rain or snow. This leaves less moisture for inland areas. But more important, the land east of the Pacific ranges lies lower than the mountains, and when the air descends, it's rewarmed and thereby holds on to whatever moisture it still contains. That's why most of our deserts exist. The rain shadow is boldly evident in the huge intermountain territory of the West. Then, as the air passes over the Rockies, it's again forced high enough to squeeze out additional moisture. East of the Rockies and in their subsequent rain shadow, the Great Plains also has a dry climate, but it's spared desert status because of moderating moisture leaking up in swirls of humid air from the Gulf of Mexico.

Globally, deserts account for 14 to 33 percent of the earth's land surface, depending on the definition.[3] Unlike typical American drylands, where aridity is largely caused by rain shadows of mountains, most of the world's deserts occur in two belts, one lying roughly fifteen to thirty degrees north of the equator and the other commensurately south of it. There, wind currents stemming from the earth's rotation and higher temperatures at the equator cause nearly permanent high-pressure zones that push away clouds. This phenomenon affects only the most southern deserts in America.

As a general rule of thumb, land with less than 10 inches of precipitation per year is considered a desert, though both rainfall and evaporation affect aridity. A more thorough definition includes areas where rainfall is balanced or exceeded by evaporation.[4] Central Alaska sees yearly precipitation of 10 inches or less, yet its green tundra is sopping in wetlands all summer long. Evaporation there happens to be low, and permafrost prevents water loss through seepage. In contrast, portions of the Southwest and southern California enjoying 15 inches of rain can truly describe a dusty desert because of high evaporation in the hot, sunny climate. In the extreme case of Death Valley, the annual evaporation rate exceeds precipitation by a whopping 120 inches—enough to vaporize a ten-foot-deep lake if by some miracle one existed.

Unlike America's other landscape types, the deserts adjoin one another in a nearly contiguous belt rather than being scattered around the country as are mountains, forests, wetlands, and to some extent grasslands. Covering about 500,000 square miles, or 14 percent of the country, the desert complex extends across all or parts of nine states, from the Columbia Plateau of eastern Oregon southward through southern Idaho, southwestern Wyoming, Nevada, much of Utah, one-fifth of California, parts of Arizona and New Mexico, and southwestern Texas.[5]

Mountains rise within much of the desert area. Some of these jut up high enough to catch snow and rain, enabling the growth of forests, grasses, or chaparral amid the desert sea, just like islands ringed by ocean. But much of the desert region is flatland, plateau, hill, or plain. Perhaps owing to movies set in the Sahara, sand dunes form a popular image of deserts. Though sand dunes do cover 20 percent of deserts globally, they account for only 1 percent of the arid land in America. Here, most deserts are, rather, a dry version of scrubland or grassland, and the characteristics of life overlap with those of these other biomes.

Reflecting the long-held notion of deserts as wasteland, publicly owned acreage accounts for more of the desert than any other landscape. The reason is simple: homesteaders didn't claim the land because they couldn't survive there. In the Mojave Desert of southern California, 20 million of 26 million acres remain in public ownership. But given the difficulty of living there and the bankrupting costs of importing water, it's amazing that any sizable acreage was claimed for private ownership at all.

A Desert of Changing Form

Four principal desert types interlock in the West. Ecologist Forrest Shreve mapped these in 1942, not according to underlying geology and landforms—which change and overlap among the deserts—but by the plants that grow there.[6] Rainfall, elevation, and latitude influence this botany. To the north lies the Great Basin Desert, typified by nineteen species of sagebrush and also home of greasewood, rabbitbrush, and bitterbrush, while juniper and pinyon pepper the mountainsides. This is the largest desert and by far the coldest, with subzero temperatures in winter. Most of the land rises above 4,000 feet, and a few peaks top a lofty 13,000.

The Great Basin Desert includes four distinct areas. Northernmost, the 50,000-square-mile Columbia Plateau resulted from massive lava flows, later cut by steep-walled canyons. Though grassland steppe best describes this zone, much of it receives less than ten inches of rain per year, and it looks like a desert. South of the Columbia Plateau lies the 210,000-square-

Green River, Utah. This and other waterways carve spectacular canyons into desert plateaus and through dry mountain ranges.

Saguaro forest in Arizona. These cacti are typical of the Sonoran Desert, our richest in plant life.

Joshua trees, California. This keystone species of the Mojave Desert is critical to many wildlife species in the Southwest.

Death Valley, California. This harsh section of the Mojave Desert is part of our largest national park outside Alaska and home to 900 kinds of plants.

Suburban Phoenix, Arizona. New roads, homes, and commercial development are consuming desert acreage at a rapid rate near Sunbelt cities.

Fortynine Palms Oasis, Joshua Tree National Park. Groundwater flows that create many oases in the Mojave Desert are disappearing because of pumping for land development.

mile expanse of the Basin and Range Province.[7] This encompasses the lion's share of Nevada, the driest state. Paralleling mountain ranges, most of them one ridge wide, alternate with broad alluvial fans and flat, land-locked valleys. Here, too, the Great Salt Lake sprawls amoebalike across northwestern Utah with its adjacent desert, as white as salt from the shaker. On the eastern edge of the Great Basin Desert, lobes of the Rocky Mountains isolate the 12,000-square-mile Wyoming Basin, in the south-western corner of that state. A high, cold territory of sagebrush, it in-cludes mineralized hills called the Red Desert. In the final section of the Great Basin Desert, red and orange sandstone accounts for the impressive 125,000-square-mile Colorado Plateau. This may be the most photogenic of deserts, with its incomparable landforms. Arches National Park in Utah features sandstone eroded by the soft but timeless force of wind. River-carved to an extreme, Canyonlands National Park shows off spec-tacular desert scenery. The Grand Canyon of the Colorado River also falls within this desert, though its plant life mixes with that of the south.

The Mojave Desert adjoins the Great Basin. Smallest of the four deserts, its 50,000 square miles run southward toward the international boundary and eastward to the Colorado River.[8] The Mojave borders the urban maw of southern California and surrounds Las Vegas, Nevada. Hot-ter than the Great Basin and with rainfall coming mostly in late winter, the Mojave is distinguished by the Joshua tree, which sports a woody trunk as much as a foot in diameter and dagger-shaped leaves. Many species associate with the keystone Joshua tree, including a genus of moth called *Tegeticula*. The female collects the tree's pollen and carries it to other flowers, fertilizing them when she lays her eggs inside the flowers' ovaries. When the moth's larvae hatch, they eat a limited number of the Joshua tree's seeds. Thus, the moth ensures the tree's fertilization, and the tree en-sures the moth's survival in turn. Red-tailed hawks perch in the Joshua tree's crooked limbs, wood rats hide in cavities among the branches, and the brilliant Scott's oriole nests high on the tree for safety. Dead Joshua trees attract termites, which are relished by the yucca night lizard.

In the Mojave, the heat-tolerant creosote bush takes the place of sage-brush. Its waxy leaves lend a distinctive oily smell to the air, especially after the rare rainfall. Clonelike rings of stringy stems growing out of a shared root mass date back an astonishing 11,000 years, making creosote one of the oldest living organisms on earth. In areas such as Joshua Tree

National Park, ungrazed by cattle, the Mojave appears surprisingly green, with California junipers, pinyons, Mojave yuccas, grasses, and wildflowers thriving in a mixed mosaic. Death Valley, an outdoor museum of desert features, includes dunes, alluvial washes, and a topographic extravaganza that soars from North America's lowest point, 282 feet below sea level, to the 11,049-foot summit of Telescope Peak. Three years might pass without rain in some parts of this desert. At Death Valley, America's highest temperature was recorded, 134 degrees, though our hottest desert overall is our southernmost.

The Sonoran Desert straddles the lower Colorado River in Arizona and California and extends to sea level through most of Mexico's Baja Peninsula, totaling 120,000 square miles in both countries.[9] About 45,000 square miles of this desert lie in the United States. Here, we see the classic icon of old cowboy movies and upscale desert landscaping—the saguaro cactus. Stately giants fifty feet high have lived a century. One cactus can store as much as ten tons of water and suck up enough moisture in a single summer rainstorm to last a year. But like so much of life in the desert, saguaros grow slowly; a young one might take fifteen years to attain a mere foot in height. Taller ones support woodpeckers, purple martins, owls, wood rats, and lizards. Other Sonoran Desert plants include the thorny stemmed ocotillo, with its crimson flowers; ironwood, with the second-densest wood in the world; and the exotic-looking fan palm, growing where water percolates to the surface and creates an oasis. With the most diverse plant life of any desert in the world, the Sonoran hosts some 2,500 species, along with a wide array of wildlife—for example, six kinds of rattlesnakes. Much of the biological richness derives from rainy seasons in both winter and summer. And unlike the other deserts, the Sonoran owes its aridity not only to the rain shadow of mountains but also to the subtropical high-pressure system that pushes clouds away. A highlight here, Anza-Borrego Desert State Park, sprawls at the eastern base of California's coastal mountains within an easy drive of San Diego. Also a part of the Sonoran Desert, the Cabeza Prieta region, at the southwestern corner of Arizona, is considered the largest unoccupied territory in the contiguous states and the largest intact desert wilderness.[10]

Finally, the Chihuahuan Desert is the second largest, but 90 percent of it lies in Mexico; only about 12,000 square miles extend into Arizona, New Mexico, and western Texas.[11] The Chihuahuan receives few winter rains but enjoys summer storms blowing off the Gulf of Mexico, and as a result it yields a rich collection of plants, including dozens of species of cactus, creosote bush, and mesquite. Yuccas, agaves, and sotols bloom brightly in the spring. An exemplar of the Chihuahuan Desert, Big Bend National Park, in southern Texas, includes lofty ranges and monolithic, rockbound canyons of the Rio Grande. Though remote by any standard, this arid borderland represents a mixing ground not only of two extremely different nations but also of the past and the future, of long-term protection and shortsighted abuse, and of wildly divergent attitudes about the purpose and fate of deserts.

Dismantling the Desert

Desert as wasteland and desert as fragile ecosystem are conflicting views people are only beginning to sort out in the decisions we're obligated to make about arid lands. Still of the old school, Utah representative James Hansen invited the Department of Energy to locate a nuclear waste dump within a proposed wilderness area at the entrance of Canyonlands National Park. "If other states won't take it, we should," Hansen said of the radioactive refuse. "Sure, there would be some buildings and a chain-link fence, but you can't eliminate the growth of the West to placate a few tourists."[12] Ironically, the waste dump would undermine the growth of the area—something the neighboring Nevada delegation knew when it opposed the shipment of nuclear waste to Yucca Mountain, northwest of Las Vegas. Nuclear graveyards are just the latest in a long line of uses relegated to the desert because nobody else wants them or because they pose dangers to society: ammunition dumps, military bases, missile-testing grounds, bombing ranges, A-bomb fallout zones, big dams, power plants, and the continent's hottest magnet for gambling and prostitution.

As American society struggles with its vision and vacillating sense of responsibility for desert land, native qualities lose ground to four agents of change—mining, urban development, off-road vehicles, and grazing. As a result of these, botanist Ronald Taylor estimated that only 25 percent of the original habitat of the Great Basin still exists, much of it degraded.[13] Other deserts have felt the effects as much or more. Aquatic species such as fish, mussels, and amphibians are the most endangered families of creatures nationwide, and aquatic species in the desert suffer the most of all.

About two-thirds of all our endangered fish species live in the desert. While 80 percent of the wildlife live within one mile of scarce water supplies, diversions, development, and cattle grazing all target desert stream bottoms.[14]

While mines yielding gold, silver, copper, gypsum, and other minerals have all scarred desert land, uranium mining has been a curse to dozens of valleys, mesas, and plains, with radioactive tailings across Utah, Arizona, Colorado, and Wyoming. On the Navajo Indian Reservation in Arizona, careless development of 90,000 acres leased for uranium extraction contaminated twenty Indian communities with radioactivity, afflicted native people with health problems, and polluted ninety miles of the Rio Puerco when a wastewater dam burst.[15] Many of the consequences of mining discussed in chapter 1 apply to desert land, where voices for moderation and stewardship have been heard even less because of the remote and waterless nature of this landscape.

Affecting far more desert acreage than does new mining, urban development is on the march. In one of the desert's great ironies, this land so hostile to settlement and human life includes some of the most rapidly sprawling cities in America. On a percentage basis, Nevada, Idaho, Arizona, Colorado, and Utah were the fastest-growing states in 1998. In Arizona's Sonoran Desert, Phoenix housed 65,000 people in 1940 and 2.7 million in 1998. Half a million arrived between 1990 and 1995 alone. Groundwater pumping to serve the phenomenal growth has depleted the underground reservoir, requiring that water of poorer quality be pumped at great expense from the distant Colorado River. Throughout the Southwest, per capita water consumption is three times the national average, lawn watering being the big culprit.[16] A booming Albuquerque, New Mexico, pumped groundwater three times faster than it could be replenished.[17] With an insatiable appetite for subdivisions and sprawl, that city pushed Congress to approve a four-lane highway through Petroglyph National Monument, one of the most extraordinary of all native rock-art sites, sacred to Pueblo Indians.[18] In 1998, supporters of the monument still fought to reroute the road.

The urbanizing trend surfaces most clearly in the neon extravaganza of Las Vegas. As if a modern-day gold rush were on, 1,000 new residents arrived each week in the 1990s. A million people now live in the casino capital of the world, and planners responding to bottomless enthusiasm for boom-time growth predict another million in the next twenty years. With everybody driving cars in the ultimate suburban culture, this relatively small American city ranks fifth in carbon monoxide pollution. Its atmospheric effluent adds to the disappointing haze at Grand Canyon National Park, 180 miles away, where smog noticeably degrades the view 65 percent of the time. With residents in this sun-bleached landscape using 360 gallons of water per day, compared with 211 in Los Angeles, Las Vegas's search for new supplies has become a quest. Water managers propose to dam the Virgin River of Zion National Park fame, draw more from the already overappropriated Colorado River, and suck dwindling underground supplies from the surrounding countryside. Such pumping robs rural areas and desert ecosystems of the groundwater and spring flows they need. In some desert areas, such as near Lancaster, on the western side of the Mojave, extraction of groundwater has caused the land to subside as much as four feet over crushed cavities that will never hold water again. Much of rural Nevada resists the Las Vegas brand of water piracy, but the political balance is shifting, and the reason is clear. A single casino hotel is said to employ more people, with a larger payroll, than all the state's ranching and agribusiness combined.[19]

While the flow of water has nearly stopped, the suburbanization of Las Vegas overflows amply down the lower Colorado River valley. Thus, the gambling city chews at the Mojave from the east while limitless growth probing out from Los Angeles has already pushed half a million people into the western Mojave. Only public land prevents a head-on collision of these two locomotives of sprawl.

Urban growth gnaws at more remote desert areas as well. Less affected only in scale, the San Pedro River valley winds from Mexico into Arizona. A natural laboratory of biological diversity, this north–south conduit between tropical and temperate regions provides habitat to 400 bird species—one of the highest such numbers in North America. The watershed supports nearly every type of botanical community in the Southwest. Recognizing these virtues, the Bureau of Land Management (BLM) established the country's first federal riparian conservation area there in 1989 and moved cattle out of the river corridor. In a telling lesson for the rest of the desert, native plant life recovered quickly. But the San Pedro's woes continue. Groundwater pumping to accommodate urban growth now depletes the river. Along with ranches, farms, and a military base, the town of Sierra Vista usurps a flow equivalent to the river's entire volume. The prognosis for the rich biology of this stellar valley is poor.

Urban growth in the desert raises some tough questions. If development inevitably occurs someplace, should it just as well happen here as anywhere else? Would the American landscape be any better off if the million people going to Las Vegas went to rainy Oregon, where they would more than double the size of Portland?

People come to the desert cities because they like the climate, but they couldn't survive without pipes and canals that import every drop of water and without air conditioners fueled by power plants gulping coal and polluting the air of a four-state region. Southwestern skies are no longer crystal blue, the way they used to be. But how different are those dependences from those of any big city? New York takes water from the Catskill Mountains, not as distant as the sources for Los Angeles or Phoenix but still many miles away. While Minneapolis doesn't require much air-conditioning, it needs far more energy for heating. If people don't mind the searing sun and parched landscape, perhaps the desert is as good as anyplace for development. But for a moment, consider a far less defensible use of desert land: irrigated agriculture.

Irrigated farming takes 85 percent of the water supply in dryland regions such as California and Arizona. While farmers can produce some of the crops nowhere else, livestock accounts for much of the acreage. Furthermore, the water going to the crops is often 90 percent subsidized, yet a third of those crops have been in such chronic surplus that the government for years paid farmers to curtail their production.[20] With booming urban growth, the trend of cities to buy both water rights and land from farmers or ranchers and then rededicate the water to new residential neighborhoods is now a major movement in southern Arizona and south-central Colorado. It will continue as the economic value of water comes into sharper focus in the desert regions.[21]

Because the desert is so fragile, we can upset nature's balance even without paving or plowing. Careless recreation can easily damage the land. A single track pressed into arid soil by an off-road vehicle might be seen for decades; the tracks of tanks practicing during World War II still scar the Mojave, and off-road vehicle use has caused dust storms that have fanned out over a hundred square miles.[22] Aside from damaging the soil, uncontrolled use of motorcycles and four-wheel-drive vehicles directly exacts a grim toll on desert ecosystems. In the infamous Barstow to Las Vegas motorcycle race, thousands of dirt-bikers obliterated life in a swath like that of Sherman's army, only the bikers did it for fun. Just by roaring through, motorcycles shattered bird nests, mulched essential wildlife food supplies, and pulverized the microbiotic crust of the soil. The Bureau of Land Management let this happen to its land until 1975, when the agency finally banned the point-to-point races.

Recreation in the deserts has become a growth industry, with both an upside and a downside. Tourism now accounts for more economic activity in Utah than any other industry, employing 69,000 workers and generating $3.5 billion per year. Recreation is a big business that depends on scenery and wildlife, and it can help people recognize the intrinsic qualities of drylands. But it's difficult to see that happening on an average summer day, when the drivers of 6,000 vehicles vie for 2,000 parking spaces at the South Rim of the Grand Canyon. Serving any tourist willing to pay and probably many who are unwilling to walk even half a mile, 10,000 helicopter and airplane flights per month drone incessantly over this great national park. River runners in the bottom of the canyon embark on an eighteen-day sojourn only to hear airplanes overhead constantly, as if this one-of-a-kind wilderness lay at the end of a runway.

While suburbs and uncontrolled off-road driving cause their share of problems to desert areas, cattle cause the most severe environmental impact. Cows graze on much of the desert acreage and affect this land far more than other grasslands because aridity prevents recovery of native plants and soil. Unlike rain-blessed prairies, the desert was never subjected to intensive grazing by large herbivores such as bison, and native plant communities are incapable of sustaining cattle grazing.

Even in presumably protected sanctuaries such as Oregon's Hart Mountain National Wildlife Refuge, ranching for years preempted native desert life on two-thirds of the federal acreage. Cows overran springs and creek bottoms and ate the grass until little more than sagebrush remained in the mid-1990s.[23] And beyond the ecological conflicts, the desert produces poorly for cattle. The average stocking rate on BLM land in Arizona in the 1980s was one cow per 200 acres. Even then, the damage still occurred; most of the public land showed static or deteriorating range conditions, marked by dead bunchgrasses and a proliferation of weeds.[24]

Owing largely to the effects of cattle, the West faces an epidemic of desertification—the spread of unproductive land stripped of native vegetation. Ecologist Reed Noss reported in 1994 that at least moderate desertification or degradation is occurring on 98 percent of the arid land in the United States.[25] A report by the Council on Environmental Quality warned that overgrazing "has become the most potent desertification force."[26]

Mirroring all that is happening in arid America, the endangered desert tortoise—an indicator of desert health—has disappeared from much of its wide homeland in the Mojave and Sonoran Desert regions. The tortoise sleeps six to nine months per year to evade the hottest and coldest weather. An adult consumes only twenty-three pounds of plants annually, and one pint of water will last a whole summer. Though its needs are slight, this living symbol of the desert may die out in most of its range within fifteen years, according to the Desert Tortoise Council.

The ancient reptile is supremely suited to its place, but millions of years of evolution have not prepared it for the uncontrolled activities of newcomers armed to the teeth with technology. Off-road vehicles kill tortoises, flatten the plants they need to eat, and collapse underground burrows. Ravens, multiplying with people's garbage, landfills, and road-kills, devour tortoise eggs. A respiratory disease, released into the wild by domestic tortoises that people turn loose when they no longer want them, takes a heavy toll.[27] But cows may pose the most serious threat. Livestock eat the plants needed by tortoises, with especially painful effects during droughts. In the Piute Valley of Nevada, a third of the tortoise population perished in one dry year because cows had heavily grazed the land before the tortoises even woke up from hibernation. The rancher using this public property paid only seven cents per acre for each of his cows—a heavily subsidized rate. One cow and calf per year eat enough plants to support 400 tortoises, so even small cuts in stock numbers would return a lot of tortoise feed to these peaceful, timeless creatures.

In theory, the tortoise and other desert life should not be in such dire straits because the high proportion of public land in the desert creates opportunities for good management. But as shown in other chapters, public land also is at risk for the "tragedy of the commons." Under this phenomenon, first described by ecologist Garrett Hardin, nobody takes care of commonly owned land because the individual won't gain from good stewardship unless everybody participates in kind, something that requires cooperation or regulation or both.[28] Self-sacrifice for the good of everybody or of the land simply means that someone else will reap the short-term gain. Put another way, the benefits of grazing an extra cow go to the owner, but the loss in depleted range is shared among all users. Even more succinctly, the benefits are privatized but the costs are communized. Yet the tragedy of the commons can be reversed as citizens with growing appreciation for deserts and for all land take greater responsibility for public acreage and encourage the same from government agencies, which are directed to properly manage these lands but are heavily influenced by people looking only to reap profits from the public estate.

Sparing Life in a Spare Land

Because deserts are less appealing in the classic sense of scenery and don't lend themselves to convenient forms of recreation, the movement to protect this land lagged behind efforts on behalf of mountains, forests, rivers, wetlands, and seashores. Only grasslands have received less conservation attention over the course of history, and that's understandable because they were homesteaded long ago and farmed to the final acre. In contrast, the deserts belong mostly to the public, and their extreme nature and stark, chromatic beauty have gradually gained a following.

President Theodore Roosevelt protected the Grand Canyon as one of our early national parks, but his reason was the canyon, not the desert that the Colorado River flows through. Woodrow Wilson designated Dinosaur National Monument principally because of its fossil treasures, only incidentally tagging on the sublime canyons of the Green and Yampa Rivers and thereby protecting a significant chunk of desert.

The establishment of Canyonlands National Park in 1964 marked one of the first great measures to safeguard the desert for its own inherent qualities. Motivated partly by the need to balance preservation with reservoir development in the Colorado River corridor, Secretary of the Interior Stewart Udall initiated this park to protect extraordinary canyons, mesas, cliffs, and plateaus that covered much of the ground between Arches National Park and the reservoir behind Glen Canyon Dam.

Now, at the turn of the 21st century, citizen efforts to conserve the land, the space, and the silence of the desert have arisen across the West. In a unique approach along the boundaries of Arizona, New Mexico, and

Mexico, the Malpai Borderlands Group, an association of ranchers, works with government agencies to protect indigenous species while continuing the ranching way of life and averting urban sprawl. Half private, half public, the Malpai's million acres include the Gray Ranch, bought by The Nature Conservancy and later resold to a foundation with conservation easements barring subdivision of the 321,702-acre spread. At a similar scale, the Conservancy bought the Dugout Ranch at the border of Canyonlands National Park in Utah. In the Chihuahuan Desert, The Conservation Fund and the Richard King Mellon Foundation acquired 40,000 acres of the magnificent Chinati Mountains and donated them to the Texas Parks and Wildlife Department.

Drylands don't always have to be publicly bought to be protected or well managed. At the northern end of the American desert, the Oregon rangelands of Doc and Connie Hatfield and some of their neighbors have become a model of reform. The owners avoid overgrazing by rotating cattle through fenced allotments and by pushing the stock out of riparian areas, where they would eat all the vegetation, trample the banks, compact the soil, and pollute the water. BLM biologists and others have promoted these principles of good management for decades, and here they've been put to work profitably by ranchers.[29] Also in Oregon, at the overgrazed Hart Mountain National Wildlife Refuge, manager Barry Reiswig moved cattle off refuge land under a fifteen-year plan of rest beginning in 1994. Ranchers objected, but within a few years a remarkable recovery of grasses and native plants could be seen—a model of change.[30]

Conservation of a different type evolved in the Mojave Desert at the Coachella Valley, southwest of Joshua Tree National Park. Exclusive real estate development there ringed sixty-five golf courses, with more under way. The self-proclaimed "golf capital of the world" sprawled beyond the posh old resorts of Palm Springs and spread eastward through the desert, with no end in sight. The population of the valley climbed from 12,000 in 1940 to 220,000 in 1988 and was expected to double again by 2003.

Directly in the path of the condominiums and golf links, the threatened Coachella Valley fringe-toed lizard required for its survival undisturbed dunes of shifting sand, its only remaining habitat at ground zero of the boom. After some contentious attempts to cooperate, the developers, government officials, and conservation representatives realized that they faced stupefying blockades for everybody unless they settled down to solve the problems at hand. Paul Selzer, a lawyer for the developers, said that when everyone finally talked in good faith, they made progress. "In that forum, people ceased being devils. . . . With an endangered species all you have to do is lose once and it's all over; the developers were sensitive to that."[31]

To buy the land needed for the lizard's survival required a lot of money. The Nature Conservancy pledged $2 million and bought 2,000 acres at the center of the needed preserve. The BLM offered $5 million in land exchanges, and the California Department of Fish and Game found $1 million. Five million dollars came from the federal Land and Water Conservation Fund. The builders eventually agreed to give up $7 million. The resulting preserve encompassed only 10 percent of the lizard's remaining habitat, but biologists hoped it would be enough. They hailed the project as a success in cooperation to solve an endangered-species impasse. The preserve is the only natural open space left in a critical niche of the Mojave Desert.

Yet saving a species nearing extinction is more complicated than one would think, and nothing is easy. The sand dunes themselves need nourishment in the form of new sand blown in from elsewhere, and evaluators of the Coachella program in 1993 discovered that a critical source of new sand lacked protection. Fortunately, it had not yet been developed, and efforts were launched to safeguard the additional area.[32]

In compromised situations such as the dispute over lizard habitat at greater Palm Springs, success in saving natural values is hard to come by, expensive, and minimal at best. Seeking to avoid the threats of extinction rather than coping with them so terribly late in the game, California conservationists in the 1980s launched an ambitious campaign to protect sizable sections of the Mojave Desert.

Under the Federal Land Policy and Management Act of 1976, the BLM had drafted a plan for its 13.5 million acres of southern California desert. But the agency recommended only 2 million acres for wilderness status—the one designation that would prevent troublesome off-road vehicle travel and new mining. This meager recommendation sorely disappointed the people who had championed the 1976 law, and then the Reagan administration slashed the proposal to a minimalist 1.7 million acres. Stonewalled by the BLM, conservationists pushed to safeguard the finest of the Mojave under congressional designation as a national park or wilderness.

Rising up against the desert protectors, the mining, off-road vehicle, and cattle industries opposed any limitations on what they could do on public land. From their group, the California Desert Coalition, spokeswoman Marie Brashear wrote off the conservation proposal as "just a huge ego trip by environmentalists who want to see how much wilderness they can stuff under their belts."[33] Some users of motorized off-road vehicles vowed to keep driving in the Mojave even if the government tried to restrict them. In a disturbing resort to violence, one man stabbed another to death in a campground following an argument about desert protection, and callers telephoned death threats to park advocates. But the plan enjoyed support from 75 percent of polled Californians.[34] Once Pete Wilson vacated his seat in the U.S. Senate and Democrat Barbara Boxer won election, the bill began to move, and after years of strenuous effort by thousands of people, President Bill Clinton signed the California Desert Protection Act in 1994.

The milestone legislation made Death Valley National Park the largest national park outside Alaska, at 3.3 million acres. It also created the 1.4-million-acre Mojave National Preserve out of BLM land—essentially a national park with hunting allowed. Another provision upgraded Joshua Tree National Monument to park status and enlarged it, though a troubling moat of development still grows to its north and south. In the largest single addition ever to the National Wilderness Preservation System outside Alaska, the act designated sixty-nine new areas, totaling 3.7 million acres. However, nagging resistance to the measure persisted and hamstrung implementation efforts. The administration finally beat back congressional renitence and funded management for the protected areas in 1997, but the agencies still had to accommodate a hash of compromises, including mining claims, private inholdings, grazing, and some off-road vehicle use.

The second great advance for desert protection in the decade came with the Grand Staircase–Escalante National Monument in Utah. Though the lower end of the incomparably carved Escalante Canyon had fallen victim to stagnant floodwaters behind Glen Canyon Dam in the 1960s, the upper portions of the canyon's startlingly vertical topography survived. From a main stem that twists and turns beneath fluted sandstone walls, tributaries finger out into plateau country, each a slickrock wonderland with soaring cliffs, cottonwood groves, shaded alcoves, delicate arches, and fern-clad grottoes.

Inspired by a report prepared by pioneering preservationist Bob Marshall, Secretary of the Interior Harold Ickes in 1936 had considered a 4.5-million-acre Escalante National Monument, but ranching, mining, and hydropower interests had quashed his plan. Through the benign graces of neglect, much of the Escalante remained a wilderness in the 1990s, and conservationists hoped for protection of a corridor linking a hundred miles of desert from Capitol Reef National Park to the Kaiparowits Plateau, near the Utah–Arizona border.

Kaiparowits—a land of rock mesas and high plateaus—had a raucous history of its own. Schemes to mine the plateau for coal were torpedoed by a conservation coalition in 1976, prompting residents of Kanab to hang environmentalist spokesman Robert Redford in effigy.[35] In the following decades, other proposals to drill for oil and gas and to bulldoze roads cropped up; the most distressing plan, in 1995, called for 650,000 acres of roadless plateau to be opened to coal strip-mining.[36]

Addressing the persistent threats, President Bill Clinton in 1996 designated 1.7 million acres of this Utah wildland as a national monument—virtually the same as a national park except that consent of Congress is not required to protect a monument. The president announced, "Our parents and grandparents saved the Grand Canyon for us. Today we will save the grand Escalante Canyons and the Kaiparowits Plateau of Utah for our children." But the fact that the federal government took action didn't mean local officials would honor it. Unimpressed by the economic opportunities of recreation, Kane and Garfield County commissioners all but declared war on the U.S. government and dispatched bulldozers into the newly created monument to scrape out roads, hoping to nip wilderness proposals in the bud.[37] In their favorite act of contempt, southern Utahans uncoiled their ropes again and hung both the president and Secretary of the Interior Bruce Babbitt in effigy.

Going the extra mile to placate opponents, the administration agreed to convey alternative federal property and mineral rights to a Dutch company that was supported by the state in its efforts to mine BLM property.[38] In the meantime, a state agency that held scattered inholdings on Kaiparowits flaunted the new national monument status and leased land to Conoco Inc. for oil drilling. But the company failed to tap marketable deposits, and in 1998 the federal and state governments signed a land swap agreement resolving some of the acrimony. While proposals elsewhere for wilderness designation and parks stalled out in the 1990s, these two advances at the Mojave Desert and the Colorado Plateau made it through, an indication that the movement to protect the best of this landscape has begun to mature.

The effort to preserve some share of the original desert continues in Utah. There, in our second-driest state, large additional tracts of public land remain roadless at the turn of the 21st century. In 1998, the Southern Utah Wilderness Alliance recommended that about 6 million acres be protected, embracing such elegant tracts as Desolation Canyon of the Green River; the borders of Canyonlands, Zion, and Capitol Reef National Parks; and the Book Cliffs, regarded as the longest continuous escarpment in the world. The state's only environmentally conscious congressman, Wayne Owens, had introduced a bill to protect 5 million acres in 1989, but then he was ousted. Representative James Hansen introduced a bill to designate a nominal 1.8 million acres but, more important, to allow dams, pipelines, and other intrusions within already protected areas. His proposal received rave reviews from rural Utahans influenced by anti-federalism, the extractive industries, and the boosterish Mormon Church. But wilderness enthusiasts turned out in force to oppose Hansen's bill at a final hearing in Salt Lake City. A filibuster led by Senator Bill Bradley of New Jersey then killed the anti-wilderness measure.

This type of debate will surface elsewhere across desert lands. Within the BLM's 174-million-acre federal estate in the lower forty-eight states— most of it desert and grassland—the agency has only 5.3 million acres protected as wilderness. Another 17 million acres officially qualify, but only 7.5 million of this was proposed for protection by the agency in 1998.[39] Thus, most of the public land of the great American desert remains open for mining, new roads, and off-road vehicle use. But the balance between exploitation and protection is changing with the growing solidarity of people who recognize the intrinsic value of our driest landscape.

The Oasis

The lure of the oasis permeates the literature of deserts. The oasis is so different from the desert yet is a part of it, at the heart of it. Amid scarcity, life thrives once again.

Riverfronts and riparian bottoms are the closest we come to oases in most of the American deserts. There, life-giving water flows down from the Rockies, the Sierra Nevada, or any of dozens of smaller mountain masses. Where they haven't been ousted by the opprobrious tamarisk—a shrub imported from Spain—native cottonwoods and willows green the shores. Birds and other wildlife follow their daily paths, and sandy beaches welcome people to camp alongside flowing water. The streamsides, however, are not true oases.

In Joshua Tree National Park, my wife, Ann, and I set off on the trail to Fortynine Palms Oasis, this time in search of the real thing: a spring-fed colony of palms in the desert. We climbed up a mountainside and switchbacked among house-sized cobbles of granite. It was midwinter, but the air felt balmy and the sun was bright. Though we passed by creosote bushes, barrel cacti, and catclaw acacias with shirt-snagging thorns, we were most struck by the minimalist life, the naked ground, the earth's sinews and bones laid bare to the wind.

As we crested a ridge top, our trail offered a view back to the valley we had come from. At the base of the mountain slope, road cuts and bull-dozed landings led to streets, gas stations, mini-malls, subdivisions, and the grid of development called Twentynine Palms. To the north, across an immense plain of aridity, specks of white marked sunlight reflected from windows—hundreds of reflections. Though Joshua Tree National Park lies 125 miles from Los Angeles, we were still clearly within its sphere of influence.

The trail topped a ridge and plummeted down its back side, where rock ribs suddenly hid us from the built-up valley. Now we felt isolated, alone again in a spare land. Then, as we rounded a bend in the trail, we saw the oasis far below. A cluster of palms filled a low spot in a ravine and climbed the slopes until cut off by rock walls. One bend in the trail took us out of view, but the next bend brought us back, again and again, closer each time.

Finally, we stepped into that room of fantasy where fat trunks of California fan palms shot straight up for forty feet to tropical tufts of green. Dead fronds remained attached but had fallen down against the trunks, thatching them with a cushion of tan leaves six feet across. Roots of the palms gripped the soil—not taproots but thousands of groping strings seeking to anchor and support the unlikely trees. Willows and a few gnarled Fremont cottonwoods also grew at this Mojave refuge, but the palms reigned supreme. Pools of water ponded in terraces one above the other, skimmed with algae that supported colonies of insects. The water trickled from pool to pool with the quiet sound of liquid poured slowly from a pitcher. Say's phoebes fluttered in and out of the leaves, rustling them, all of it so tropical. At other oases in the park, including Lost Palms and the Oasis of Marah, the pools have disappeared owing to pumping of groundwater nearby, which has lowered water tables by sixteen feet. But not here, not yet.

Utterly enchanted, we felt blessed to be in this exquisite place, so full of life in a desert where life comes hard and lean. But the scars of disrespect saddened us. A fire had burned through the trees. Palms are adapted to fire; the Indians burned oases as often as every four years because the trees then bore better fruit.[40] Twentynine Palms has burned three times since the 1940s, though the last fire was an act of arson, four years before we visited. The trees had survived, but into the satiny black of the burned trunks, beautiful in their own right, the next wave of vandals had carved their initials. An aluminum can and a plastic bag bobbed in a pool. We picked them up, wondering why those other people had not felt a sense of reverence or at least respect when visiting such a rare place. Like so many of the landscapes of America, this one expressed strengths and qualities and supported a whole circle of life, but here, that circle lay in a delicate microcosm. Why the disrespect? Was it ignorance about the land, or carelessness, or insensitivity to what makes life on earth possible? Was it because people see their own landscape all the time and therefore take it for granted, or was it because so many people never see the natural land at all and therefore have little idea of what it is, what it does, or why it's necessary?

We lingered at the oasis until twilight and then reluctantly left, passing again through its green curtain and back into the desert, where the colors faded in sunset's dimming glow. Sharply etched shadows disappeared as the light softened, and then the brightest stars dotted the deepest blue of the Mojave sky.

CHAPTER 5

LIFELINES OF RIVERS

AT A LIKELY LOOKING pool in the Roanoke River of Virginia, shaded under a canopy of silver maples so thick that the light beneath them looked green, my brother-in-law, Steve Schmitz, cast a spinner out onto the eddy line. Besides being a good bass stream, the Roanoke supports the largest number of fish species on Virginia's Atlantic slope. It marks the northern end of a rich zone of aquatic fauna that typify southern Appalachian waters—the ones that have not been heavily dammed, channelized, or polluted. We couldn't see the fish or mussels or crayfish, but indicating that they were there, a kingfisher rattled its call and darted from one leggy sycamore limb to another. Serene turtles basked on rocks at the waterline and plopped into the river when they noticed us. In lanky, slow-motion strides, great blue herons stalked the shallows for minnows and crustaceans. Every minute of the day, the murmuring current swept a rich load of nutrients and food past eddy lines, where the detritus settled out to be gobbled by redbreast sunfish, largemouth bass, grass pickerel, shorthead redhorse, and yellow bullhead.

Most fish bite early in the morning, and there we were in the heat of the day, so we gave up on fishing and instead jumped in ourselves, lying back to let the gentle current whisk us downriver while the canoe drifted on its own. Up to my neck now, I had a better view of the river and thought about just how important the flow of water can be. As an immediate gift, the bubbly chill dropped my body temperature back into the comfort zone. The wide Appalachian stream granted communities along its way their drinking water. Like mother to child, it nourished an intricate web of life under its surface and along its shores. It made a large region livable for both people and a swimming, crawling, soaring, browsing, pecking, fabulous array of creatures.

Everything that lives needs water, and rivers are the water supply of the earth.

Buoyed up by the vital liquid, I stared at the sky and thought about where I was—in a stream, moving slowly to someplace else. I thought about how this river links the high divide of the Blue Ridge Mountains with the seashore of the Atlantic Coast. It winds through a humid forest for most of the way and then glimmers past farms sown in corn, oats, and tobacco, through towns of red brick homes built of Piedmont clay following the Civil War, and over ten dams that interrupt the river's flow from the Appalachian headwaters to Albemarle Sound. This animate centerpiece of the land flows either from or to everything. Watching treetops quietly slip by in my peripheral vision and occasionally grounding my feet on gravel shallows, I couldn't help but think of the river as the connecting artery that links all its landscapes together and defines them as one big organism.

River Wealth

The rivers of America flow with beauty, power, and magic. They carry the water from mountains, forests, grasslands, deserts, and lakes back to the seashore; the rivers close the hydrologic cycle on which all creatures depend. From tiny trickles where splattering rain has barely begun to coalesce to the mouths of America's fifteen watery behemoths that each disgorge 50,000 cubic feet per second or more, the rivers shine as highlights of the land.[1] They glisten, tumble, bubble, and roar. All the time, they move. They change color: silvery blue, emerald green, golden brown. The rivers lend life to everything they touch.

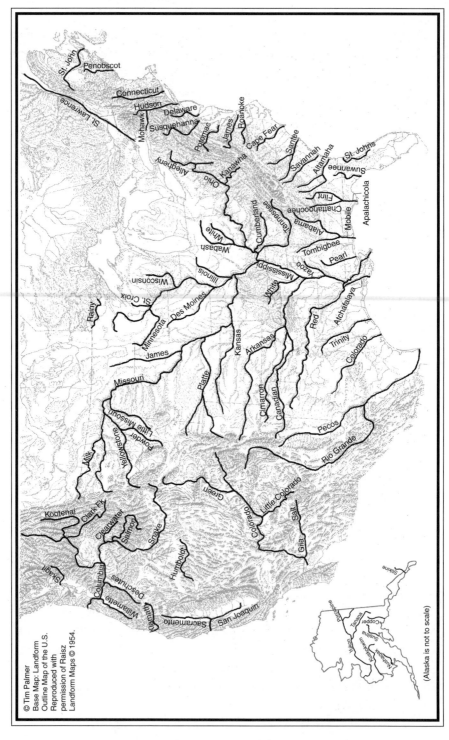

(Alaska is not to scale)

We need our rivers. We can't live without them. From New York City to Los Angeles, they supply half our drinking water, and the other half comes from groundwater, inextricably linked to the surface flow. Fish, insects, algae, and the tiniest plankton stack up as fundamental building blocks of the largest ecosystems, like the essential foundation of a home.

In so many ways, rivers serve life so well. Consider this example: water is one of few substances that when frozen become less dense, not more. Ice occupies 9 percent more space than the water it's made of. That fact may seem like just a curious quirk of physics and chemistry, but it's why ice crystallizes on top of rivers and lakes. If ice sank, it would freeze out the bottom life that survives under stones in streambeds during winter—the biomass on which fish and all the rest depend.

Bonded to the flow as tightly as willow roots grip damp soil, the riparian, or riverfront, community of water-nourished plants is critical to 70 percent or more of the land-based wildlife.[2] This includes everything from our largest ungulate, the moose, to the Richardson vole, a mouselike mammal that scurries to water and swims away at the slightest provocation. Riverfronts in temperate regions overflow with life, and in arid country, rivers are even more important for their scarcity. In Nevada, 80 percent of the wildlife species depend directly on the riparian zone, though it covers less than 1 percent of the land.[3] Even more obviously dependent on rivers, the freshwater fishes of North America may be the richest in variety among all temperate regions of the earth; 790 species live here, with the greatest numbers in the East and especially the Southeast.[4] A world center of freshwater diversity, the United States ranks first in species of crayfish, mussels, and snails, as well as stone flies, mayflies, and caddis flies—favorite foods of trout.[5]

Close to the daily lives of many people, the rivers help define our communities. A stream of some kind graces almost every city, town, and village, from Alakanuk, Alaska, to Miami, Florida. Along with the wildlife that depends on riverfronts, I belong there. We all belong there (though expensive homes on floodplains do not). Our ancestors, going back hundreds of thousands of years, lived along riverbanks—places with appeal as basic and ingrained as genetic coding.

The rivers are the lifelines, and even more basic to America, they have given our land its shape. They jettison away the silty whittlings of soil. The flow of water reduces the surface of North America by an average of one foot every 10,000 years, but this is done selectively, in the carving of canyons and the sculpting of valleys.[6] The erosion will one day reach clear to mountaintops and include everything, bones and all. In that sense, the rivers are supremely powerful.

No one has calculated the rivers' worth in dollars and cents, and no one really can, but streams of all sizes underpin economic health.[7] A good water supply ranks as the most essential infrastructure for homes, towns, farms, and factories. Thirty-one million freshwater anglers generated billions of dollars in America's economy in 1991.[8] Greenways for river recreation deliver wealth in all regions and brighten cities such as Sacramento, Boise, Hartford, and Washington, D.C.

Rivers hold practical importance of many kinds; yet the appeal goes beyond, to something elusive, something understood only by seeing and feeling the special qualities of animated water. The rivers move, and so the eye settles on them. Many of the streams run clear, so we see into them, through them. They sparkle in the sun and cast reflections at quiet pools. When I'm lucky enough to camp near one, its soothing voice lulls me to sleep at night. When I get a headache, I sit by the river and let it "stream" my pain away. The rivers hydrate our bodies and nourish the life of the earth. They can literally carry us away. In a boat, an inner tube, or just a bathing suit, we can navigate the streams with little effort, lofted by the current on a fine ride to wherever the water goes.

To imagine a river basin or watershed—meaning all the land that drains into a particular stream—I close my eyes and picture the blackened, flattened, two-dimensional silhouette of a big oak tree in winter. The girthy trunk describes the river's main stem. Outer twigs represent the smallest tributaries, the whole picture a veinwork of streams as branched and vital as the old oak in real life. And like the oak, this river tree is just one in a forest.

Out of sight, raindrops on the opposite side of the mountain coalesce and flow to a neighboring river. In similar patterns repeated all the way across the continent, a series of these divides spawns rivers whose headwaters border one another but whose flows pour in opposite ways, to differing landscapes. This image of linkage entices me further. I unfold a map and with my finger trace a route from east to west by going up and down the drainages: from the Atlantic Ocean, I travel up the Susquehanna River, then down the Allegheny and Ohio, then up the Mississippi, the Missouri, the Yellowstone, and Atlantic Creek to Two Ocean Lake. This small body of snowmelt has a double outlet, enabling water to flow off either side of the continental divide. I follow the westbound flow down Pacific Creek to the Snake River and the Columbia, which takes me to the Pacific Ocean. Though it involves steep gradients and waterfalls, this is a continuous water passage across America. If I move my finger north or south, I can travel by different rivers. These were once, in fact, the conduits of early American exploration, commerce, and adventure; Lewis and Clark's journey to the Pacific was made mostly by water. The map of the United States thus becomes a diagram of achievable fantasy; by combining river and overland travel, we can eventually reach anyplace, including the amber-colored streams of the upper Midwest, the snaky swamps of the South, the snowy backbone of the Rockies, and the grizzly wilds of Alaska.

A River Tour of America

In New England, rivers rip from glaciated ground and over waterfalls dating to continental ice sheets that blocked the earlier streams and forced them into new routes. Clear water foaming over gray boulders, a green backdrop of northern hardwoods and conifers, a mountain route quickly running out to sea by way of villages and old industrial towns—these are the northeastern rivers. In many of them, salmon once quivered to the brim, but wild spawners now return to only seven small streams. Current reintroduction efforts may bring the Atlantic salmon back to waterways, including the Connecticut River, New England's largest.

Down the eastern backbone of the Appalachians, the tangled green of waterfront forests shades steep-sloped rivers. These streams tumble out of our oldest mountains, through sandstone gorges, onto foothill terraces, and then across farmed outwash plains. Teeming with life where they haven't been dammed, crowded by development, or poisoned by acid from coal mines, these rivers flow through a temperate land. In mountain-walled valleys, limestone bedrock and its life-giving chemical breakdown products yield our greatest numbers of fish and mussel species. These streams are not just beautiful but biologically wondrous with freshwater fauna.

On the Coastal Plain—lowlands near sea level from New Jersey through Texas—rivers coil as slow-moving lifeways trucking water from the interior. Some meander through baldcypress swamps and marsh grass, and wetlands might finger back from the banks for miles. Blackened water produced by dissolved organic material in swamps, white sand brought from decomposing quartzite in the Appalachians, and green jungles on the floodplains combine in tricolored river corridors—black, white, and green—dazzling. Overflowing annually into adjacent swamps, the rivers here have some of the least developed shoreline in America. The wetlands feed nutrients to the rivers, which in turn supply estuaries enormously productive as fisheries in the ocean.[9] It's all one great, seamless system of land, water, and life.

Gridded into farms throughout inner America, the Midwest is still gullied by rivers with pushy brown flows that drain the farms and swell into giants as well known as the Ohio, Wabash, Illinois, Minnesota, and Mississippi Rivers. From the north, woodlands and wetlands near Canada spawn hundreds of clear-water and blackwater streams that plunge into the Great Lakes. From the south, rivers in the limestone hills of Kentucky and Tennessee twist out to the Mississippi, and a set of Appalachian-style streams drains the Ozark and Ouachita highlands in Missouri and Arkansas. Here in the Midwest, blue catfish once weighed 300 pounds; the sprawling Mississippi basin still houses several hundred species of fish.

The Great Plains incline slightly, as a tilted table might, from the Rockies toward the Mississippi, and its rivers strike parallel routes across the alluvium washed down from the mountains. Long, lightly developed streams riffle in low flows through grasslands and cottonwood ribbons that give life to a whole region. Biological mixing grounds, valleys such as Nebraska's Niobrara allow the East to meet the West, resulting in a mingling of species and the interbreeding by which new species evolve.

Deep snows of the Rocky Mountains melt into an extraordinary set of rivers that span from the Columbia, which begins in Canada, to the Rio Grande, which rises among the peaks of Colorado before scribing the country's border with Mexico. Two emblematic wild rivers, the Selway and the Salmon, grace the mountains of Idaho. The upper Snake, Yampa, and North Platte Rivers host some of the finest remaining cottonwood forests in the West—crucial to the region's wildlife. The mix of mountain and river scenery is nowhere so perfectly blended as where the Snake River curves in front of the Teton Range. The rivers of this region support otters, moose, elk, and colonies of beavers.

West of the Rockies, desert rivers feed water to an arid land. The Owyhee, Green, Colorado, Dolores, San Juan, and Virgin Rivers cut scenic masterpieces of basalt or sandstone canyons deep into plateaus, and in early summer they peak with silty runoff from faraway mountains.

Sierra Nevada rivers burst from granite high country, cascade over waterfalls, slice brilliant canyons, penetrate shaded conifer forests, and finally stream across an oak-clad savanna before they empty into grasslands of California's Central Valley. No other region presents such a showcase of crystalline water boiling through rapids, and the rivers of the Sierra also nourish a vestige of Central Valley wetlands, essential for the Pacific Flyway of waterfowl. These rivers supply America's most industrialized belt of agriculture and dozens of cities that continue to grow, with no end in sight.

In the Northwest, streams bubble down from green mountains pummeled by rain. Volcanic snowcaps melt into white water from northern California through Washington, and smaller streams drain mossy woodlands of the Coast Ranges. These are the rivers of the Pacific salmon and steelhead, legendary fish that live in the sea but spawn in the rivers. They once fed a whole culture, but dams blocking their way and habitat destruction have reduced the fish to near extinction levels. More than anywhere else, the rivers here create a regional identity with their full-bodied flows through conifer forests, countryside, and cities.

In Alaska, a third of America's freshwater flows from a fifth of the land, and the rivers are as big and diverse as the state. Salmon still swim up thousand-mile streams, and the runoff of rain forest, volcano, ice field, and tundra twists and shines across the place that native people call the Great Land. The finest remaining wild waterways anywhere include giants such as the Yukon, nearly as untouched as the Mississippi was in 1750. Hundreds of rivers here show little sign of the 21st century, but they are a rare set of streams in our country.

Troubled Waters

As long as it rains, a world without rivers is unimaginable, but a world without healthy rivers is what most people see every day. About 40 percent of the surveyed stream mileage in the country fails to meet state standards for swimming or chemical criteria for human health.[10] Half the

stream mileage fails the test of biological health, which includes consid-
erations such as the ability of the water to support a full complement of
native fish.[11]

Since passage of the Clean Water Act of 1972, cities and industries have
made great strides in cleaning up pollution from sewage and industrial
plants. But the legislated goal of having fishable and swimmable waters
everywhere by 1985 has proved elusive. We haven't even come close. The
country's overall water quality remains poor, owing first to polluted runoff
from farms, logging tracts, and other large areas of land and second to an
epidemic of toxic waste from the chemical, pesticide, and electronics age.[12]

Sixty-eight percent of the contamination in our streams comes from
polluted runoff. Control of this is difficult because it involves not just
water but everything we do to the land.[13] For example, farming. Silt from
agricultural runoff isn't just a matter of a little mud in the water. Rather,
overloads of silt and sediment block sunlight from beneficial aquatic
plants; transport phosphorus, which causes smothering blooms of algae;
interfere with the breathing and sight of fish; and clog gravel beds, where
a flow of water and oxygen is needed for spawning and for creatures such
as stone flies, on which other life depends.[14] The effects of polluted runoff are insidious and often unexpected.

In one disturbing case, a toxic organism in the Pamlico River poisoned
University of North Carolina researcher Howard Glasgow. Rashes and
headaches led to memory loss, emotional rages, and debilitating neuro-
logical disorders that literally knocked the man off his feet. The toxic
source was *Pfiesteria piscicida,* Latin for "fish killer." This single-celled
dinoflagellate does not have to be ingested via drinking water to wreak its
hideous effects; simply breathing the air associated with it can cause problems.[15]

Though this species has long inhabited warm lowland waters, scientists
believe that the *Pfiesteria* outbreak stemmed from an overload of nutri-
ent-rich, algae-producing waste associated with a boom in North Carolina hog production. One pig produces four times the waste of a person,
and agribusinesses now raise 1,100 swine in a single building. Many of
these buildings make up a modern pig operation. One factory cesspool
can hold the waste equivalent of a large city. North Carolina alone has to
accommodate 9.5 million tons of pig manure per year—far too much for

the land or water to absorb. Running off into the rivers, the hog waste feeds explosive blooms of algae and, in turn, *Pfiesteria*. About his illness, Glasgow reflected, "My friends say I've become the canary in the coal mine."

This alarming toxin warns us that the health of people and other creatures depends on river health. And the effects of poorly controlled hog farms go far beyond fish kills. Thirty percent of private wells in the lowland areas of North Carolina register pollution. One spill from a hog-waste lagoon that released 25 million gallons of feces and urine in 1995 not only killed 10 million fish but also closed 364,000 acres of coastal wetlands to commercial shellfishing. By 1997, the dreaded *Pfiesteria* had infected eastern tidal waters and closed fisheries as far north as the Pocomoke River in Maryland.

Not much better than a factory farm for pigs, the average modern poultry barn generates four tons of litter per day. In the Potomac headwaters alone, 900 of these factories operated in 1997. In addition to a mountain of manure, each barn disposes of about 5,200 dead birds per year. A single barn requires 40 to 160 acres for adequate disposal of the waste—land that is not available—and so manure-laden runoff pollutes the rivers.[16] Finally recognizing the problems of industrial animal operations and overcoming resistance to controls aimed at protecting its citizens, the state of North Carolina belatedly adopted a moratorium on new swine factories. But without federal controls requiring that minimum standards be met everywhere, agribusinesses simply gravitate to the states least likely to regulate them. Among this group, Missouri endured pollution spills at 63 percent of its hog and chicken factories between 1990 and 1994. In Utah, a sweetheart deal between the legislature and the industry prevents citizens from suing agribusinesses to reduce offensive odors—a mephitic problem of knockout proportions across the new hog belt of America.

Defending his company, a spokesman for Monticello Pork in Illinois maintained that hogs have been raised in rural areas for many years and that "what's coming out of our buildings is fertilizer."[17] But people living nearby disagree when the stench of the livestock factories drives them from their neighborhoods and countryside. It's farmers in rural areas who now lead the fight for better regulation. They see the hog and chicken factories as a gross perversion of agriculture—one that few of these men, who have spent their whole lives in animal production, had ever begun to imagine.[18]

As a result of lobbying by agribusiness and farm organizations, federal law requires no treatment for animal waste, though nationwide it amounts to 150 times the volume of human sewage and impairs 35,000 miles of rivers.[19] Six thousand livestock feedlots and poultry farms were unregulated by the federal government in 1997; only a fourth of them came under state purview. Seeking to fill one of the most egregious gaps in the pollution control system, in 1998 the federal Environmental Protection Agency proposed rules for feedlots but faced opposition from congressmen decrying "unnecessary" regulations and federal interference.

While polluted runoff, including animal waste, has stopped us far short of reaching legislated goals for swimmable waters, the other half of the unmet challenge in halting water pollution involves toxic chemicals. Highly poisonous even in minuscule amounts, toxins have been dumped untreated into rivers and groundwater and often go undetected in sewage plants and at clandestine dump sites. Pesticides combine the intractable difficulties of polluted runoff with the virulence of toxic wastes, and the problem is getting worse. Since Rachel Carson wrote *Silent Spring* in 1962, warning us about pesticides, we've doubled the amount in use.[20] Applicators continually ratchet up the dosage and toxicity as insects adapt to the chemicals; 500 troublesome pests are now regarded as pesticide resistant. Carcinogens and neurotoxins in the chemicals affect not only birds and wildlife; farmers and their families exposed to the oily sprays and acrid dusts of this industry contract cancer at six times the normal rate.[21] Toxins sometimes make water undrinkable even after expensive treatment.

For all the publicized success in cleaning up the pollution of heavy industries, the Environmental Working Group found that chemical plants, pulp mills, and other manufacturers still discharged 1 billion pounds of toxic chemicals into American waters between 1990 and 1994. This data center found that another 450 million pounds of toxins were simply flushed untreated through sewage plants. And even more dumping went unreported. Because of exemptions for chosen industries and small businesses, only about 340 of the mind-boggling 73,000 chemicals used in commerce were reported.[22] Among the most alarming problems, radioactive waste from fifty years of weapons production leaks into the ground-water and seeps toward the Columbia River at the Hanford Nuclear Reservation in Washington.[23]

Today's polluters will haunt the generations to come, just as polluters of the past diminish our world today, costing us dearly in terms of health and money. Here is just one example: during a thirty-year period, the General Electric Company poured 2 million pounds of nondegrading polychlorinated biphenyls (PCBs) into the Hudson River, a toxic legacy now residing in sediments of the river and estuary. A 1997 study by the U.S. Fish and Wildlife Service found that tree swallows feeding on midges that breed in the PCB-laced mud suffer problems with reproduction and feather development. Herons and terns may be afflicted as well.[24] When General Electric abandoned its plant in 1982, it left the public with a $280 million cleanup problem.[25]

The old, abandoned sources of pollution pose enough trouble, but clear violations of federal and state laws continue uncontested every day. A General Accounting Office report in 1997 found that more than 40 percent of Ohio's polluters regularly violate the terms of their permits. As prescribed by law, many states, including Ohio, have authority to enforce federal Clean Water Act requirements, but that doesn't mean they do it. State primacy too often means state discretion over what gets enforced and on whom. The federal Environmental Protection Agency announced that Pennsylvania reported only six of sixty-four major air pollution violators in 1996, suggesting that under political pressure, officials in charge of the state's air and water inspectors turned a blind eye to pollution.[26]

In a bald-faced affront to accountability, twenty states, including Michigan, Idaho, and Texas, passed laws to keep industrial violations secret from the public if polluters monitor and identify their own problems.[27] The ostensible public benefit in this ludicrous special-interest scam is that it saves agency personnel some time and money; of course, no matter what the job, not doing it saves somebody some time. No surprise: when the results of self-reporting were monitored, industries were found to dramatically underestimate their discharges, even in states without the shield of confidential reporting.[28] Politicians enacted these travesties of the public's right to know by espousing anti-regulatory rhetoric and promising to get big government off the little man's back. Similarly, a New York State policy of "self-policing" by industry in 1994 consisted of drastic cut-

backs in state inspections to avoid "interrupting production." Other cut-
backs and whitewashes of the anti-regulatory era have plagued Connecticut, Minnesota, Virginia, and other states, with resulting pollution of
rivers.[29]

When it didn't cut regulations outright, Congress in the late 1990s
seemed obsessed with divesting authority to state governments, and it's
no coincidence that both River Network and the National Wildlife Federation found poor enforcement at the state level to be the weakest link
in the chain of pollution cleanup. Nineteen states were found to have
failed in their Clean Water Act responsibilities; the others were rated as
poor or weak. Not a single state had done a good job, according to a
National Wildlife Federation study. Both groups launched programs to
involve citizens in the arena of state responsibility, with a determination
to bolster grassroots pressure on the agencies.[30]

For most people, the bottom line regarding water quality isn't who
regulates it or how but whether tap water is drinkable or not. Nearly 30
percent of community water systems reported violations of health standards between 1986 and 1991.[31] In 1997, the Natural Resources Defense
Council and the Environmental Working Group analyzed federally collected data and found that 45 million Americans drank water contaminated with fecal matter, parasites, toxic chemicals, pesticides, disease-
causing microbes, lead, or other contaminants exceeding federal health
standards. Those problems came from the pollution dumped into our
rivers and groundwater despite laws that say it shouldn't be happening.

Though everyone knows that water is fundamental to our existence, a
survey done by American Rivers found a troubling lack of public awareness about pollution and other river issues. But 94 percent of the respondents expressed concern for their tap water, and 99 percent worried about
what their children had to drink. "For healthy water supplies we need
healthy rivers," said Kevin Coyle, president of the group in 1994. To bring
home his point, he added, "Each night my little girl plays a game. She says
she won't go to bed unless I carry her up the steps. So I say okay. She
climbs on my back, and up we go, and each time we do that I think about
the fact that 70 percent of her body weight is Potomac River."

Clean water advocates fought off a drive by the 1997 Congress to
weaken the Safe Drinking Water Act and even managed to gain some improvements.[32] But even here, it's the chemical age. While our drinking

Pine Creek, Pennsylvania. This Appalachian stream has managed to retain outstanding qualities because much of its watershed is protected as state forest land.

West Branch, Susquehanna River, Pennsylvania. Though this river flows through wild, forested country, its water is polluted with acid from coal mines.

Suwannee River near Luraville, Florida. Rivers of the southern Appalachians, Coastal Plain, and Deep South are exceptionally rich in species diversity and aquatic life.

Niobrara River, Nebraska. One of the finest rivers of the Great Plains, the Niobrara's corridor serves as a mixing ground for native plants and birds of the East and the West.

Snake River, Wyoming. A quintessential river of the Rockies, the Snake provides rich riparian habitat.

East Rosebud Creek, Montana. Plunging down from summits of the Beartooth Range, this stream links the high country with the lowlands of the Plains.

Green River at Island Park, Utah. Transecting two great landscapes of America, this river cuts through the Rockies and then crosses 300 miles of desert.

Cattle feed lot, Colorado. A major cause of water pollution, erosion, and loss of riparian habitat, these cattle could easily be kept out of the stream by proper fencing.

Lower Suwannee River, Florida. As this real estate sign attests, loopholes in regulations allow building on floodplains that will be inundated again and again.

Producing minimal hydropower and mainly serving barges that carry surplus grain to Asia, four dams on the lower Snake River are driving the Northwest's salmon to extinction.

water laws focus on tactics such as chlorination and filtration, we often lose sight of the key task—to keep rivers and groundwater unpolluted in the first place.

The Health of Whole River Systems

Analyzing a wide spectrum of stresses on our rivers, the National Research Council estimated that in addition to pollution problems, artificially low flows hurt 40 percent of our stream mileage, while siltation, bank erosion, and channelization alter 41 percent of the total.[33] Also looking broadly at America's portrait of river health, the National Park Service surveyed the country and found that only 2 percent of the stream mileage meets the criteria of the national Wild and Scenic Rivers Act, which requires that designated rivers be of outstanding quality and relatively unaffected by pollution, dams, or development.[34]

Causing a lot of the problems, 75,000 dams six feet or greater in height have been built across America, blocking nearly every major stream outside Alaska.[35] About 5,500 of the dams rise more than fifty feet. Even the renowned Salmon River of Idaho has a small dam that barricades upper reaches at a fish hatchery, and the Yellowstone, often called our longest free-flowing river outside Alaska, has four significant diversion dams. Some entire regions don't even have one section of free-flowing river 100 miles long. Nationwide, only 145 damless reaches of 100 miles or more can still be found outside Alaska, and many of those rivers have diversions, levees, floodplain development, and pollution.[36] Such widespread damming has been a traumatic change where every one of America's 3.6 million miles of rivers and streams were undammed only a few hundred years ago.

Not just benign instruments of progress, the dams flood entire valleys and canyons beneath the flat pools of reservoirs. At these sites, whole aquatic and terrestrial ecosystems plus the homes and history of entire communities may as well have been on the *Titanic*. And beyond the loss of all that's permanently flooded, dams block the migration of seagoing fish such as salmon, steelhead, and a dozen other species; they alter water temperatures so much that native fish die; they trigger algal explosions called eutrophication that decrease oxygen and smother invertebrate life; they eliminate the seasonal cycles of high and low water under which whole communities of creatures have evolved; and they make possible diversions that undermine the health of streams below the dams.[37]

Diversions for irrigation and hydropower alone degrade tens of thousands of miles of streams. Irrigation companies have nearly dried up the entire Snake River—the West's third-largest river—by shunting the water off into three enormous canals bound for farms. The Colorado River is drained dry before reaching its salt-polluted mouth, just across the border in Mexico, at the Gulf of California. This fact would be regarded as a national tragedy if the international border were located only a few miles farther south. The problem affects smaller streams throughout the West, and even on the Connecticut River, power plants render some sections of the great eastern artery almost dry. Leaving some water in the rivers for fish, wildlife, and water quality could often protect stream life without impinging greatly on other uses, but rules for doing this have been enacted at precious few streams.[38]

Whether for irrigation, hydropower, domestic, or industrial purposes, 11 percent of North America's total freshwater runoff is withdrawn for human use, and too often these diversions damage the health of the streams.[39] The city of Virginia Beach now proposes to divert water from the Roanoke River—the river where this chapter began—a loss that could cripple the middle river and the Roanoke River Wildlife Refuge.

Urban growth affects rivers not only through the withdrawal of too much water but even more through the construction of roads, suburban neighborhoods, and vacation homes along the water's edge. Shoreline habitat turns into pavement, riprap, and mowed lawns. The combined effects of development, farming, and grazing have damaged or destroyed 60 to 80 percent of the riparian corridors of the United States.[40] Left alone, these riverfront zones serve as home to wildlife, absorb floodwaters, purify runoff, and recharge groundwater. Knowing all that, it's easy to see that a river is more than just water sluicing between two banks; a river is the combined current, gravel beds, shorelines, riparian habitat, and lowland periodically reclaimed during floods. All these riverine members serve important functions, if allowed to do their jobs.

Not only does waterfront development preempt the floodplain's natural, free work of filtering runoff and accommodating overflow volume, but it also puts people in jeopardy and guarantees property damage when the inevitable floods hit. The hazards arise not from high water, which is as timeless as rain, but from people building homes where swollen rivers are bound to flow. Levees, roads, and development compound the difficulties by preventing runoff from spreading out. Instead, they force flood levels higher. Throughout the United States, 179 million acres lie on the hundred-year floodplain—the land likely to flood at least once each century. That's less than 8 percent of America. With the threat of floods now well known, one might think we'd gravitate to some of the other 92 percent of the land when we build houses and invest our money, but by the late 1970s, 3.5 million to 5.5 million floodplain acres had been developed for housing and urban use. It's no coincidence that annual flood losses have increased by 1.5 to 2.5 percent per year.[41] In 1993, the Great Flood of the Mississippi broke all records for damage. In 1996, the president declared West Virginia a federal disaster area four separate times owing to floods. In 1997, storm runoff in California filled some of the country's largest reservoirs and spilled in uncontrolled releases below them, breaking levees, forcing the evacuation of 100,000 people, and ringing up $1.6 billion in losses.[42] Though we immortalize the dust bowl's choking of ten Great Plains states as the quintessential natural disaster, flooding has been worse. In the 1990s alone, it hit forty-five states, with record damage costs of $37 billion.[43] In spite of billions of dollars spent trying to control the rivers, flood losses—adjusted for inflation—have nearly tripled since 1951.[44]

In trying to cope with these natural events—modern-day but biblical in proportion—we've done the worst possible thing. Instead of regulating private development so that it stays above the predictable rush of floods, we've tried to control the floods themselves by damming the rivers and erecting levees. And the deceiving part is that we've been somewhat successful. A lot of engineering and construction projects have effectively quelled many small and medium-sized floods. We've done this well enough that people have forgotten about the hazards. After flood zones have been "protected" by dams and levees, local governments have even rescinded hard-earned restrictions on home building along some rivers. Under this seductive but mistaken sense of security, we've paved and populated the lowlands only to have the really large floods overtop the dams, breach the levees, and wreak damage unimagined by our ancestors who first settled the river towns. Taxpayers foot the bill through disaster relief, replacement of public facilities such as roads and sewer lines, flood insurance payments, and other subsidies, not to mention the initial cost of the dams and levees themselves—an expense that people at the time thought would solve the problem in one shot rather than make it worse.

In American culture and politics, it has been acceptable to spend billions of taxpayer dollars ineffectively in trying to control nature but unacceptable to control the actions of people who insist on building in the path of a flood. The pattern continues. The city council of Fresno, California, approved a subdivision of luxury houses in the bed of the San Joaquin River only a month after four-foot floods ripped through the site.[45] Elsewhere in California, even though communities had adequate flood mapping and warning, 58,000 homes were planned on acreage that had flooded in 1997. These are not cases of ignorance; developers are simply getting the favors they want from local governments.

The dams and levees give people a false sense of security, and what little security there might really be decreases all the time as mud fills in the reservoirs. Because the silt transported by the rivers settles out in the flatwater, flood-control dams gradually lose their capacity for storage. Some, such as Little Pine Creek Dam in Pennsylvania, overflowed with silt twenty-five years ago. The U.S. Army Corps of Engineers reported that in a single storm, Kaweah Reservoir in California received half the sediment expected in a fifty-year period.[46] At Lake Austin in Texas, silt decreased storage capacity by 96 percent in a mere thirteen years. Solutions to this problem, destined to make white elephants out of most dams, are limited to raising the level of the structures to buy a little more time or pumping sediment from the reservoirs, which is prohibitively expensive.[47] The only real solution is to construct new buildings away from flood hazards and to relocate old development on higher ground.

If our society embraced this strategy wholeheartedly, the life span of the reservoirs we've already built would give us some time to restore all but the most urbanized floodplains, which would then be more easily protected by levees. Rather than regarding our hard-earned though shortsighted investment in flood-control dams as the solution, we might do well to regard it as expensively borrowed time that can now be used to correct land-use mistakes of the past. This daunting task begins with a simple but effective floodplain zoning ordinance in every community.

High water resoundingly shows that the rivers' sphere of influence envelops the floodplain, and likewise, the influence of what we do even on mountaintops extends down to river bottoms. The health of our streams might be regarded as a report card on everything done to the land; the patterns of runoff tell us so much about how we care for our forests, tend our farms, build our roads, recycle our waste, and respect our neighbors' property downstream. As early as 1782, recognizing that logging caused water to run off faster—worsening floods and leaving little flow for the dry seasons—J. Hector St. John de Crèvecoeur wrote of grist mills standing on dry ground where twenty years before there had been plenty of water: "This effect does not surprise me. Our ancient woods kept the earth moist and damp, and the sun could evaporate none of the water contained within their shades. Who knows how far these effects may extend?"[48] Now we know: the effects extend from the top of the watershed to the bottom—everywhere.

More than most rivers, the Mississippi exemplifies the connections between what people do to the land and what happens to the rivers. In its lower reaches, 150 major chemical and petroleum industries discharge into 150 miles of river, victimizing the people in poor southern towns nearby. Receiving more toxic waste than any other body of water, this grand artery once called the Father of Waters is now known as Cancer Alley. Upstream reaches have their own set of problems: in the tributary basins of the Midwest, farmers have drained millions of acres of wetlands. To plant more acreage with crops that are in chronic surplus, farmers have piped or ditched their fields to carry away storm water. But this has aggravated flood hazards below, caused increased runoff to spill onto the land of downstream farmers, and indirectly driven flood insurance and disaster relief accounts deep into red ink.

Along the Mississippi, levees have been thrown up to repel floodwaters, leading towns and whole states to war with one another in the one-upmanship of higher walls. In an earlier era, runoff spread out on the floodplain, recharging groundwater, lessening flood damage, depositing fertile soil, and feeding one of the most critical wetland and wildlife corridors on the continent. But now the floods rise higher in their straitjacket of levees until the structures fail or are overtopped, a human-made disaster that resulted in $19 billion in flood damage in 1993 alone.[49]

With its vast watershed, its industrial-scale wastes, its channelized headwaters and walled-up shorelines, the Mississippi River offers a megasample of the land-and-water relationship, but the same bonds apply everywhere. The Willamette River of Oregon carries industrial toxins and foul runoff, requiring expensive treatment for a waterway that would otherwise be Portland's most economic source of new drinking water. The Columbia basin's salmon, once supporting a $1.2 billion industry employing 25,000 or more people, are approaching extinction.[50] The ancient forests of Oregon have been logged, and with the loss of that forest we've lost a free, natural system for maintaining clean streams critical to public water supplies. Everyone downstream misses the spongelike forest floor that once soaked up more floodwaters than the most expensive big dam could ever begin to do. Up and down this northwestern artery, hot debates over flooding, drinking water, endangered salmon, and the last old-growth forests send Americans a signal we would be fools to ignore: the watersheds of this land are in deep trouble.

Beyond the direct effects on people, distressed river systems such as the Willamette and the Mississippi result in sharp losses in biological diversity. Zoologist Larry Master reported that 36 percent of America's fish species are extinct or imperiled, as well as 67 percent of the mussels and 64 percent of the crayfish. One-quarter of the amphibians are in danger.[51] Among 2,000 sizeable watersheds in America, 1,300 have been so damaged that they contain at least one imperiled species of fish or mussel.[52] These are the most threatened families of creatures in the country. In Alabama—a hotbed of biological diversity—dams on the Coosa River alone drove twenty-seven species of aquatic snails to oblivion, probably the largest single extinction catastrophe in American history.[53] Aquatic creatures are more endangered but less noticed than those on land; we can't see the life in the rivers, so we're unaware of the losses when they occur.

Scanning the host of river problems with a nationwide perspective, American Rivers annually names twenty waterways as those most endangered. This call to arms typically includes streams such as the Hudson River in New York, where toxins linger; the Snake and Columbia Rivers, where the world's greatest migration of chinook salmon now populates the endangered species list; the Rio Grande, where cities of 800,000 people just across the border in Mexico treat sewage not the slightest bit; and the Penobscot River in Maine, where a proposed hydropower dam would have undercut expensive, decades-long efforts to restore Atlantic salmon.[54]

Reappearing on the list year after year, the American River lies upstream of Sacramento, California. Here, the Bureau of Reclamation planned Auburn Dam, a $2.2 billion structure to deliver water costing twenty times what farmers would pay. The reasons for building this public-works monolith change with the shifting winds of politics and natural catastrophe. Given the boosters' current aim of flood control, the dam's cost would equal the combined expense of Grand Coulee and Hoover Dams, adjusted for inflation. Yet improvements at levees and at an existing dam promise greater flood protection at one-tenth the cost and have gained the support of the Sacramento Area Flood Control Agency and the Sacramento City Council. The reason the Auburn proposal continues is that Congressman John Doolittle—when not talking about balancing the federal budget—works overtime to siphon millions of tax dollars into one of the most wasteful water projects ever contemplated in American history.

Auburn Dam may be the worst, but when political rhetoric turns toward cost cutting, austerity, and the shrinking of government, consider some of the other unnecessary subsidies that damage our rivers. In the past quarter century, we've spent $140 billion on U.S. Army Corps of Engineers flood-control projects and on disaster relief and preparedness, most of it flood related, but flood damages now cost $4 billion per year.[55] Government disaster relief payments for floods during the 1990s totaled $15 billion to $30 billion.[56] On top of that, a federal flood insurance program covers losses of people who buy flood insurance, but nearly half of the payments go to only 2 percent of policyholders, who suffer high water repeatedly. They take the federally subsidized payments but lack the incentive or will to move out of harm's way.[57] The program's debt stood at $917 million in 1997.

If that's not enough to raise the ire of a cost-conscious tax cutter, consider the water subsidies for western agriculture. Scores of western rivers have been converted to reservoirs and thousands of miles of streams have been dried up by diversions to irrigate crops. To do all this, the taxpayer picks up the tab—typically 90 percent of the cost of the water—which has totaled billions of dollars over the years.[58] Trying to grow many of the same crops, farmers in other regions suffer when taxpayers foot the irrigation bill for arid-land farmers, many of them big corporations. Building

LIFELINES OF RIVERS   185

absurdity onto largesse, 30 to 40 percent of the subsidized water goes to raise surplus crops, which other farmers have been paid not to grow.[59]

Nothing, however, is more subsidized than the barging system on rivers. Of $786 million budgeted by the government for barging facilities, taxpayers have shelled out $700 million. Without the subsidies on locks, dams, and channelization for barges on the lower Snake River, rail transport would be cheaper.[60] And without the dams built for barging, the salmon of that basin would likely be in good shape, along with the enormous economy and food supply that those fish made possible. The principal commodity carried by the barges is grain on its way to Asia. In this perverse cycle of subsidy, the taxpayers are actually paying to drive one of our own sources of food—the salmon—to extinction while other government money is spent in trying to save the fish.[61] And on the Mississippi, new locks and dams for commercial barging will cost billions of dollars, nearly all of it to be paid by taxpayers.[62]

The federal subsidies for floodplain real estate, western irrigation, and barging all cost money and all destroy rivers. The waste has gone unnoticed in the hype of growth and development, but today, that is changing. As we enter the 21st century, more and more people seek better ways to care for the earth and its crucial lifelines of water.

A Movement to Save Rivers

The Clean Water Act of 1972 and its subsequent amendments give encouragement and hope. This federal law mandated that cities and industries clean up, and it provided federal money to help communities tackle the job. The law has enabled hundreds of streams to recover from blind abuse.

Along the Ohio River, a new generation of anglers reel in pike and bass where my grandfather and I hooked only carp and catfish. The Blackstone River of Rhode Island, once among the most polluted streams in America, has become a model of recovery, as have the Merrimack, Concord, and Nashua Rivers in Massachusetts. The Environmental Protection Agency has required 63,000 industries and municipalities to treat their waste and reports that 90 percent of the point sources of pollution from sewage plants and industries have been cleaned up, at least to some degree. To help pay for this job, the agency spent $54 billion and states spent another $128 billion on sewage treatment plants between 1972 and 1989; since then, another $19 billion has gone out in loans for municipal plants. And the investment has paid off; sewage pollution has decreased by 46 percent, even with a 30 percent increase in the amount of waste being treated.[63] The statistics of success are impressive; while only 36 percent of our rivers were rated as safe for swimming when the Clean Water Act was passed, 60 percent now are.

Feeling the pinch of the federal law, polluting industries and related groups paid big money to elect anti-environment politicians in the 1990s. The resulting House of Representatives in 1995 passed a budget bill slashing $760 million from clean water programs and reducing the already minimal Environmental Protection Agency (EPA) enforcement budget by a fourth. Avoiding the embarrassing exposure of an open debate on this popular cause, members of Congress tried to attach seventeen riders onto unrelated bills in their efforts to hamstring the cleanup of water. They tried to exempt favored industries, stop new regulations against radioactive elements in drinking water, and withhold information from the public. The motivation for this retrograde group in Congress was clearly not the public interest. Rather, House members voting to undercut clean water efforts each received an average of $54,669 for their next reelection campaign from political action committees affiliated with lobbyists seeking to undercut the Clean Water Act.[64] But the public outcry was too great, and the worst cuts failed to pass the more moderate Senate. In 1997, nineteen of the congressional representatives who voted to gut pollution laws lost their seats to challengers promising to protect the environment. But still running scared, the EPA scaled back any expectations that the legislated goal of clean water for all the country's rivers would be met; in a 1997 report, the agency lamely stated, "On the whole, we have managed to hold the line or prevent further degradation."

Yet simply holding our ground is becoming quite the challenge because of endless growth. After agricultural runoff, municipal waste remains the second most serious water quality problem, and an estimated $137 billion will be needed simply to sustain existing treatment levels until the year 2012.[65] Federal expenditures for environmental work, however, have been reduced almost continually as a percentage of the federal budget since the 1970s.[66] Somehow the shortfall will have to be addressed, and new action is required to deal with polluted runoff, which has mostly escaped federal mandates. One encouraging sign here is that farmers, water suppliers, and government agencies in hundreds of projects nation-wide now cooperate in prototypal efforts to improve the water in agri-cultural areas. In central Iowa, for example, the Des Moines Water Works depends on the Raccoon River, which has a watershed that also houses 6,300 farms. A local project encourages farmers to leave buffer strips along streams, apply rest-rotation in grazing, and reduce pesticide use.[67]

In the East Coast *Pfiesteria* belt, money set aside under the 1996 Farm Bill was used to idle 100,000 acres along North Carolina rivers where farm waste laden with nitrogen was overloading the river systems. Though it accomplished important work, this program shows how the costs of pollution on private land continually burden the public. Because better regulation has little support in Congress, the taxpayer ends up footing the bill for pollution that never should have been allowed in the first place.

While much remains to be done to clean up our waters, other people are working on a second front of river protection: floodplain manage-ment. The principal tool—floodplain zoning—can halt further develop-ment of lowlands along rivers. The challenges, however, are legion. The National Flood Insurance Program commendably requires zoning in order for landowners to receive insurance and federally backed mort-gages, but the regulations are riddled with loopholes. Ordinances usually ban new buildings only from the worst "hazard" areas—far less than the land likely to flood every hundred years. Developers may "flood-proof" buildings by putting mobile homes on stilts or, worse, by constructing houses on earthfill that destroys additional habitat and displaces even more floodwater. It would be far better simply to locate new development on higher ground.[68]

As a landmark of promising change, a White House commission in 1994 reported that we need to reduce flood hazards through land-use controls and relocation of flood-prone development. Levees should be set back from waterways, and regulations should recognize hazards beyond the hundred-year floodplain.[69] The commission repeated what flood pol-icy reformers such as Gilbert White had been saying since the 1930s.[70] But this time, in the wake of the 1993 Mississippi floods, the recommenda-tions fell on fertile ground. Congress earmarked $600 million for reloca-tion out of a $6 billion relief package. The 900-person town of Valmeyer,

Illinois, moved to a bluff. Upriver and down, landowners relocated single homes and whole neighborhoods. Eight thousand homes and businesses were moved from the floodplain—10 percent of the flood-damaged structures. Governments acquired 50,000 acres for floodplain and wildlife habitat, most of it from farmers. And for future disasters, Congress earmarked 15 percent of relief funds to "predisaster mitigation," such as relocation of repeatedly flooded homes. The law set aside $20 million per year for relocation funded by flood insurance premiums, and it established insurance discounts for communities that go beyond the minimum standards of floodplain zoning.[71]

After fifty years of trying to control rivers by building dams and levees instead of respecting the inevitability of floods, the times have changed, or at least the stage is set. In the aftermath of the 1997 West Coast floods, *Los Angeles Times* editors recognized that the "days of massive new dams and control projects are over." The chorus of public opinion no longer calls for the tiresome approach of simply building more dams.[72]

Rejecting the old channelization and levee response as well, Napa County, California, devised a plan to restore natural river channels in order to lower urban flood levels. In 1998, the Clinton administration proposed that $25 million be spent on this type of alternative to dam and levee building. With sixty projects waiting in the wings—all of them likely to save the taxpayers money in the long run—the administration hoped to raise annual funding to $100 million by 2002.

Beyond water quality and floodplain management reform, people are pursuing dozens of strategies to solve the menacing problems of damaged rivers and watersheds. Exciting prospects lie with the relicensing of hundreds of old private hydroelectric dams, especially in New England, the northern Midwest, California, and the Northwest. Many of the fifty-year licenses will soon expire, and now the old dams and diversions must meet environmental standards.[73] This is a once-in-a-lifetime opportunity to correct some of the past damage by reinstating healthier flows below the dams, improving water temperature through dam operations, installing fish ladders for migrating species otherwise blocked by the hydroelectric plants, and in some cases eliminating the dams altogether. After a ten-year battle, the Federal Energy Regulatory Commission required its first dam removal in 1998. On Maine's Kennebec River, Edwards Dam had blocked nine fish species from their spawning grounds since 1837 for a trifling 3.5

megawatts of electricity.[74] The ramshackle old dam was removed in July 1999. Other dilapidated dams were pulled out of several rivers in Wisconsin, and larger dams were slated for demolition on the Elwha River in Washington—a once great salmon stream that could become great again, though Senator Slade Gorton of Washington blocked funding for the Elwha restoration in 1998 after the Clinton administration refused to relegate decisions on other dam removals or revisions to Congress.

While a few of the most useless and harmful dams are being taken out of rivers, water in some thirsty reaches is being put back in. At scattered sites such as the Umatilla River in eastern Oregon and Ash Meadows National Wildlife Refuge in Nevada, some flows are being returned to streams that had been dried up for years by irrigation diversions.[75] In another sign of change in both the Northeast and the Northwest, conservation and fishing groups have waged intensive efforts to restore anadromous, or seagoing, fish including salmon, steelhead, and shad. One success here lies on the Susquehanna River, where the states of Pennsylvania and Maryland along with regional utility companies signed a long-sought agreement in 1993 to provide fish passage facilities at three old dams.

Covering the gamut of issues, interest in better care for rivers and their watersheds is booming nationwide—a groundswell that every politician should be aware of. The Clean Water Network now includes 1,000 member organizations from environmental, sporting, labor, religious, and other groups.

American Rivers, which formed in 1973 to urge protection of our finest waterways in the National Wild and Scenic Rivers System, expanded its interests and became the nation's principal river conservation group.[76] Now it lobbies for effective federal laws, fights major threats to waterways, and urges better care for hometown streams as well as the continent's largest arteries and remaining wild rivers. In 1998, the president of American Rivers, Rebecca Wodder, said, "Our conservation programs are geared toward restoring the self-renewing processes of our nation's rivers—from headwaters sending clean water downstream, to floodplains that act as filters for pollutants, to the river's most basic rhythms that sustain life. Healthy rivers will support the biological communities, including people, that depend on them."

Responding to the opportunity of having healthy rivers everywhere, people all across America are forming small organizations to protect their local rivers. In 1990, 500 groups were known to be working on river conservation in the United States. A 1996 survey found 3,000 such groups.

Attempting to avoid the problems that often result in stalemates among warring factions, residents in many regions are now forming watershed councils to inaugurate discussions about their rivers and land. Under this model, representatives from all points of view meet with the common goals of continuing to live in their chosen communities, protecting what remains, and restoring some reasonable part of what has been lost. Promoting this approach in 1998, Joy Huber of the Rivers Council of Washington said, "When people come together, they find they have common goals and a shared, undeniable dependency on water and soil."

Committed river conservationists have formed statewide river organizations in half the states, spearheading efforts to lobby legislatures and to help local groups be effective. California, Idaho, Washington, Wisconsin, New Mexico, Ohio, Massachusetts, and New York have strong programs. But much of the country remains untended. Little activity is found on the Great Plains or in the South. Yet in Alabama, Don Elder, a trumpet player with the City of Birmingham Symphony Orchestra, built the Cahaba River Society into an effective group for stewarding one of America's biologically richest streams. Other Alabamans built on this effort by forming a statewide organization. In 1998, similar statewide groups were formed in North Carolina and Georgia.

River Network, a national organization based in Portland, Oregon, helps these local and state groups across the country. Founder Phil Wallin said, "The solutions to river degradation, like the problems, are primarily local. The solutions must be created by citizen activists, valley by valley and stream by stream." River Network hopes to see a river conservation organization in every major watershed.

By working in their own river basins, people acting under River Network's model for the future might regain some of the control that has been lost to the forces that brought us a polluted Mississippi and a population of salmon on the brink of extinction. With an activated citizenry as stewards of home territories, perhaps we'll begin to see changes in the way landowners, communities, and governments care for all the land and water of America.

Making a Difference

Personifying the movement to better care for rivers, Bob McCullough has spent a lifetime working for change, and his success is enough to hearten anybody who cares about water.

The grandson of a timber baron who had logged the Appalachian Mountains of northern Pennsylvania down to bare ground, Bob grew up fishing in his backyard streams of Pine Creek, Cedar Run, and other tributaries to the West Branch of the Susquehanna. A strapping young man, six feet two, with a confident gleam in his eye and an ever-present smile, McCullough served in World War II and eventually returned to his hometown area. Though blind in his left eye and with only partial vision in his right, he regarded this problem as a minor handicap; he could still fish and work. "The big problem," he reflected in a 1998 interview, "was still ahead of me."

For thirty years, McCullough sold cars to make a living and to raise three children, but in his spare time he fished for trout. Tying on his flies by feel because he couldn't see the leader, he specialized in night fishing. "I can't see much in the daytime anyway, so night fishing leveled the playing field with the other guys," he joked.

As the years passed, McCullough noticed more and more about his rivers. While the devastation of logging had wreaked havoc on mountain streams, some had recovered with the vigorous regrowth of eastern forests. But in the 1950s and 1960s, McCullough began to see pollution from sewage systems, a growing clutter of trash in open dumps, a boom in floodplain development, and new strip mines chewing up the mountains for coal. "There were so many problems it was unbelievable," he said. "And few people back then cared."

Using his considerable sales abilities, McCullough convinced people to care. He helped to organize a local chapter of Trout Unlimited and the Pine Creek Watershed Association. "You have to push and push and push," he said of technique, "but always in a way that people understand. The people up Pine Creek could talk fishing, so that's what we did. Pretty soon they agreed we had to do something about sewage waste, or mobile homes on the floodplain. But you have to talk to people, each and every one of them."

Just as important, McCullough developed rapport over the years with professionals working in the environmental agencies. He built friendships with technicians, who then fed him information that otherwise would have languished because of political resistance and upper-level bureaucrats who didn't want to rock the boat. And he also became friends with officials at the highest levels in the agencies. That way, when they heard from McCullough, they felt they had to do something.

Eventually, the Lycoming County Planning Commission hired McCullough for his skills in explaining environmental programs. Better than anyone else, he could take the heat at public meetings where, long before the so-called wise use movement of rabid anti-environmentalists had a name, mobs of angry landowners attacked plans for everything from closing an illegal dump to zoning the floodplain.

With his instigation, salesmanship, and persistent badgering of officials, McCullough helped launch programs to test septic tanks and town sewage plants along Pine Creek and to fix the ones that didn't work. He got the state to buy important open spaces; within a decade, these totaled thousands of acres along waterfronts that otherwise would have been developed. He coaxed local governments into the flood insurance program until all fifty-two townships and towns in the county had floodplain zoning.

He did all this by serving on task forces, taking politicians and newspaper writers on field trips, organizing fishermen, sitting in country kitchens and listening to people, arguing with bureaucrats who weren't doing their jobs, supporting those who were, and never, ever giving up. "I couldn't have done any of it without Miriam," Bob said of his wife. Because Bob's sight was so poor, Miriam drove him to hundreds of night meetings and read him thousands of pages of letters and reports.

In retirement at age seventy, McCullough increased the pace with what may be his greatest accomplishment: he and a few other people formed the Pennsylvania Environmental Defense Foundation and set out to bring towns and industries on rivers all over Pennsylvania into compliance with water quality laws. "It's very simple," Bob said of his strategy. "They have to follow the law. We have most of the regulations we need, but there's never been any shortage of political favors in this state, and so big industries and whole cities get off without doing what the law says. That hasn't always been true, but that's the way it is in 1998."

With lawyer John Childe filing suits whenever McCullough or the foundation's director, Jim Barr, discovered violations, the organization won case after case and cleaned up stream after stream. Through the settlements, they raised money and gave it to local conservation groups to watchdog their areas.

"Finding the violations is easy," McCullough explained. "The phone rings at night. Somebody on the other end says, 'Hey Bob, take a look at the July 25 surveillance report on your favorite coal company.' Then they hang up. The guys out there doing the work would get nowhere through their own legal channels, but they know they can depend on me and Jim and John."

In 1998, after Miriam died, Bob didn't attend as many night meetings as he used to, but if you ask him how it's going, he says, "Hey, if it's not going, I get out and push!"

The foundation's brightest success came at Babb Creek, a rushing stream of the north-central Pennsylvania highlands that for a century had run Day-Glo orange, first with iron and acid from old deep mines and then from whole mountainsides of strip mining. After trying to get state officials to enforce requirements of the company's discharge permit, the foundation filed suit and won a negotiated settlement that stopped the mining, required reclamation, and levied a fee, to be deposited in a trust fund. Using this money, state engineers drew up a plan to neutralize the acid with limestone. The Army National Guard and volunteers, including local teenagers, enlisted in the construction effort. Babb Creek's pH climbed from 4.5 to 6, and mayflies and trout began to return after a hundred-year absence.[77] "On Babb Creek," McCullough said, "the cooperation of state and federal agencies and other groups has been great. Now we're going after half a dozen other acid streams. And you know what? We're going to bring them back to life."

Reflecting on his success, McCullough said, "Too many people work until they hit a wall, and then they try to go through it. You can't do that. If you hit a wall, you have to go around it."

With fifty years of experience in working to stop pollution and restore streams in his native state, McCullough said, "We *have* made progress. Our streams in northern Pennsylvania are better than they were fifteen years ago." He has the advantage of living in a region where the growth rate is almost zero, so the hard-earned victories of conservation are not simply undone by the weight of more people and more development. With the satisfaction of a life well lived, McCullough said, "In this part of the country, we've saved some of the best for the next generation."

Like Bob McCullough, more and more people are finding that to reclaim the heart of our country, we need to go to the rivers. They bring life to the land and at the same time reflect all we do to the land. Rivers are the pathways that lead us to everything else, and if we want to protect and defend America, the stream out the backdoor is a good place to begin.

CHAPTER 6

IMMERSED IN LAKES AND WETLANDS

O<small>N A DAY</small> carefully chosen for its calmness, I paddled out from shore, and I entered what seemed to be a whole separate sphere of earth. Deeper, colder, cleaner, a place of extremes, Lake Superior dwarfs the other lakes. The world's largest fresh-water body in surface area, it reaches out 350 by 160 miles, and its blue-green depths plunge to 1,333 feet. Unable to see the whole thing, I wanted at least to taste the flavor of this great American lake. I had planned a three-day outing but carried enough food for five days in case I became stranded by a wave-tossing storm.

When I launched, the gravel underneath me shone like a buried trea-sure of varnished beads, millions of them, replaced in deeper water with egg-shaped rocks of pastel colors, as if dyed for Easter and piled up by the uncountable thousands. Then huge rocks armored the bottom, rocks I could only guess to be the size of cars. I couldn't tell how far down any

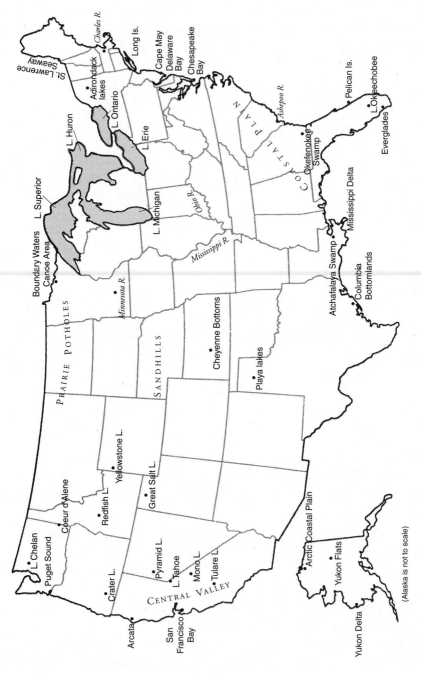

LAKES AND WETLANDS OF THE UNITED STATES
(selected place names)

(Alaska is not to scale)

Charles R.

Long Is.

Cape May
Delaware
Bay
Chesapeake
Bay

Adirondack
lakes

St. Lawrence
Seaway

L. Huron

L. Ontario

L. Erie

L. Superior

COASTAL PLAIN

Ashepoo R.

Pelican Is.

L. Okeechobee

Okefenokee
Swamp

Everglades

Boundary Waters
Canoe Area

L. Michigan

Ohio R.

Mississippi Delta

Mississippi R.

Atchafalaya Swamp

Columbia
Bottomlands

PRAIRIE POTHOLES

Minnesota R.

SANDHILLS

Cheyenne Bottoms

Playa lakes

Yellowstone L.

Coeur d'Alene

Redfish L.

Great Salt L.

L. Chelan

Puget Sound

Crater L.

Pyramid L.

L. Tahoe

Mono L.

Tulare L.

Arctic Coastal Plain

Yukon Flats

CENTRAL VALLEY

Arcata

San
Francisco
Bay

Yukon Delta

of it was. Only a few strokes from land, the lake bed had dropped deeper than the length of my paddle, and now I floated a hundred yards out, gazing at the shoulder-to-shoulder crowd of big underwater boulders. As I drifted farther, the rocky, gray shores receded, along with an escarpment of cliffs and the earthy, green comfort of north wood conifers. Behind me, that weather-pounded lakeshore looked like the coast of Maine. Ahead of me, it was all water.

The lake appeared still, but it wasn't. It respired with movements as regular and steady as the expansion and contraction of my lungs. When I looked down, the bottom warped in and out of shape as if seen through old, wavy glass. The cause of this distortion, a silent buoyancy, lofted me up and eased me down in an effortless ride on the pulse of swells pumped by offshore winds I never felt.

I could have stayed a long time, as the water does. Runoff entering Lake Superior from its tributaries in the pinewoods and voyageurs' canoe country lingers in the lake for an impressive 200 years. Average "residence time" extends to 500 years for the entire Great Lakes system. Whatever flows in and whatever people dump in stays for the ages before spilling out into the St. Lawrence River and then the Atlantic Ocean.

Beyond a rugged headland, I paddled my boat to a protected cove, and among cliff faces, I found a crevasselike enclave just twice the size of the canoe. I couldn't resist. Inside, with glimmers of reflected light dancing on rock walls, I discovered a placid, green room, though it would be a battering thunder hole during storms. Thirsting for whatever was next to come, I moved on and later camped at a surf-worn spit by the mouth of a small river, up against an edge of birch and spruce, alone in a lush waterfront wilderness.

That evening, sitting on the shore of the westernmost, northernmost Great Lake, squarely at mid-continent, I felt the tranquility I associate with so many lakes. The setting disc of sun burned through a flaming horizon, and the surface of Lake Superior grew truly calm, compelling in its peacefulness. The stillness and the spaciousness of simply looking out over water—a lot of water—made me feel placid and at ease, yet somehow it held the promise of unlimited possibilities.

Part of the lake-based satisfaction is looking out at a blank wilderness of space, and space. The horizon of water offers a clean slate. Nothing else on earth looks quite so empty, but on second thought, not empty at all.

It's full—full of water and everything water contains. The lake view is almost hypnotic to many who prop up their feet and stare, from Champlain in Vermont to Lake Washington bordering Seattle, from Itasca in Minnesota to Okeechobee in Florida. A man with a special affinity for ponds and small lakes, Henry David Thoreau, wrote, "Nothing so fair, so pure . . . lies on the surface of the earth." We've enshrined Walden Pond as the site of a classic in American literature, and Thoreau's book about it became a philosophical underpinning to the conservation movement. The moist, balmy breeze, the soothing swish of waves lapping on shore, the crisp coolness of an afternoon plunge—all these draw people to lakes, among the most beloved getaways on earth.

When the storm blew in off Lake Superior, it built in menacing fury that commanded my respect and had me wondering when I'd ever be able to paddle home. The wind first roughened the surface, making it look like sticky frosting patted with the flat side of a knife. Then the waves began to roll, finally building to breakers as they pounded ashore through a night that kept me awake in its tossing restlessness. Grounded the next day, I hiked to the top of a rocky knoll, where, whipped by wind, I could see out across whitecaps forever. The lake was so big that it was hard to imagine the sparse population of its basin having any effect. It does, of course, but compared with most others, Superior is a lucky lake.

A year after my voyage in the northland, now at the southern end of the country, in Louisiana, I readied myself for another sampling of America's flatwater. There, in Atchafalaya Swamp, I paddled my canoe through a flooded forest. Not clear but black, the water carried organic detritus in various stages of suspension and rot, the surface a fluid mirror reflecting big trees reaching for the sky. Several feet of water submerged the bases of the fluted, buttressed baldcypress trees.

My friend and guide Charles Fryling paddled ahead of me, confidently leading the way through the maze of Deep South woodland, slaloming between tree trunks, slopping through eddies solid green with duckweed, ducking under branches fuzzed with the curls of epiphytes—lichens that live off the air but anchor themselves on the limbs of trees. The fecundity of the swamp overpowered me, and in its heat I stopped to splash water on my face and listen to the *cluk-cluk-cluk* of a flicker, the single-stroke drum roll of a pileated woodpecker rapping on resonant dead wood, and the jungle calls of a dozen birds I didn't know.

Wildlife of shy temperament retreated from our soupy path, reminding me of my first wetland experience. Swamps or marshes could scarcely be found in the Appalachian hill country where I grew up, so it wasn't until high school, when I borrowed the family car and drove down to some lowlands, that my friend Ogi and I discovered "swamping." Cattails lined the shore, and lanky birds I had never seen hunted in the shallows. We tested the water, cool but pleasant in the month of May. We scanned the surface for snakes. Shirtless and satisfied we'd be spared, we inched in up to our waists. Feeling our way along, we waded deeper, never quite knowing what the next footstep would bring. Without needing to discuss what we were doing, we each realized we could walk or swim with just our eyes and nose out of the water, and thereby explore the swamp with stealth. We hoped to go unnoticed as we eased across the basin toward a great blue heron, a magnificently strange bird to me at the time. With our eyes at water level, perspective was strangely foreshortened, and the bird seemed to grow to pterodactyl dimensions while we inched our way ahead. Then the heron whooshed up with its guttural alarm, *Gwaak! gwaak!* Ogi and I were inexplicably thrilled to be soaking wet, hidden, and immersed in this new, unknown landscape.

Now, thirty years later in the Atchafalaya—the big time of swamps— I cautiously watched for alligators. I didn't see any twelve-foot, plated bodies but rather a pair of silent, sullen eyebrows barely breaking the surface in ale-black water. Our largest reptile had refined "swamping" to an art form. Underneath the walnut-shell mimicry of the eyebrows, two big eyeballs subtly followed my motions, left, right, or dead still.

To keep up with Charles, who had been there perhaps two hundred times during years of dedicated effort to promote protection of the Atcha-falaya, I pulled my way through a narrow channel in a willow–tupelo forest and then into an open pond brightened by water lilies, the floating green pads like big, green poker chips dealt out across the surface. Here, feeding on bugs that hovered near the waterline, fish jumped erratically, some of them large, and some gaining impressive air before splashing back home. Suddenly, the water split apart at the side of my canoe. A fish materialized from thin air and instantly arched its slick body to make the turn back downward. But its powerful trajectory carried it like a little rocket over my canoe, and it landed with a fleshy thud in the bottom of the boat. Desperate for water, it flopped and batted my gear with its broad tail. I wetted my hands and on the third try managed to pin it down and gain a slippery grip. Then I returned the squirming mass of swamp-muscle to the Atchafalaya.

As beautiful as Lake Superior, the swamp expressed the opposite in many ways. Intimate instead of vast, it brewed with life and death and decay, while the lake had tingled with cold crispness, its life quite spare. In between these two significant American water bodies, all manner of lakes and wetlands brighten the countryside, from vernal pools croaking with frogs to salty landlocked seas. Lakes are known as an archetype of beauty and wetlands as a hotbed of life, but both offer far more.

From slick algae at the bottom of the food chain to toothy northern pike at the top, lakes add a whole new dimension to the freshwater eco-system, different from rivers. They come in many types: the enormous Great Lakes, high-country tarns left over from mountain glaciers, north-ern lakes gouged out by the larger continental glaciers in flatter terrain, alkali-ringed lakes shimmering in the deserts, ponds lacking the wind-swept shorelines that give full-grown lakes their seductive beaches, and lowland lakes nourished by overflowing rivers, seaside lagoons, and satu-rated water tables.

Most lakes have wetlands affiliated with them around the edges, but wetlands also exist separately. Defined by the presence of water either part-time or full-time and by soil and plant species that indicate frequent saturation, some wetlands produce more biomass per acre than any other type of ecosystem.[1] Like lakes, they come in all shapes and sizes. Estuarine wetlands at the edge of the ocean include intertidal zones and salt marshes—open, grassy lowlands where tides recycle and mix seawater with freshwater. Mangrove swamps—impenetrable thickets of short trees on stilted roots—resemble brush piles in shallow seas along tropical coasts. Freshwater wetlands include naturally acidic rain-fed bogs of the north; fens, which host diverse plant life watered by both surface water and groundwater flows; and marshes, where cattails, sedges, grasses, and other sun-loving aquatic plants thrive. Swamps are wooded wetlands, whether flooded stands of red maple in the north, the willow–tupelo–sweetgum combinations of warmer climes, or baldcypress—the quintessential mossy swamp of the Deep South. At mid-continent, glaciers left tens of thou-sands of prairie potholes scattered across the northern Great Plains. Rip-arian wetlands pool on the floodplains of rivers everywhere, especially our largest waterways. In the far north, the tundra is mostly soggy land where meltwater in summertime accumulates on top of the great saucer of permafrost. Wetlands of all kinds now cover about 5 percent of America outside Alaska and 6 percent of the world's land surface.[2] Each type hosts its own array of plants and animals; each carries out key functions in the greater circle of land and life on earth.

The Value of Lakes and Wetlands

Lakes, along with seashores, rank as the most popular landscapes for recreation and tourist retreat, from the crowded beach at Presque Isle on Lake Erie to the high country backpackers' paradise of the Rockies. Lakes also provide for an intricate complex of life, with game fish such as striped bass, lake trout, and walleye near the top of the food chain. Our lakes were once so rich that commercial fisheries bustled at Lakes Erie and Ontario in the Northeast and even at Tulare Lake in the semiarid San Joaquin Valley of California. Clean, shining lakes are among Americans' favorite places, and people value them as strongly and intuitively as they value any kind of landscape.

The worth of wetlands is more subtle and hidden than that of lakes, but they're every bit as rich in depth of purpose and beauty of natural function. Swamps, marshes, and their kin not only provide for ecosystems of extraordinary, unparalleled abundance but also offer a whole set of services to other landscapes and to people. The original 221 million acres of wetlands outside Alaska once formed a life-support system for the rest of the country, and the acres that remain still try to do the job.

Wetlands purify water. They might be regarded as holding ponds full of plants and animals that treat waste for free. Excess nutrients that would quickly overload a lake or river and cause a smothering carpet of algae are systematically processed in wetlands. Bacteria break down nutrients, aquatic plants bloom and grow, and insects and invertebrates eat the plants and zooplankton.

Mussels in wetlands and lakes act as filter feeders; some can process twelve gallons of water per day, turning excess nutrients into muscle flesh, which is then eaten by gulls, muskrats, otters, and other predators on up the food chain. Grazing creatures, including crayfish and dabbling ducks, clean up excess algae and other wetland vegetation, and the small grazers become dinner for fish, kingfishers, bitterns, ospreys, herons, eagles, minks, raccoons, alligators, bears, and people, with a robust, healthy, balanced system the result.

A thousand-acre marsh can purify the nitrogenous wastes of 20,000 people—an impressive credential to anyone who pays bills for sewage treatment. Taking advantage of wetlands as nutrient processors, the city of Arcata, California, provides primary treatment for its sewage but then carefully rations it out into a chain of ponds and marshes, where nature completes the cleanup job far better and more cheaply than technology ever could, with big benefits to wildlife. Arcata and some other communities utilize wetlands' natural processes in a planned and structured way, but just by being there, the average wetland treats water pollution constantly.[3]

Excess sediment, America's most ubiquitous water pollutant, oozes off farmland, cattle range, logging tracts, road cuts, and suburban construction sites, carrying nutrients and phosphates from the soil and transporting other chemicals and waste. But when the silty runoff flows through wetlands, the mud settles out and contributes to the soil and nutrient base of a partly terrestrial system, which can assimilate it. Forested wetlands in farming regions remove 80 percent of the phosphorus and 90 percent of the nitrogen from the water that flows through them.[4]

A creation of the glaciers, the prairie pothole wetlands of the corn belt purify water in an especially efficient way. Landlocked by higher terrain, these low depressions collect runoff that eventually seeps into the ground or evaporates. Coming in all sizes, the shallow potholes become small lakes in the spring. Then the water subsides to leave a flourishing greenery of cattails, sedges, and salad greens for ducks and other wildlife.

Farmlands, which now blanket the region, discharge silt and chemical waste in their runoff. Much of this once flowed into the pothole wetlands, where the silt settled and the runoff soaked into the ground to reemerge later as spring flows that fed the rivers with a steady tap line of good water. It made a fine, free system of water filtration, capable of accommodating a lot of cultivation on the prairie.

But wanting to grow corn on every last acre, farmers not only cultivated their arable fields but also went on to fill the wetlands, drain them into ditches, and punch outlet pipes through the banks or swales that had served as natural pothole dams. Instead of settling, the silty water now runs straight to a stream. All this has crippled the native system, and grossly polluted rivers are the result. The Minnesota River once ran so clear that you could pluck mussels from its white, sandy bottom; now, it looks like chocolate milk edged in brown ooze as it sluices away the equivalent of one dump-truck load of soil every five minutes to the Mississippi River, where the soil disguised as water is not wanted.[5]

The loss of pothole wetlands not only turned good water into sludge but also aggravated flooding downstream. Where the heavy rainfall and snowmelt once lay trapped in the potholes for steady, gentle release lasting well into the dry season, it now flashes off through drain tiles and plastic pipes, creating the floods that destroy farms, property, and homes downstream. "Twenty-five years ago it took three weeks for runoff to get to the Mississippi," said Jim Heinecke, manager of Big Stone National Wildlife Refuge, at the headwaters of the Minnesota River. "Now it takes three days."[6] Through an easement acquisition program, Heinecke's agency seeks to reinstate some of the wetlands' flood-abating functions of old, though money to do this is short and resistance great. But consider the alternatives: the Minnesota Department of Natural Resources estimated that it would cost $1.5 million to replace the water storage capability lost when only 5,000 acres are drained.[7]

Not just in the prairie potholes region but wherever wetlands exist, they help to control floods. The Natural Valley Storage Project of the Army Corps of Engineers protects marshes along the Charles River upstream of Boston and offers better flood control at far cheaper prices than any dam and levee system could ever do. Hydrating during floods, 8,422 acres of wetlands later release the absorbed water slowly to the river. The Charles River wetlands save $17 million per year in avoided flood damages.[8]

Stopping floods of a different sort, wetlands along seashores accommodate the shock waves of hurricanes and ocean storms. Along with sand dunes, they guard the continent as a front line of defense, and they protect the land that lies behind them by accommodating surges in water level. Especially wide in Louisiana, this wetland buffer averages twenty-two miles, and every inch is needed, a fact that's becoming more apparent each year as the Mississippi Delta wetlands disappear.[9]

Here is the unfortunate chain of events: made up of mud brought down from uplands by the Mississippi River, the Delta has always been subsiding because the immense weight of the silt—30,000 feet deep in places—depresses the Coastal Plain and packs the soil under its own pressure.[10] Counteracting this in a balanced system, an unchecked Mississippi River has historically delivered 440 million tons of new silt each year. So even as the Delta marshlands subsided, incoming silt, spread out annually on top, maintained an equilibrium.[11] But now, with levees and channelization creating faster currents in the lower river and preventing its frequent overflow, the silt flushes out to deep waters of the Gulf of Mexico, leaving nothing to compensate for the continuing subsidence. The coastal marshes are literally sinking into the sea. Salt water intrudes inland, storms hammer communities that once enjoyed the salt marsh buffer, fisheries die out because their nursery grounds disappear, and the Mississippi-delivered silt wreaks havoc on the deepwater ecosystem of the Gulf because it settles in offshore waters, where it's not supposed to be. The only real solution—though no one is holding his breath on this—is to reinstate the natural function of the river in delivering its annual allotment of silt, which for eons stabilized and sustained the coastal wetlands. In so many ways such as this, the rivers, wetlands, and seashores are connected, as are all the landscapes of America.

At the Gulf shore and nearly everywhere they exist, wetlands serve as nurseries for myriad creatures. The U.S. Fish and Wildlife Service estimated that up to 43 percent of endangered species rely on wetlands for some part of their life cycle. According to the Environmental Protection Agency, wetlands are among the most biologically productive ecosystems in the world and are comparable to tropical rain forests and coral reefs in the diversity of life they support.[12]

Oysters, for example, come not from the deep sea but from tidal wetlands. Along the Gulf coast, they attach themselves to the roots of mangroves, which sprout wherever shifting sand or muck is available. Not only oysters but also 60 percent of all commercially harvested shellfish need wetlands.[13] In the Southeast, 96 percent of the commercial harvest and half the recreational catch of all fish and shellfish depend on coastal wetlands. Even in their waning condition, the marshes and swamps of Louisiana produced $244 million worth of commercial seafood in 1991.[14]

In southern Florida, the wetlands of the Everglades once provided nurseries for shellfish and fish and delivered the freshwater supply needed for a luxuriant underwater prairie of sea grass in the shallow Florida Bay, essential to the region's commercial fishery. But low and polluted flows resulting from sugarcane farming and diversions north of the Everglades have killed off the grasses and led to a crash in the fishery. Now, unemployment plagues a whole industry that once thrived because healthy wetlands had served it, like some great gift of the gods.

Wetlands and lakes are where ducks live, and the potholes of the upper Midwest alone produce half the waterfowl of the continent. But wetlands don't have to pass the "duck test" of having enough surface water to land a mallard. Even wetlands that dry up for part of the year fill vital ecological niches. In places such as New England, these vernal pools offer sanctuaries for frogs, salamanders, fairy shrimp, and other morsels that elsewhere would fall prey to fish but here are available to mammals and birds, which thrive. However, more and more roads now separate the vernal pools, acting as death traps for amphibians and other wildlife migrating in their slow, vulnerable gait away from the pools in summer.

Many other wetlands hold water year-round, supporting fish that in turn eat mosquito larvae. But if ditches divert the water before it flows into the wetlands, the perennial pools dry up, the fish perish, and the mosquitoes multiply out of control. At Rumsey Marsh in suburban Boston, where mosquito clouds became an irksome problem for residents, reinstatement of sufficient water and fish habitat resulted in a 90 percent reduction of the mosquitoes and eliminated the need for pesticides.

Healthy wetlands are also valuable for recreation. The Okefenokee Swamp alone generates an estimated $55 million in tourist revenues annually to a couple of rural Georgia counties.[15] Nationwide, 3 million waterfowl hunters contribute $670 million per year to the economies of wetland regions.[16]

A study conducted by the University of California found that the state's remaining 454,000 acres of wetlands deliver quantifiable benefits to society worth $10 billion per year.[17] Other studies indicate that coastal wetlands are worth $800 to $9,000 per acre for fish production, recreation, storm protection, and water treatment.[18] And the figures don't include the beauty of sunset over water or the value of quiet escapes with binoculars in hand or walks with husband or wife, children or dog. They don't count the sound of geese overhead announcing the coming of spring and fall or the opportunity for children to go "swamping" in their own neighborhoods.

A Watery Brilliance

As the most striking feature on the map of America, the Great Lakes are a fitting place to begin a tour of the flatwaters of our country. This legacy of glacial scouring holds one-fifth of the world's freshwater and 95 percent of the U.S. supply. Lakes Superior, Huron, Michigan, Erie, and Ontario, along with broad connecting rivers called the St. Marys, St. Clair, Detroit, and Niagara, cover 95,000 square miles. Millions of vacationers from the Midwest and East throng to these lakes, and 10 percent of the U.S. population and one-fourth of all Canadians live along their shores.[19] Though the lakes are large, they drain relatively small watersheds—the water surface itself accounts for half of the Great Lakes basin above the St. Lawrence River. For comparison, an average lake in America draws from a watershed six times its size.[20]

The Great Lakes owe their existence to the ice ages, when glaciers depressed the crust of the earth as much as 1,500 feet and left moraines as barricades at the southernmost advance of ice. In fact, most of the lakes in America began with glaciation and lie in the north. Both continental and mountain glaciers muscled their ways southward or downward from their sources of snow, scraping out low spots as they went. When the ice melted, water collected in these depressions. Like the blade of a bulldozer, the glaciers also pushed enormous piles of rock and dirt ahead of them, and where the ice advance stopped, moraines spanned whole valleys, functioning as natural dams.

In the Northeast, the lake-making glaciers advanced southward nearly to the Ohio River valley. Their stellar legacy includes the lacustrine country of Maine, where topographic maps show as much water as land in some regions. Disc- and amoeba-shaped bodies of water speckle the north woods in an intricate network of windswept lakes and tree-shaded ponds. Similarly studded with flatwater gems, the Adirondack Mountains shelter whole chains of lakes, including the Saranac Lakes, linked by rivers and enjoyed by people whose ancestors built rustic cabins in a comforting old style of logs and stone.

Bogs, swamps, and marshes appear all over these northern regions, many of them old glacial lakes now filled with sediment from erosion of surrounding land. And even when the glaciers didn't scour out lake beds, they often made enough of a depression to collect groundwater. Rotting

Lake Superior. The largest of all our lakes, Superior is also the cleanest and least developed in the Great Lakes chain.

Atchafalaya Swamp, Louisiana. An abundance of wetland life thrives in this hardwood swamp near the mouth of the Mississippi River.

Round Pond, Maine. Thousands of lakes, ponds, and wetlands were carved by glaciers across the northern states.

Okefenokee Swamp, Georgia. Baldcypress trees here are regrowing after logging and fire cleared the forest early in the 20th century.

Great egret, Withlacoochee River, Florida. Wetlands provide for hundreds of bird species and some of the richest of all habitat for wildlife.

Atchafalaya Swamp, Louisiana. Our greatest wooded wetland was threatened by drainage canals, channel-ization, and clearing for farmland. Much of the swamp is now protected.

Wetlands along Silver Creek, Idaho. Riparian wetlands are vital to the life of rivers, the quality and supply of groundwater, and 70 percent or more of wildlife species.

Lake McDonald, Montana. Lakes formed by mountain glaciers are among people's favorite destinations for recreation.

Water hyacinth, Florida. This exotic weed has infested lakes, wetlands, and rivers and has crowded out native life.

Pearl River, Louisiana. Despite regulations intended to limit development in wetlands, parcels such as this continue to be drained, filled, and built upon.

vegetation then accumulated as organic sludge. Without completely decomposing, it formed the peat that underlies north-woods bogs and hosts acid-loving plants such as cranberry, rhododendron, sheep laurel, black spruce, and tamarack.

To the south, marshes sprawl where eastern rivers meet their sea-level estuaries. The mouth of the Connecticut River; Hackensack Meadows, near New York City; and Delaware Bay, with its great populations of migrating shorebirds, are just a few examples. Marshlands fringe the 200-mile-long Chesapeake Bay, though not as much as they did before home owners began riprapping miles of shoreline with rocks in an effort to extend their lawns and protect their homes.

South of the glacial advance yet still above the Coastal Plain, most of the "lakes" on today's landscape are in fact reservoirs—human-made impoundments resulting from cement or earthen dams blocking rivers. Large reservoirs are especially common in the Appalachians, the Midwest, the south-central states, and California. Unlike lakes, with their natural shorelines, windswept beaches, round-stone cobble bars, and lush, green fringes of hydric plants, reservoirs lap up against hillsides where water had never collected before. They erode steep banks and fluctuate in level daily, according to operational plans of the Army Corps of Engineers, the Tennessee Valley Authority, or electrical utility companies. Reservoir levels are often backed up high into the brush in springtime and later dropped low for hydropower, flood control, or irrigation. Where this happens, a "dead zone," or bathtub ring of mud, rock, and rotting timber, encircles many of the reservoirs for part of the year, playing havoc with both aquatic and terrestrial life that otherwise might benefit at the flatwater edges of lakes.[21]

Not counting Alaska, two-thirds of America's wetlands lie in the South.[22] Beyond Delaware Bay, the unglaciated Coastal Plain spreads out and coastal marshes fatten to fifty-mile widths in South Carolina and Georgia. With waving fields of yellow cordgrass and salt grass, these salt marshes flood twice a day under tides. Farther from the ocean, brackish marshes of mixed salt water and fresh water support needle rushes and three-cornered grass. Freshwater marshes lie inland, with bulrushes, sedges, and cattails, and beyond them, slightly higher in elevation, bald-cypress trees shade dark swamps. One of the largest and most majestic of these, Okefenokee Swamp spills across southern Georgia with blackened water that grew baldcypress giants logged early in the 1900s. A new forest is now recovering. Sizable acreage of the Okefenokee falls within a national wildlife refuge, but E. I. du Pont de Nemours and Company (DuPont) proposed that 38,000 adjoining acres be mined for titanium, a fate that could disturb essential groundwater flow, pollute the swamp, and strip twenty-acre sections of wetland at a time. As of 1999, agencies and conservation groups were searching for ways to buy out DuPont.

The Coastal Plain is also veined by meandering rivers with swampy floodplains up to ten miles wide. Here lie some of the wildest parcels of eastern real estate; to find roadless or untouched country in the Southeast, don't look for rugged mountains; instead, look for flat, saturated bottomlands.

As the southernmost extension of the Coastal Plain, Florida has just emerged from the ocean, geologically speaking; at the time of European settlement, 54 percent of it was lake and wetland, the largest proportion among the states.[23] Not counting the Great Lakes, Lake Okeechobee, in south-central Florida, is the largest eastern lake, and it is the essential water supply for wetlands that once defined Florida from that point southward. The ultimate wetland for waterbirds, the fifty-mile-wide Everglades and adjacent Big Cypress Swamp constitute the largest freshwater marsh in the world.[24]

Other wetlands streak or flood the entire Gulf coast, where rivers overflow onto broad riparian flats. Flowing down the midrib of America, the Mississippi River swells over its banks regularly and supplies groundwater to a wide corridor on the interior Coastal Plain, which begins far inland, near the mouth of the Ohio River, and runs for 550 miles to the Gulf of Mexico.

Back up at the Mississippi's source, in the northern Midwest, the legacy of the continental glaciers appears again, with amber-stained lakes rich in tannin from rotting plants. In northern Minnesota, paddlers flock to the million-acre Boundary Waters Canoe Area—a thousand lakes in the largest protected wilderness between Idaho and Florida.[25] Minnesotans' license plates say "Land of 10,000 Lakes," but in fact 15,292 have been counted; some14,000 more lie in adjacent Wisconsin. Just as ubiquitous, bogs make this north country what it is.

Like thousands of oval mirrors, small lakes and wetlands dot the prairie pothole country of Minnesota, the Dakotas, eastern Montana, and the prairie provinces of Canada. Depending on the wetness of the year, 2 million to 7 million ponds can be found, most of them kettles—depressions left by blocks of ice melting in the waning centuries of glaciation. In addition to the prairie potholes, four other wetland complexes spice up the Great Plains: the Sand Hills wetlands of northern Nebraska, the Rainwater Basin of Nebraska, the Cheyenne Bottoms of Kansas, and the playa lakes of northern Texas, probably excavated by scouring winds that moan across the Great Plains.[26] Waterfowl depend on all these watering holes.

Lakes of the western mountains glimmer like glacier-carved jewels against backdrops of amazing grandeur. Thousands of these lie scattered through the high country. A few road-accessible paragons include St. Mary and McDonald Lakes in Glacier National Park. Endangered sockeye salmon—once swimming in red-and-green masses but now reduced to a few fish—still struggle to reach home at their Redfish Lake spawning grounds in Idaho. Yellowstone Lake is the largest high-elevation water body on the continent.

Though beavers inhabit many regions, the valleys of the Rockies have long formed their stronghold and remain the best places to see these clever, tree-chewing dam builders. At the time of Europeans' arrival in America, 60 million to 400 million beavers shaped a whole landscape by creating teeming ponds, swamps, and marshes. Trapped nearly to extinction, the furbearers have made a comeback, and some of the wetland richness has returned.

Looking like mirages but in fact the real thing, dozens of lakes sparkle in the deserts of the West. Some draw migrating birds to brine shrimp and billions of alkali flies buzzing over the salty, landlocked waters. Largest is the Great Salt Lake—next to the Great Lakes, it is America's largest lake in surface area, but its average depth is only thirteen feet. In the cycle of the ages, this crusty-shored landmark shrinks and swells, depending on runoff. Though seven times as salty as the ocean, it hosts millions of shorebirds and waterfowl.

Great Basin lakes include the stark expanse of Pyramid Lake in northern Nevada, where a rare sucker, the cui-ui (*kwee*-wee), survives, but tenuously because diversions to hay fields have lowered lake levels. In the 1990s, conservation groups, Indian tribes, and the federal government succeeded in buying back some of the needed water for Pyramid Lake.[27] Hundreds of other lakes in the Great Basin Desert swell with water during spring runoff and then shrink into white-bedded salt flats in summer. At Mono Lake in California, a million birds congregate on their semiannual migrations. At the shoreline, towers of tufa rise in spires, domes, and castle-turret designs. The eerie formations result from underwater springs pumping out calcium-rich compounds that precipitate and eventually pile up in free-form sculptures that are exposed to air once evaporation and diversions lower water levels.

A showcase of California's Sierra Nevada, Lake Tahoe compels people to simply stand and stare at its startlingly blue color. Our second-deepest lake, it bottoms out at 1,685 feet and contains more water than all the other lakes and reservoirs in California combined. Tahoe's vivid blue has deteriorated, however, because nutrient buildup allows algae to grow. If unchecked, the algae will gradually turn the mountain masterpiece green. Clarity has decreased from 108 to 70 feet and continues to worsen by a foot and a half per year. In 1969, state and federal governments charged the Tahoe Regional Planning Agency with protecting the lake, and the epic struggle between people determined to "keep Tahoe blue" and those with development interests has raged ever since.[28] At higher elevations, hundreds of other Sierra Nevada lakes reflect the exquisite golden light of that range.

Farther west, winter downpours and the flush of snowmelt once flooded 4 million acres of California's Central Valley, and this inland sea supported millions of waterbirds on the Pacific Flyway. Today, 10 percent of the wetlands remain. The Central Valley drains out to San Francisco Bay via the Sacramento–San Joaquin Delta, once a million-acre wetland but now scratched and cordoned off with drains and levees for agriculture. Farming here will ultimately prove futile because the delta continually subsides owing to lack of new silt deposits and oxidation of peat soils that dry up and blow away when plowed.[29]

In the Pacific Northwest, Oregon's Crater Lake owes its life to the explosive volcanic eruption of Mount Mazama 7,000 years ago and the subsequent collapse of the peak. The resulting seven-mile-wide caldera filled with water to a depth of 1,931 feet. In Washington, wetlands ring the perimeter of Puget Sound, and inland, the landmark of Lake Chelan has been raised by a dam, but not by much, so this gem of the North Cascades still looks fairly natural.

Alaska, glinting with hundreds of thousands of ponds and lakes,

includes wetlands as large as entire states, owing to a geographic empo-
rium of permafrost, glacial scouring, seismic shifts, and a landscape so
recently formed that drainage patterns lack the articulation that comes in
time with erosion. About 175 million acres—43 percent of the state—is
lake and wetland, exceeding all the rest of the country's wetland acreage
by a wide margin. Countless ponds spangle the Yukon Flats, the Arctic
Coastal Plain, and the Yukon-Kuskokwim Delta with animals and birds
and insects in a cornucopia that can no longer even be imagined in the
once rich Midwest, Deep South, or Northeast, where so much of the
wetland estate has been lost.

Polluted, Drained, and Developed

During the past two centuries, a relentless barrage of sewage, farm waste,
and toxins has been dumped into our lakes and wetlands; their dimensions have been shrunk by diversions, their outlets dammed, their shorelines girded with roads, their frontages chopped up for building lots. Pollution makes even more trouble in lakes than in rivers. Without any current for transport and dilution and without riffles for aeration, the waste
sits and accumulates in flatwater and lake-floor sediments.

Many of the egregious problems of stinking sewage and multicolored
effluent spitting from the pipes of industries have been fixed, thanks to
the federal Clean Water Act. But other problems remain, glossed over in
lax enforcement by the states. Now, toxic substances and chemical poisons, usually impossible to see or smell, may be even worse than the old
problems, and harder to solve.

Take the case of Coeur d'Alene. This lake of northern Idaho fingers
out in bays beneath piney mountains, laps at the streets of its comfortable
resort town, and draws people for vacations and conferences. Pleasant
relief comes with a dip in the clear water on a hot summer day, and you
might think you were in the high mountains of the Rockies. But behind
the veneer of a booming tourist trade, the water's reflective surface hides
one of the more appalling toxic dumps in America. A century of hard-
rock mining on tributaries has left a legacy of lead, cadmium, arsenic, and
other deadly elements in the top eleven inches of sediment—75 million
toxic tons of it. Mining companies did the damage, and the local newspa-

per and high-rise resort—under joint ownership—have downplayed the lake's pollution.[30] But the Coeur d'Alene Tribe pushed for cleanup.

The Indians' action in 1994 should have come as no surprise. Twenty years before, health officials testing children's blood in the mining town of Kellogg found lead at 6.5 times the Environmental Protection Agency's "level of concern." Men working at the smelter died of kidney disease at four times the normal rate. Swans and other wildlife still perish outright when they graze on contaminated lowlands. Lead, cadmium, and mercury sink into lake sediments, but low oxygen levels can release those metals back into the water, and low oxygen levels occur as a result of farm and lawn fertilizer runoff, lake-bottom bark buildup from sawmills, and pollution with human waste. Meanwhile, 300,000 residents downstream, at Spokane, drink from Coeur d'Alene's outflow.

State environmental agencies had sued the mining companies, but the legislature, in the arms of the industry, refused to continue funding the legal challenge. Officials had to settle for $4.5 million to begin fixing damages estimated at two hundred times that amount. The tribe, recognizing that it could not depend on Idaho to enforce state water quality responsibilities, sued to restore the lake. A similar federal lawsuit for $1 billion followed in 1995. If successful, it will launch one of the largest toxic cleanup efforts ever. Idaho's senior senator responded to this possibility with a federal bill to limit the amount of money the mining companies would have to pay.[31]

While mining waste alone transformed Coeur d'Alene into a model of abuse, neglect, and deception, the Great Lakes have suffered it all, in enormous amounts and with international consequences. Once one of the biological wonders of the continent, the lakes supported an abundance that is now unfathomable. In the mid-1800s, fishermen netted whole boatloads of walleye and bass at will. Atlantic salmon by the millions spawned at Lake Ontario; the last was caught in 1890. In 1950, anglers raked in 20 million pounds of blue pike, a magnificent species driven to extinction by the end of that decade. Four other lake-dependent species also hit the grave of extinction, and five others were listed as threatened or endangered.[32] The total commercial catch in Lake Erie plummeted from 1 million pounds at the end of the 1800s to 4,000 pounds in 1964. That great lake was subsequently pronounced "dead," a casualty of sewage and industrial spill, its oxygen levels at zero, its shallows matted in rotting algae, its remaining fish deformed or sick with blisters and sores. Ecologist Barry Commoner called Lake Erie "the most blatant example of the environmental crisis in the United States."[33]

Chemists have found 900 known or suspected toxins in the Great Lakes, and only a few would be enough for alarm. Two hundred toxic dumps crowd the Niagara River, which links Lake Erie with Ontario. Mist from the famous Niagara Falls—America's most photographed natural feature, visited by 5 million people per year—is suspected as a cause of the area's high rates of cancer. Throughout the Great Lakes states, residents have received a higher dose of toxins than has any comparable population in North America, and agencies have issued advisories limiting the eating of twenty species of fish.[34]

The push to curb sewage and conventional industrial wastes in the 1970s helped the lakes but failed to deal adequately with the full effects of toxins. The federal government banned further production of PCBs, used to insulate electrical equipment and to manufacture paint, ink, and insecticides, but the chemicals refuse to break down over time and continue to poison water supplies. Likewise, dioxin from wood preservatives, from the burning of plastics and fossil fuels, and especially from paper mills contaminates lakes, wetlands, and rivers. Some of the hazards are well known, but we're only beginning to learn about other effects.

Surveying the health of the Great Lakes, zoologist Theo Colborn noticed a puzzling and alarming trend. Though many adult fish, birds, and mammals appeared to be healthy, she again and again encountered severe problems with offspring—declines in mink populations, unhatched eggs of raptors, deformities and deaths in young birds. Predators as varied as lake trout, bald eagles, otters, cormorants, snapping turtles, terns, and coho salmon all showed strange symptoms of disease, and they all had buildups of toxins in their flesh. Though immeasurable in the water itself, the chemicals had accumulated from animal to animal up through the food chain until tissues of top predators had up to twenty-five times the amount found in the water. Expanding her studies beyond the Great Lakes, Colborn found a worldwide epidemic of hormone disrupters resulting from poisonous chemicals in our water. Exposed through plastics and pollution, humans are vulnerable to the same effects.[35]

As accumulators, lakes store not only toxins dumped into them but also chemical fallout from the atmosphere. Toxicologists believe that the smokestacks and tailpipes of industries and cars are the largest source of degradation throughout the Great Lakes basin and now cause more problems for the lakes than all the pipes that still deliver polluted water.[36] And at Lake Tahoe, where exhaustive efforts to cut water pollution are still inadequate, a troublesome amount of algae-nourishing nitrogen comes from car exhaust in the traffic-clogged basin.

In lakes and rivers near agricultural and industrial areas, dioxin, DDT, and PCBs are now regularly suspected in the health problems of wildlife and people; officials know that these chemicals cause serious problems because they've been well studied. But the unknown is greater, and each year manufacturers introduce a thousand new chemicals, mostly without adequate testing and review. The chemical companies do the tests themselves, and they often do their own reporting on effluent that they dump. Thousands of these substances end up at the bottoms of lakes.

Pollution comes from the complex chemicals of industry and also the commonest sources. Take the jet ski, for example. The two-stroke engines of these recreational craft discharge one-fourth of their fuel unspent, including benzene and toluene. The noise of these machines buzzing in circles on an otherwise serene lake may be annoying, but that's nothing compared with the toxic wake they leave in the water. The Tahoe Regional Planning Agency finally banned two-stroke engines as of 1999. In an effort to regulate jet skis nationwide, the Environmental Protection Agency compromised to cut pollution by 75 percent by the year 2006. But the remaining 25 percent—a significant additive to the country's waters—could have been avoided. Four-stroke motors run forty times cleaner than the old two-strokes, but the industry resisted this option because it would have cost 15 percent more.[37]

The threats to lakes and wetlands go beyond the noxious pollution that once choked Lake Erie and beyond the chemical poisons that rivet themselves to human tissues. Invading species brought here from distant countries lack predators in their new environment and proliferate at phenomenal rates, pillaging whole ecosystems. An example is the sea lamprey, which invaded the Great Lakes above Niagara Falls via the Welland Ship Canal beginning in 1830. The lampreys attach their rasping mouths to living fish and then suck out vital fluids. Biologists developed poisons, barriers, and traps for this parasite and effectively reduced its numbers by

90 percent.[38] This was no small struggle, but in other cases, it seems impossible to get rid of exotic pests.

Hydrilla, a stringy aquatic weed, gains an advantage over native plants by photosynthesizing in low light, growing a gangly ten inches per day and ultimately shading out native plants and clogging waterways with spongy mats firm enough for ducks to walk on. Somebody dumped this African and Asian weed into Florida waters in the 1960s, and the pest now has a stranglehold on lakes and rivers as far away as the Pacific Northwest. Nobody knows where its effects will end.

Even scarier, the hitchhiking zebra mussel arrived, as did hundreds of other unwanted organisms, in ballast water of ships that plied the Great Lakes after the much-celebrated St. Lawrence Seaway opened in 1959. One of the more effective facilities for inadvertent mixing of worldwide flora and fauna, this system of locks, canals, and dredged channels turned Great Lakes cities as far away as Duluth, Minnesota, into seaports and turned the lakes into entirely different and degraded ecosystems. More than 140 species of exotic algae, plants, and animals now pollute the Great Lakes.[39] Discovered only in 1988, the thumbnail-sized zebra mussel invaded the lakes and quickly spread to river systems of the East and Midwest. Filtering out phytoplankton, it outcompetes native species and globs up in masses several feet deep on any hard surface. At one water intake structure for a power plant, 20,000 zebra mussels were crowded onto each square foot.[40] The zebra mussel fastens onto the shells of native mollusks and as a result has smothered virtually all Great Lakes mussel species. Uniquely diverse populations of the southern Appalachians are now being victimized in the same way.

Even more insidious, each hungry zebra mussel processes a quart of water per day, filtering out nutritious plankton and other solids. While this may seem like a solution to turbidity problems, it's not. The zebra-induced clarity of Lake Erie has increased beyond what it would be without any pollution at all, and limnologists now worry that too much ultraviolet radiation is reaching fish and aquatic life that evolved in a more shaded environment.[41]

Exotic species have besieged wetlands as well. Under the guise of beauty, purple loosestrife's showy flowers and coarse stems crowd out the native life of marshlands from coast to coast. Yet sales of this pariah as a decorative plant remain legal in all but a dozen states.[42] In Ontario, release of an Old World beetle thought to eat only loosestrife has resulted in a 95 percent reduction of the renegade plant; it is hoped that the beetle will die out once its job is done.

While pollution, exotic species, and shoreline development pose the central problems of lakes, outside Alaska draining and filling have completely eliminated 54 percent of our wetlands—arguably the most damaged of all landscapes in America.[43] Others share serious problems, but most escape such total eradication. The rate of loss has slowed in the past two decades, but absolute losses continue, owing to land development and agriculture. In Florida, where 46 percent of the wetlands have been destroyed, 11 species have disappeared and 117 are at risk. Most of the Midwest's great wetland forest ecosystems, which once spanned northern Illinois and Indiana, are gone. Nowhere is the damage worse than in farmed Iowa, which has lost 98 percent of its wetlands.

Waterfowl populations mirror the decline of their wetland habitats. Ducks and geese of the Pacific Flyway need California marshes, but 4 million acres have been reduced to 80,000 in refuges and 300,000 in private ownership. Much of the latter lies in rice farms or duck hunting clubs, but the hunting clubs are now liquidating.[44] At San Francisco Bay, 95 percent of the tidal wetlands have been lost.[45] Crowding of birds at the few remaining areas invites outbreaks of avian cholera and botulism— epidemics equally troublesome in the playa lakes of Texas, where birds congregate because they have no choice.

The wetlands that remain suffer from low water, diverted flows, pollution, and urbanization at their edges. In the West, irrigation diversions that intercept the snowmelt of high mountains have completely dried up wetlands and lakes once rich in life, including the twenty-six-mile Winnemucca Lake in Nevada, scarcely damp today. Tulare Lake, in the San Joaquin River valley of California, is now nothing but a lot of pesticide-ridden cotton fields and waste ponds full of foul runoff. U.S. Fish and Wildlife Service biologists have estimated that up to 10,000 birds per year may be dying from exposure to the poisonous effluent in these ponds.[46] Wastewater from agriculture goes unregulated even when it is toxic to wildlife or people.

Stillwater National Wildlife Refuge in Nevada—a marsh that has accommodated 300,000 waterfowl on the Pacific Flyway—has been desiccated by ranch diversions that sluice water out of the Carson River to grow hay. The water that does trickle toward the refuge from farmed fields leaches poisonous salts out of the desert soil, as well as mercury, arsenic, boron, and selenium. A congressional appropriation to buy back water rights held by farmers afforded some relief by restoring minimum flows to Stillwater.[47] But the same kinds of poisons kill or deform birds at a dozen or more refuges that receive their water from the waste-making end of irrigation ditches, most notably at Kesterson National Wildlife Refuge in central California.[48] Leachate from irrigated land elsewhere in the West will eventually render not only the terminal wetlands hazardous but the agricultural land useless as well. A 1990 report of the San Joaquin Valley Drainage Program warned that within fifty years, more than 460,000 acres in California's Central Valley will be too salinized to grow crops.

The ultimate case of preemption by agriculture is seen in the Everglades, America's most famous wetland, which is partly safeguarded within Everglades National Park at the southern tip of Florida. But much of the Everglades never received protection, and the combined intrusions—from suburban Miami to corporate sugarcane farms—destroyed half the original 2.9 million acres. As if this loss were not enough, sugarcane farms now dump deadly wastewater, which flows into the national park. With most flows of good water diverted through canals and ditches, the life force of the swamp depends on pathetic drainage via road culverts rather than the twenty-mile-wide sheet of runoff that once seeped smoothly and slowly southward from Lake Okeechobee. This greatest of wetland-based national parks has seen a 90 percent reduction in wading birds since 1930 and endangered status for the Florida panther and American crocodile.[49] Unlike many forgotten swamps and marshes, however, the Everglades have been the object of intense restoration efforts, as discussed later in this chapter.

The 1990s Siege on Wetlands

With a singularly troubled fate, wetlands are part land, part water; part private, part public. Legal precedent typically regards land as private property and water as public property. But in the duality of wetlands, the edges of ownership and responsibility blur and tangle. Efforts to cope with this duality have led to one of the great natural resource conflicts of our time.

However moderate their effects, laws governing wetlands and attempting to curb the losses have been a flash point in attacks by developers and agribusinesses wishing to roll back environmental regulations. Their lobbying dramatizes what are sometimes fictional tales of small landowners facing an anonymous government denying people the use of their property.[50] In fact, section 404 of the Clean Water Act calls for the Army Corps of Engineers to forbid or limit the loss of wetlands, but the agency rarely denies requests to drain or fill. Among 90,000 projects as of 1992, the Corps approved 80,000 permits with little or no review, according to agency reports. Only 0.5 percent of the permit applications were turned down (a few states do a better job).[51] Simply having regulations on the books weeds out some nonqualifying plans to drain or fill. But for developers who persist, loopholes can often be found, and the loss of wetlands proceeds almost unabated in regions lacking citizen watchdog groups to monitor enforcement.

The Columbia Bottomlands, along the Brazos River of Texas, offers a window to the political influence at play. The city of Lake Jackson, south of Houston, planned a golf course on 200 acres of prime wetlands and forest important to dwindling numbers of songbirds on their migration between Central America and North America. The U.S. Fish and Wildlife Service and the Texas Parks and Wildlife Department challenged the city's permit application to the Army Corps of Engineers. But Republican majority whip Tom DeLay—the local congressman—inserted provisions into a completely unrelated congressional appropriations bill forbidding the Corps to deny the permit. It was subsequently issued in 1996. DeLay's bill also prohibited the U.S. Fish and Wildlife Service from creating a proposed refuge—the best chance to compensate landowners for not being able to drain the wetlands and mow down the valued green ash, pecan, and elm woodlands. Having rolled over the Corps and its permitting process, Texas developers next turned their eyes to additional wetlands on which to plat out nearby subdivisions.[52]

Congressman DeLay shows us how political influence works, but one doesn't normally need friends with pull to evade federal wetland regulations. As an official exemption, "Permit Number 26" for years allowed any loss of up to ten acres if a wetland was "isolated" from a river or lake. Lacking any pretense of biological or hydrologic rationale, this developers' gift from the Reagan administration forfeited 70,000 to 90,000 acres of wetland per year, making a sham of regulation.[53] Though this category of permit was discontinued in 1998, the proposed policies to replace it were even worse, expanding the "isolation" criteria to include all wetlands but those in the tidal zone.

Not satisfied with this, the so-called wise use and property rights movements targeted wetland rules for outright abolishment. An association of developers, oil companies, agricultural conglomerates, drainage contractors, and timber corporations called itself the National Wetlands Coalition. Fronting as a conservation group but parroting the rhetoric of private-rights advocates in order to gain populist appeal, this industrial association's goal was to eliminate section 404 of the Clean Water Act. In 1989, Vice President Dan Quayle and a group of congressmen tried to redefine wetlands to exclude 60 percent of the acreage addressed under the program.[54] Continuing the fight against regulation in the 1990s, industries doing the developing and draining sent new Republican congressmen to office to push the coalition's agenda, which would have allowed widespread losses including elimination of most of the remaining prairie potholes. Political action committees lobbying for weaker wetland laws gave $25 million to candidates between 1990 and 1995, not counting money from individuals. Congressmen voting to gut regulations in 1996 in effect received $17,000 per vote from the anti-wetlands cabal.[55] A "takings clause" in the same right-wing agenda would require the government to pay developers not to drain, fill, or pollute wetlands that are now ostensibly protected. Up against big money, supporters of wetlands fought off the worst attempts to dismantle the regulations, and they succeeded because they had broad public support; a 1994 survey by Times Mirror Magazines, Inc., found that 53 percent of respondents thought wetlands protection should be stronger; only 9 percent thought efforts had gone too far.[56]

Another line of attack on wetlands is the popular ruse of "mitigation." Under this model, developers can eliminate a wetland if they "create" another one somewhere else. But functioning wetlands depend on functioning hydrology, native soils, and an interlinked biotic community, from microbes to predators, which doesn't just happen wherever a bulldozer scrapes out a pond. In Florida, a survey found that only 5 percent of mitigation projects succeeded.[57] In Ohio, the Environmental Protection Agency reported that natural wetlands significantly outperformed created wetlands.[58] Historian Ann Vileisis likened these trades of real wetlands for artificial ones to the trading of "real money for Monopoly money."[59]

Under the mitigation banner, a developer doesn't necessarily have to "create" a new wetland but can protect an existing one by buying it and turning it over to public ownership. This provides welcome security for one area but still results in an overall loss of wetlands. One solution to the mitigation scam is to allow credits for restoring real but previously damaged wetlands rather than for "constructing" new wetlands. This type of repair has potential, especially in salt marshes. Real solutions, however, involve halting additional wetland losses in the first place through a mix of government controls and public and private investments in wetlands.

Stewardship and Recovery

By the late 1960s, the decline of the Great Lakes had become a symbol for the environmental movement and an exemplar of heedless waste. Near its mouth at Lake Erie, the Cuyahoga River, blazing in grease- and debris-eating flames in 1969, was a figurative image of the time. The holocaust of burning water seared itself into people's minds. It jolted Americans into questioning, How could it have come to this?

With rare solidarity, citizens throughout the region allied themselves with the goal of cleaning up the Great Lakes. But that didn't mean it would be easy. Owing to the differences between states and nations, cities and counties, industries and agriculture, working across political lines became paramount. Groups such as Great Lakes United—a coalition of 200 sportsmen and environmental and civic organizations—spurred people to action in one of the most complex models of environmental protection ever attempted.

With great fanfare in 1972, the United States and Canada adopted the first Great Lakes Water Quality Agreement, though troublesome toxins escaped notice amid the revolting stench of sewage outfalls still needing correction. Phosphates in laundry detergent were banned; this helped the lakes, but the agreement wasn't enough. In 1976, officials closed Lake Ontario to all fishing. Then, in 1977, the disturbing toxins that poisoned people in their own basements near New York's Love Canal made the press, leading to a revised Great Lakes Water Quality Agreement the next year. Long before similar broad-based approaches gained acceptance, this document challenged its signatories to an "ecosystem approach" and maintained that "restoration and enhancement of the boundary waters cannot be achieved independently of other parts of the Great Lakes Basin Ecosystem." Although the agreement called for the "virtual elimination" of toxins, it lacked teeth and required neither nation to enforce the compact.[60] In what had become a fairly consistent pattern, the momentum to correct abuses lasted only as long as the media's attention span following sensational events, such as the hideous Love Canal exposé.

The sad state of affairs called for further arm-twisting, but with states competing with one another for industrial favor in the "race to the bottom" of regulatory effectiveness, the appropriate coercion could come only from the federal government. Agencies there could level the playing field among states and elevate the minimum thresholds of quality without penalizing any one state. The Reagan administration responded to this challenge by disbanding the Great Lakes Basin Commission in 1981, declaring that "we know all we need to know" about the Great Lakes and attempting to eliminate research funding. Enforcement was put on the back burner or simply stopped. As a result, the epidemic of toxic wastes worsened. Facing intense pressure from citizen constituents, Congress in 1987 overrode Reagan's veto of a revised Clean Water Act and directed the Environmental Protection Agency to establish a national program office for the Great Lakes. With this as an explicit point of responsibility, reform was more likely to succeed.

Progress has come in fits and starts, but several billion dollars' worth of investment in cleanup have resulted in Lake Erie's return as the most biologically productive of the five lakes—status it had long held because of its warmth and shallowness. Not far below the site where the Cuyahoga River roared in orange flames, a revitalized lakefront now accounts for 3,500 tourism jobs in the Toledo area; lake-based recreation pumps $8 billion per year into Ohio's economy. Counts of bacteria and algae are down by 90 percent from 1968. Lake Erie is now the new walleye capital of the world and offers an excellent smallmouth bass fishery as well. But with nagging persistence, fish consumption advisories stay in effect for 97 percent of the shoreline, reminding people that the accumulated toxins haven't gone away.[61] In 1995, the lake states finally signed a new, hotly contested Great Lakes Water Quality Initiative, which called for control of twenty-two toxic compounds.

While reform at the Great Lakes has taken years and a real cleanup will take many more, victories at some smaller lakes have come with a resounding clarity of success that invites celebration. In Seattle, at one of the country's larger urban freshwater bodies, disgusting mats of blue-green algae infested Lake Washington, which was unable to accommodate the outfalls of eleven sewage treatment plants. The city relocated the plants, and by 1975 the lacustrine showcase had recovered much of its original quality.

In California, a tougher challenge awaited where Mono Lake's thirteen-mile oval of saline water had steadily succumbed to the urban growth of Los Angeles, even though it lay a seemingly safe distance of 338 miles away. By intercepting streams that feed the lake and then piping them southward, the city reduced Mono Lake's level by nearly fifty feet. A rich and unusual complex of life would certainly have been lost if it weren't for a few people who took decisive action based on deep personal commitment.

The effort began with an underdog's vision of determination when David and Sally Gaines, who spent a summer studying the lake for the National Science Foundation, became appalled at the biological disaster in progress and formed the Mono Lake Committee. They labored without pay for years, but with some enthusiastic friends they built an effective organization to battle for restoration of the lake. In a landmark case, the Supreme Court of California ruled that the Public Trust Doctrine must be applied to Mono Lake; even though Los Angeles had bought water rights, it had not bought the right to ruin the lake, which is irreplaceable public property. The court ordered a better balance between diversions and public interest. Undaunted, Los Angeles appealed and the battle raged on. Fishing groups invoked long-forgotten laws requiring minimum flows in California streams and added a breath of freshwater to Mono. Eventually worn down, having lost the scientific arguments, the court cases, and the larger contest for public support, the Los Angeles Department of Water and Power agreed in 1994 to restore flows and make up for the lost supply through conservation and replacement efforts. The state required minimum lake levels and a two-thirds reduction in diversions. After a twenty-year campaign that included the untimely death of David Gaines when his car was hit by a pickup truck on an icy winter road, Mono Lake began to return to its old magnificence.

On the shores of Mono Lake and Lake Washington and at other lacustrine sites, American society has grappled fiercely with the issue of protecting our lakes since the 1960s, and the resolve to tackle the problems—especially pollution—has gained greater momentum than in most other environmental initiatives. People want clean lakes, and they've pushed lawmakers to deliver.

The movement for wetlands has proven to be harder. While these landscapes provide essential services to people and function as fountainheads to whole ecosystems, they lack the swimming-beach, vacation-home appeal of lakes. Buggy, boggy, of little recreational value in the traditional sense, swamps and marshes have been places that most people just didn't care about. But fundamental shifts in attitude and understanding have turned all this around; there has been a phenomenal change in the way Americans regard this landscape.[62]

In an impressive trend, the rate of wetland losses dropped from 450,000 acres per year in the 1980s to 117,000 in 1997, in part credited to provisions of the Clean Water Act and to a "swampbuster" section of the 1985 Farm Bill that denies federal support funds to farmers who convert remaining wetlands to cropland.[63] Despite substantial loopholes in both laws, the regulations have helped to direct new farming and development elsewhere.

Recognizing wetland regulations as a means of protecting adjacent property, water supplies, flood control capability, and habitat, some state and local governments have also made important strides. Between 1965 and 1977, state legislatures adopted ninety-four laws setting minimum development standards for sensitive areas including wetlands. Meanwhile, local governments adopted 1,000 wetland and 1,400 lake and stream protection programs.[64] With intensifying pressure from developers, realtors, and private-rights groups in nearly all the municipalities, the task of keeping those laws on the books and enforcing them now locks wetland advocates into perpetual surveillance.

Knowing that regulations can do only part of the job, even when the public recognizes the "commons" aspect of wetlands, agencies and conservation groups have bought many important tracts outright. Ever since

President Theodore Roosevelt established the first refuge, on Florida's Pelican Island in 1903, wetlands have formed a centerpiece of the National Wildlife Refuge System. With 514 units in 1998, the refuges total 92 million acres—an area larger than that of the National Park System, though 83 percent of the refuge land lies in Alaska.[65] Just a few of the protected highlights include the Yukon Flats and Yukon Delta National Wildlife Refuges in Alaska, the Klamath Basin National Wildlife Refuge Complex in California and Oregon, the Aransas National Wildlife Refuge on the Gulf shore of Texas, and a tidal tract at Cape May National Wildlife Refuge, New Jersey.

Beyond administering the refuges, the U.S. Fish and Wildlife Service has taken other crucial steps. Recognizing the link between waterfowl and wetlands, the agency and a host of cooperating public and private parties drafted the North American Waterfowl Management Plan. This seeks to restore wetlands along migratory flyways at a massive scale.[66] A record low population of ducks in 1985 proved to be a strong impetus for the plan, and with several wet years and some strategic success, waterfowl numbers increased through the early 1990s.

The state of Florida has also taken exemplary initiative to conserve wetlands, with a combination of bond and tax programs that has led to the protection of about 11 million of the state's 35 million acres of land and water since 1990. A real estate transfer tax funded much of this—a logical approach for a state awash in profits from leapfrogging development. Florida conservationists believe that protecting 6 million more acres is critical, at which point 49 percent of the state would be protected—a model for the nation. Also of pathbreaking note in that wet state, Congress allocated $300 million to the Army Corps of Engineers to begin fixing damage inflicted when the same agency draglined the meandering Kissimmee River into a ruler-straight canal, one of the more egregious losses of wetlands in the 1960s. Officials planned to begin restoration in 1998.[67]

Conservation groups have also protected wetlands by buying them. Putting money where it counts, Ducks Unlimited set aside 7 million acres in the United States and Canada, most of it in the prairie potholes. In one of its many wetland projects, The Conservation Fund helped the U.S. Fish and Wildlife Service buy 18,000 acres of marsh along Lake Pontchartrain near New Orleans in 1996. In South Carolina, a combined effort of state and federal agencies, Ducks Unlimited, and The Nature Conservancy resulted in protection of 122,000 acres in the Ashepoo-Combahee-Edisto Basin salt marshes. Fifty-eight percent of the land remained in private ownership, with landowners selling easements to some parcels and signing conservation agreements for others, indicating their intention to keep the land open. At hundreds of other sites, large groups such as the National Audubon Society and small ones such as The Wetlands Conservancy in Oregon have bought swamps, marshes, and bogs to protect their intrinsic worth. The challenge is substantial; 75 percent of the wetlands in the forty-eight states are still in private ownership, and many will remain a target for development.[68]

Beyond saving what's left, restoration of wetlands holds promise for the future. On Long Island, New York, people are seeking to fix 10,000 acres of salt marsh by plugging old drainage ditches and reinstating tidal channels. The restored flows will turn back an invasion of giant reeds that has outcompeted other native grasses. Reintroduced killifish will prey on mosquito larvae. This project by federal, state, and county governments along with Ducks Unlimited follows on the Fish and Wildlife Service's success at the nearby Seatuck National Wildlife Refuge, where waterfowl numbers tripled following restoration of tidal flows.[69]

At the local level, people in neighborhoods as urban as Queens in New York have turned out to restore damaged wetlands. A onetime dump and industrial site at Jamaica Bay had been given to the city as a sanctuary, complete with rusted cars and junked construction scraps. In 1994, Audubon Society volunteers smashed cement slabs with sledge hammers, dragged the debris away, and reinstated native plants. At more and more landscapes across America, people are finding that restoration efforts such as this serve not only ecological needs but also human ones, with neighbors working together to heal special places near home.

At the other end of the activists' spectrum, upper-level federal and state negotiations with a whirlwind of high-stakes maneuvering sought to restore the beleaguered Everglades. Resisting reform, big sugar companies reaping millions of dollars as a result of tariff protections have been the principal source of pesticide-laden flows spilling into Everglades National Park. After a bitter campaign centering on the ruse of job losses, the industry beat back a statewide vote to require a penny-per-pound tax on sugar to help taxpayers foot the bill for pollution treatment. Rankled that the burden was left to state and federal governments, Joette Lorion of Friends of the Everglades said, "Why should taxpayers be made to pay a billion dollars to clean up after big sugar, just because the agencies don't have the will to enforce the Clean Water Act and make the polluters pay?"[70]

Though stung by this heavily financed defeat, Everglades activists persisted in their efforts. Scientists and political negotiators tried to break through the mesh of diversions, canals, flood-control distributaries, pollution outfalls, superhighways, airports, municipal aqueducts, corporate crop fields, and platted subdivisions in the swamp. Restoration aimed to set aside a buffer of open space from runaway urbanization, to increase water storage, and to reduce agricultural pollution. The Water Resources Development Act of 1996 split the cost of restoration and water quality improvements with Florida. Vice President Al Gore announced a federal commitment of at least $1.5 billion in one of the country's most ambitious attempts to restore a landscape.

The case of the Everglades clearly illustrates the cost and difficulty of correcting problems after the fact, where an eye to prevention would have served much better. Hope remains that some semblance of the integrity of the Everglades can be saved—a modest goal for one of the few national parks set aside not for its scenery but mainly for its birds and greater ecosystem. If the momentum can be sustained, in another twenty years we might see an Everglades as lively and raucous with birds, animals, and fish as it was before the big sugar companies polluted the water and before booming Miami sluiced life-giving flows away from this greatest wetland in America.

Dedicated to a Better Way

An expanse of watery marshes rims the edge of Puget Sound in Washington, and recognizing the value of places such as this, a progressive legislature in the 1970s passed a law to reduce property taxes if owners agreed to leave their wetlands be. County assessors, however, took little interest in the program. Almost nobody signed up.

The stage had thus been set when Seattle-area artist Christi Norman decided to register her streamside marsh in the program. "It was complicated to follow through with what should have been a simple process," she recalled. "I had to talk to five separate agencies to find out if my land qualified. Twice the county lost my paperwork, but eventually I had my marsh enrolled."[71]

Drawn by an interest in her local environment and motivated by what she saw as a worthwhile endeavor, the potter and ceramicist launched a new career working for the local branch of the Audubon Society. "We developed a program to help landowners apply for the tax-incentive program. Once you knew what to do, it wasn't difficult. But the application intimidated landowners enough that most wouldn't follow through. So we helped them to the finish line."

While Christi Norman and other Audubon Society staff members and volunteers guided people through the paperwork maze to protect wetlands, the state legislators who had passed the tax incentive measure and other progressive laws were replaced by a group more concerned with pleasing developers, and the new cadre set out to undermine the environmental gains of the past. "We saw the political challenges coming," Norman explained, "and succeeded in expanding our program. The National Audubon Society adopted our work as a model of grassroots organizing and gave us the extra help we needed."

To confront a hostile legislature plotting to rescind wetland laws was Norman's new job. She recounted, "To gather what might be construed as 'evidence,' the legislative committee scheduled wetland site visits and hearings. The members had every intention of spotlighting people who say that our regulations are unreasonable, illogical, and simply the work of a faceless bureaucracy somehow out to get the landowner. So we called up a group of wetland scientists and asked them to accompany the committee wherever it went. Most of the scientists were willing to take time off without pay to do this." Plagued by people who knew what they were talking about, the legislators were unable to keep these nonpartisan experts away. "Everywhere the committee held a visit, at least three scientists showed up, and they kept the discussion scientifically honest. No one could get away with saying that wetlands weren't important."

Instead of the litany of mistreatment at the hands of arrogant government officials, the legislators encountered a lineup of respected local citizens who had been alerted by the Audubon Society's grapevine to explain their views. Several were veterans of the tax incentive program. Others simply favored reasonable regulation of the area's marshes and swamps to protect water quality and wildlife and to promote flood control. "With those people in the room, an individual who had been warned five or six times about his violation of a twenty-year-old state regulation and then fined for wetlands encroachment was less likely to get away with complaints about a heavy-handed bureaucracy." Norman concluded, "The committee never got the ammunition it was looking for. That made it difficult for them to go back and say that the people of Washington didn't want wetlands protection. We still had political battles to fight, but public support shined through."

Multiplied by the hundreds, efforts such as Christi Norman's reflect a new ethic about the lakes and wetlands of America, one that grows even while the forces of change grow as well.

CHAPTER 7

AT THE EDGE OF THE LAND

F ROM THE inside of America, high in the mountains, I've worked my way down to the outer edge. There, near the seashore, is where most of the people live, and like the mountains, it's where others are drawn to look, to relax, and to enjoy the land and water of this country.

In my pilgrimage to outer reaches of the Atlantic shore, I boarded a ferryboat. It's not that Ann and I couldn't have driven to the ocean—hundreds of roads lead to thousands of beaches and outline much of our country's shoreline. But ever since returning to the northern end of Cape Hatteras after a twenty-five-year absence, I've feared "condo mania" wherever people can drive to the water. We wanted to see the shore itself, bare and blustery wild, something like what my ancestors must have seen when they first set foot in America, on a beach in New England.

At first light, we had left the van parked just a few feet above a tidal marsh that spread like a yellow prairie across slough-veined flats. Now, sunrise over the Atlantic Ocean ignited half the sky in rippled orange while the loaded ferryboat droned across the water, a mix of black and white people on board. In the fiery light, several miles eastward, lay Georgia's Sapelo Island, and already I began to sense the feeling of a miniature world that only islands convey, the feeling of separation and release from everything else on earth.

In the day's new light, with moist wind in my face and a tufted crown of trees etching the island's handsome, low profile, I realized the mainland had been my fortress. That bulwark of mountains and forests had reared me, nourished me, and protected me. Now I was leaving it, going to a barrier island whose primary purpose in the working drawings of the earth was to absorb the shock waves of storms.

Not the usual saltwater retreat, Sapelo had been settled by southern planters and slaves. Now, nature once again has gained the upper hand. An island plantation was deeded to the University of Georgia as a biological research station—the site where ecologist Eugene Odum completed pathbreaking studies of energy flow in salt marshes, finding them to be the most productive ecosystem acre for acre, outperforming alfalfa fields by a factor of seven.[1] At the northern end of the island, a community of African Americans remains where it's been since Abraham Lincoln abolished slavery. The residents' distinctive accent is a result of island isolation.

We stepped off the boat; checked in at the research station, where we had telephoned ahead to arrange our visit; and shouldered our day packs. With happy anticipation, we set off for the seashore on the eastern side of the island.

After a few miles' walk on a rutted road, the sound of booming breakers filled the air. The lane wound through salt-tolerant shrubs that stabilized old dunes and then onto a wide plain of sand ramping down ever so gently to the suds line of high tide. Herded by a stiff autumn wind with a fetch running hundreds of miles offshore, waves piled high, and three or four broke simultaneously across the shallows. Salt spray misted the air, and as I breathed it deep into my lungs, it awakened something inside me; it was like inhaling the invigorating vapor of a waterfall along a mountain stream. And yet it was more than that. Something supremely elemental in

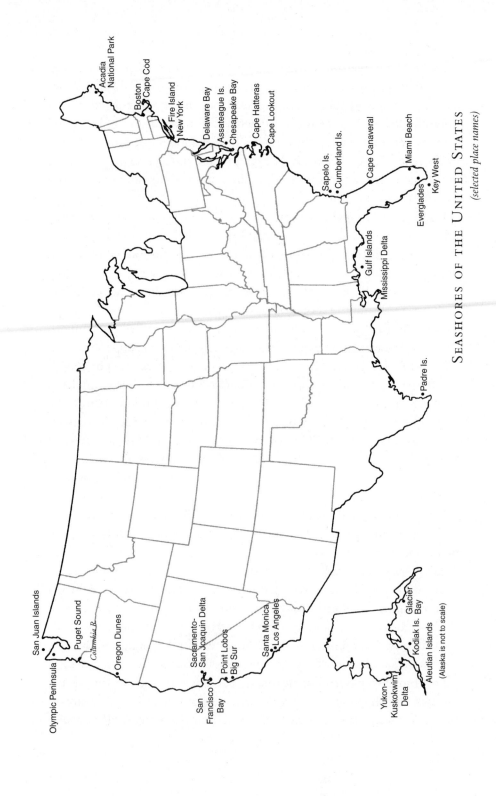

SEASHORES OF THE UNITED STATES
(selected place names)

Acadia National Park
Boston
Cape Cod
Fire Island
New York
Delaware Bay
Assateague Is.
Chesapeake Bay
Cape Hatteras
Cape Lookout
Sapelo Is.
Cumberland Is.
Cape Canaveral
Miami Beach
Key West
Everglades
Gulf Islands
Mississippi Delta
Padre Is.

San Juan Islands
Olympic Peninsula
Puget Sound
Columbia R.
Oregon Dunes
Sacramento-San Joaquin Delta
Point Lobos
Big Sur
San Francisco Bay
Santa Monica
Los Angeles

Yukon-Kuskokwim Delta
Glacier Bay
Kodiak Is.
Aleutian Islands
(Alaska is not to scale)

the fertile salt air touched a vague connection. Swept clean by wind and water, the beach stretched up and down the coast for miles, and at the waterline, where the sand was firm, we strolled northward.

We could have walked and walked, but as always, we ran out of time. Eventually, we had to turn around in order to catch the boat back home, back to the mainland. But for a few short hours, the seashore entranced me. I felt the coolness of sand sifting underfoot, the massage of the Appalachians' pulverized quartz rolling in a billion grains beneath my arches. The surf had washed ashore a whole landscape of feldspar in tan and gray. The foamy rinse of the highest waves caught me now and then and, for just an instant, claimed me as part of the ocean. I could freely cross that line from land to sea, a line that made me realize I had roamed out of bounds. I had left the continent. Sandpipers probed in the same tidal zone, and sanderlings scurried along double-time at the waterline. Herring gulls shrieked, pecked at flotsam, and soared like kites on the wind.

The obvious fact overwhelmed me: right here, North America ended. Or it began, depending on your point of view. Looking out to sea, I recognized that nearly all I've ever seen of the world lay behind me. But the infinity of water out ahead now impressed me just as much. The endlessness of it drew my eyes away. It's easy to stand on the beach and stare for hours at vastness, at emptiness, at the intersecting planes of water and sky three miles away, where the curvature of the round earth rolls under and conceals the rest of the world as completely and mysteriously as the waters hide everything under their surface, living or ghostly.

While mountains speak to an exuberant sense of spirit, and forests to security, grasslands to openness, deserts to silence, rivers to liveliness, and lakes to serenity, the oceans speak in an altogether different tone. Here, the unconscious is called, black or brilliant in the whiff of a mood. The contrast of land to sea enthralls and provokes, and it draws up long-forgotten thoughts and memories, like water pulled up from a deep, open well.

As a child, at Stone Harbor, New Jersey, I rode with joy on my father's broad shoulders when he waded out into the sea. When the waves washed in, the water surged up to his chest. Then it mercifully receded again. He kept going farther, deeper, farther. It was fun until he said, "Tell me when you see Ireland." Whatever Ireland was, I knew it lay beyond sight, which meant we'd have to go out *there,* out beyond the horizon line. I knew he was kidding, but at that tender age I was struck with a humbling and even horrifying awareness of forever, and of oblivion. I had no words for this, only feelings. The ocean, like the starry sky at night, went on endlessly, and the idea of experiencing that—of going there, of coming untied from the land—it all gave me the creeps. It sent a shiver through my supple little spine. "Let's go back, Dad." He finally turned around, and I couldn't wait to grip the firm earth under my feet again.

There at the seashore on that sunshiny day when my dad and I left the land behind, I learned one of the simplest yet greatest of all ecological lessons: the land is finite. There is only so much, and then there is salt water. I now consider this the fundamental lesson of the seashore. It's one reason the story of Noah has had such resonance for thousands of years— we cannot take land for granted. A corollary follows quickly: because the land is finite, it's precious. When I dropped off my dad's shoulders onto wet but solid sand, I yelled with glee and went running up the beach to my mother and to the land I loved.

Now at sea level again on Sapelo Island, I also realized that elevation zero is the Common Denominator: everything someday ends up in the oceans. There's no escape, no return, no hiding it. Nothing but big islands, really, the continents drain into the seas, and the water cooling my feet that day was the water of the world: the Altamaha River, which spilled into the sound just to the south; the Mississippi River, down around the curve of the Gulf of Mexico; the Amazon River, from the other hemisphere; the Ganges River, from the other side of the globe. They all flow to the oceans. In that ocean water we might see the pickings of rock and soil from a river hundreds of miles away, the chemicals leached from a million ancient bones in decay, the nutrients of fallen leaves from trees long since dead in the Appalachians, and the acrid pollution from a sewage plant in Savannah, Georgia, or maybe DDT still used in Latin America and flushed northward in the Gulf Stream.

At the seashore, we look out to strange worlds. Because it's where the continent begins and ends, it's a starting point and a finishing point, like birth and death. It marks limits of many kinds. The seashore holds us in like the walls of a very large home, or like the fence around a property we're reluctant to leave.

Ingrained in the European tradition, I had always pictured the Atlantic shore as seen from the water—east to west. That's how my father's ancestors saw it, arriving by sailboat in 1637, according to family lore. Likewise for my mother's great-grandfather: Andrew Gremer took passage for America as a fourteen-year-old to evade the German draft during Otto von Bismarck's second war with Austria in 1870. On the other side of my mother's family, Mary King and Michael Halpin fled the Irish potato famine by coming to America. Just as my relatives must have done on those exciting days of arrival, I had always imagined looking *in* from the Atlantic shore. Likewise, steeped in the myths of westward discovery, of Lewis and Clark, and of California dreaming during my youth in the 1960s, I always imagined looking *out* at the Pacific. But now at Sapelo Island, gazing out to sea for long moments, I put the continent behind me and faced away from the land. America was really home to me, and the idea of arriving here from across this ocean to the east seemed more foreign than the idea of arriving from underground.

Complementing this edge-of-sea experience, a few years later I sat bobbing in an oceangoing kayak and gazing in from the Pacific Ocean to a mountainous mass of the most rugged seashore imaginable. We were paddling in Glacier Bay, Alaska, and looking for a spot where we could safely run aground on mainland America.

Glacier Bay was everything that Sapelo Island was not. We paddled for a week in fjords that had been filled with glacial ice only a hundred years before. The sea, deep turquoise and ice-cold, spouted with humpback whales, barked with seals, and danced with Dall porpoises surfacing and plunging as if in fast motion, sleek sea mammals painted black and white like little orcas. The Coast Ranges jutted up from beneath the water's surface to icy heights of thousands of feet. Mount Fairweather, seen from the West Arm of Glacier Bay, soars to 15,300 feet directly from sea level. At a comparable distance inland from Sapelo Island, the rise in elevation might be 10 feet. Yet as at Sapelo, this was the seashore, the edge, where our love affair and ambiguous relationship with the land of America begins and ends.

We camped one night near the base of McBride Glacier, keeping a safe distance because calving walls of ice create local tidal waves, gulping whatever's onshore. We also kept our distance out of respect for mother seals who, seeking safety from predators, give birth and rear their pups on floating icebergs near the glaciers. The bergs eventually float free of the inlet and drift on the vagaries of wind and tide. A bald eagle sat on one of the floes and drifted past our camp, eyeing us sternly from his moving perch.

Far up the inlet, the tides could be described only as extreme. While mid-Atlantic tides might rise by a few feet, in Glacier Bay they fluctuated by twenty-four. The waterline was a deceptively temporal feature. Because brown bears roamed those beaches, we cooked and ate in the intertidal zone, where the scent of food would soon be flushed away. One night, we had to move dinner three times to higher ground to avoid being flushed away ourselves—the sea advanced another horizontal foot with each hungry wave. That far north, the sun hardly set in June. It dipped below the horizon in the northwest and then popped up a few hours later in the northeast, allowing us to explore until late and navigate all night long if we chose not to sleep.

All those forces at the edge of the earth filled us with zest and awe. The moon pulled the tides, the sun thawed the ice, the waves battered the cliffs, and an earthquake even shook the ground and roared under our feet, all of it with the rhythm, the power, the timelessness of great forces acting on the wild earth.

We paddled deep into the fjords until we were stopped by ice—the glacial ice that had scoured down from the mountaintops since the beginning of the Pleistocene—the force of frozen water that had shaped so much of America. At elevation zero, the glacier had finally lost its push and rotted in the corrosive waves of the Pacific. Waterfront ice turned to slush while the stones and silt, pushed there by glaciers, paused for one final moment on their journey to the sea.

Living at the Edge of the Earth

Most Americans live near the shoreline, 55 percent of the population in counties fronting the coasts and the Great Lakes.[2] New York, Philadelphia, Baltimore, Charleston, Savannah, Miami, New Orleans, Houston, San Diego, Los Angeles, San Francisco, and Seattle—all lie at sea level, in the coastal zone. And in between the cities, the oceanfront has been built out almost everywhere topography allows.

The megalopolis sprawling between Boston and Washington, D.C., is a seashore phenomenon of 35 million people. With few lessons learned, we're replicating it along the eastern coast of Florida, across the Gulf shores, up the southern quarter of California, and on the eastern side of Puget Sound in Washington. Some people flee the masses of humanity and gravitate instead to interior enclaves of the mountains, forests, and deserts, but the opposite flow continues to drain people from the staid interior and deliver them on the shores of booming economy, from Marblehead to Sarasota, from Long Beach to Bellingham.

It's not the coast per se that draws most people to oceanfront counties today. Rather, new development owes more to past momentum than to current enterprises in fishing, shipping, or immigration, which by nature cling to seashores. And even though most Americans live near the coasts, few live *on* them. The cities abut the water as a matter of economic convenience and historical coincidence, but most people now don't even see the water on a day-to-day basis and rarely get their feet wet.

Yet in some oceanfront suburbs, people pay a million dollars for a postage-stamp lot with a view. At expensive coastal resorts, gates block public access and seawalls cordon the surf from elevated swimming pools that curiously overlook plenty of space to swim in the ocean.

Though diminished by three centuries of development, the natural seashore still offers wealth and usefulness beyond all imagining. For starters, seashores fortify the continent against storms, which roar out of the Tropics as hurricanes and plow into the coasts with wind, rain, and rooftop-tall breakers. Waves can strike with twenty tons of pressure per square yard, and it's the shore that takes these massive hits. Our nation's front line of defense is not the often-cited battery of missiles and bombers but rather the beaches, dunes, wetlands, and rocky cliffs that bear the brunt of wind and water wearing every day on the land.

The barrier islands and dunes of the Atlantic shore are a good example. They owe their existence to sand washed down from the mountains. Rivers deposit the sand on the shallow continental shelf of the ocean, but waves, in the present era of rising sea level, then push the sand back, piling it up onshore. Meanwhile, the wind blows this sand into dunes. During storms, the ocean cuts passages between some of the dunes, isolating them from one another and from the mainland. Like drifting snow, the sand is blown downwind, and the dunes inch that way also; in effect, they roll over themselves, slowly migrating while new sand is washed and blown in to take the place of the old. Like floodplains along rivers, the dunes are a dynamic landscape. Though the change is constant at the local scale, the big picture is one of stability, with one dune succeeding another.

When storms strike the Atlantic shore, dunes break the onslaught of twelve-foot seas and rip-tearing winds. This works well provided the dunes have not been leveled for roads or building sites or shorn of shrubs such as yaupon and ground cover such as marram grass, sea oats, and pennywort, which collectively stitch the sandpiles together with roots as deep as thirty feet. Without these plants, the dunes not only would migrate too fast but would at times blow away and cease to exist at all. Intact, the system of dunes makes life behind it possible; it safeguards homes, neighborhoods, and whole cities.[3]

Protecting inland life and investments isn't the only thing the barrier islands and other seashores do. Far from it. The oceans contain five-sixths of all the biomass on earth, and the seashores and estuaries are the critical mixing zone between ocean life and the terrestrial world.[4] A lot of ocean biomass is edible by people; seafood is the largest single source of protein on earth. Commercial fisheries of the United States in 1991 grossed $3.3 billion in dockside receipts, which fed $27 billion in fish processing and sales.[5] But fish are not a product of the ocean alone; two-thirds of the commercial species depend at least in part on estuaries—the zone of mixed freshwater and salt water near land. Those shallow waters support everything from microscopic plankton, essential in the greater food chain, to giant sea turtles that nest on barrier islands and manatees the size of buffalo loafing in tepid bays. Three hundred species of birds can be found along the shorelines.[6]

One morning as I strolled along the oceanfront in Oregon, I was reminded of the seashore's impressive web of life. I was joined by a seal. While I walked southward, the seal flippered and porpoised through the water alongside me, so close I might have swum to it myself in a few short strokes.

Plenty of other life could have distracted me just as well—the bizarre transparency of jellyfish, the clever retreat of hermit crabs, the laughable body language of an orange-beaked oystercatcher, the baggy jowls of big-billed pelicans, whose wing beats miss the wave tops by no more than a fraction of an inch at most. But the captivating thing about the seal was that we made eye contact—almost *steady* eye contact. With the brotherhood of mammals and a shared evolutionary history that involved both of us living on land at one time, we had a connection, or so it felt to me. Old Irish folk traditions held that people could become seals and vice versa, and I can see where my forebears got the idea. The seal seemed so human with its furry little head, big dark eyes, inquisitively tufted eyebrows, and whiskers wet with salt water. After accompanying me for half a mile or so, the seal found better things to do, such as diving for a meal of fresh fish.

The seal, near the top of the food chain, personified the community of life that thrives only along the seashore. While animals of the grasslands might resemble those of the forest or desert, nothing even approximates the artistry and productivity of the animate world at the ocean's great edge.

A cross section of many natural shorelines shows freshwater ponds cordoned off from the sea by dunes and squawking with abundant bird life; brackish marshes serving as nursery grounds for oysters and a plethora of small fish; groves of windswept, salt-tolerant trees where songbirds take cover and raptors roost; dunes where tenacious plants dig deep with roots that stabilize the sand for a while; and finally, the mysterious workings of the sea itself.

Once, wondering what the tiny bubbles burping from wet sand indicated, I dug my hands into an otherwise sterile-looking beach. Awestruck, I came up with two fistfuls of sand crabs—harmless oval-shaped crustaceans half an inch long—so plentiful that the squirming little critters seemed to make up half the volume of the earth at my feet.

Just like the seal that disappeared without saying good-bye, the sellout crowd of crabs indicated to me the multitude of life that goes about its business just out of sight at the seashore. Low tide offers another window to a family tree of invertebrates: purple urchins, green anemones, orange starfish, red-capped crabs, blue-shelled mussels piled on top of one another as deep as your hand can reach. Whole cities of barnacles cement themselves to the rocks, where they sift the salt water for organic particles too small to see. Underlying all this is a lush lawn of seaweeds—some waving like prairie grass in the tidal shallows, some flat stemmed like a thousand leather belts, some beaded with float-bladders that pop when you step on them. The low-tide zone at an uncombed American shore is literally thick with life. Walking there, even with the utmost care, you can't help but crunch on creatures and wade in them with every step you take. And every bit of it feeds other unseen life, as if in a great old-growth forest with deep water lapping at the treetops. This edge where land meets water shows the nourishing power of both elements, and the friendly seal was the handsome bearer of that message to me.

Beyond these intricate systems of ancient creation, people just love the seashore. Whether it's the sandy flats at Atlantic City or the volcanic headlands of Hawaii, people flock to the oceanfront, and they come for many reasons. In 1880, physician John H. Packard published *Sea-Air and Sea-Bathing,* imploring people to breathe the salt air for their health. "Upon most persons the effect of breathing this air is tonic and invigorating, producing an immediate sense of exhilaration, improving the appetite, and promoting digestion."[7] While it may not be the cure-all that Packard prescribed, most people agree: ocean air makes us feel good. We suck it deep into our lungs and feel recharged. After the Civil War, vacations to the shore became popular among the middle class, and they have remained so, with millions of people hitting the beaches each summer like a mass migration of lemmings that at the last moment decides to stop at the waterline and celebrate life instead of blundering fatefully in.

The ocean shores pull at us with an irresistible attraction. As Anne Simon wrote in *The Thin Edge,* "Here where the sea is shallowest, land is lowest, rivers slowest, there is a dynamic interchange between water and earth, a phenomenon often believed to make passions run higher, emotions keener, the sense of well-being quickened. We come closer to our primitive selves on the thin edge, at once nurtured and excited by it."[8]

For recreation, the seashore may be the most popular natural landscape of all. Images of vacationing in a beach house brighten many childhood memories. Revitalized urban waterfronts in virtually every coastal city draw crowds to the water's edge, however artificial it might be, however much the emphasis has changed toward spending money rather than "sea-breathing" under Dr. Packard's prescription. At the seashore, people still literally immerse themselves in the forces of nature, splashing in the foam, swimming beyond the breakers, riding the roll of waves. By the millions we walk the sandy beaches, and we also fish, sail, run, kayak, birdwatch, sunbathe, play volleyball, pitch horseshoes, and simply sit in wonder at the watery space before us.

Striking a chord within the psyche, the waves at the seashore roll in and out like a slow but steady heartbeat. The sun thaws the tension in our backs. The breeze whistles its tune in our ears. The foam bubbles like champagne around our feet. We can cool off when we're hot, run free on a great playground of sand, and relax with the music of eternal surf when we're tired and need a rest.

Circumnavigating the Country

My visits to Sapelo Island and Glacier Bay offered only two glimpses of America's 90,000 miles of coastline.[9] In the Northeast, Maine boasts one of the most jagged shores, with deep inlets, rocky peninsulas, and islands studding offshore waters. An airline distance of 230 miles becomes 3,750 when the convolutions of the Maine shoreline and its estimated 3,000 islands are followed—greater than the distance from Bangor to San Francisco.

Continental glaciers in New England scraped coastal land to bedrock and depressed it under the weight of the ice. Then the land rebounded, rising back up above sea level, but not enough to expose the old Coastal Plain. Instead, the northeastern edge remains rugged, with picturesque headlands of rock, a seashore seen in all its glory at Acadia National Park.

The southward advance of the glaciers ended in southern New England, leaving a legacy of sandy moraines forming Cape Cod and the entire landmass of Long Island. From New Jersey southward, the mid-Atlantic shore combines mile upon mile of sandy beach with serpentine inlets of rivers that filter their way out through sea-level wetlands. Chesapeake Bay ranks as the continent's largest among 900 estuaries.[10] From North Carolina to Florida and especially along the coast of Georgia, the Atlantic shore is graced with coastal marshes as far as the eye can see, a Great Plains of the watery South.

The barrier islands—skinny sandbars parallel to the coast and just offshore—begin in Massachusetts but reach full flower off the coast of Maryland; then they run with only minor interruption all the way to Mexico. Chincoteague Island, Cape Hatteras National Seashore, and Tybee Island typify 300 isles with a combined oceanfront of 2,700 miles.[11] In Georgia, homes and condominiums occupy only three of the state's barrier islands; in a fortunate twist of fate, early northern industrialists bought up most of the Georgia islands as winter retreats, and in recent decades their descendants have deeded over their land for parks. Miami Beach, once just another barrier island, consisted of a spit of sand 200 feet wide ridged by low dunes. Developers converted that modest landscape into a filled-in complex of glittering high-rise hotels located in one of the most hurricane-susceptible areas one could imagine.[12]

South of Miami, at the tropical tip of Florida, the mangrove swamps begin—dense thickets of ten-foot shrubs on root-stilts knee-deep in water. Other mangrove swamps can be found along the Gulf shores of Louisiana and Texas.

A chain of islands arcing for 130 miles out into the Gulf of Mexico, the Florida Keys are our only living coral barrier reef, the third-longest in the world.[13] Coral reefs worldwide are among the richest ecosystems, support about 30 percent of all marine species, and are distinguished as the largest animal-made structures on earth.[14] A railroad linking the keys by bridges and causeways opened the coral-ringed, mangrove-covered islands to tourists in 1912. Far greater changes came when the railway was converted to a road in 1938. The keys' hardwood hammocks—lowlands raised slightly above sea level—support diverse plant communities, but 60 percent of them have been developed.[15] Beyond the road's end at Key West, a continuing string of coral islands survives, sanctuaries to the wildlife of tropical America as it once extended across the entire chain of keys.

At this southern tip of Florida, the 28,673-mile Atlantic shoreline of the United States ends and the Gulf of Mexico begins. People think of the western side of Florida as the wilder coast, though a perpetual real estate boom is changing that image into a wistful memory. To the north, an arc of seashore where the Florida Peninsula turns westward into the Florida Panhandle marks the only true jungle in the United States, a subtropical forest of broadleaf trees and tangled undergrowth soaked in warm rainfall. Much of it has been clear-cut in the past decades, but fine reaches of shoreline remain, with mirror-flat waters of the Gulf to the west and the thick, green glory of southern forest to the east.

Though still in the empire of sand, the 22,081-mile shoreline of the Gulf coast, complete with inlets, tidal rivers, and barrier islands, differs from the Atlantic shore to the east. Hurricanes roll in off the Gulf of Mexico, but the waters here are usually calm, a pale blue prism over chalk-colored sand. Growing urban populations share the habitat with one of the country's greatest commercial fisheries, and a few remaining enclaves of wildness still support black bears and rare red-cockaded woodpeckers.[16]

The Mississippi Delta—one of only two extensive deltas in America

Sapelo Island, Georgia. This barrier island, along with forty-four others that are protected along the Atlantic and Gulf shores, remains with its dunes and its ecosystem intact.

Daytona Beach, Florida. Much of the American shoreline has been built up, but fifteen states now have at least some type of setback regulations for new development.

California coast north of San Francisco. Rugged with headlands and sea cliffs created by earthquakes, the West Coast rises up dramatically from the sea.

Elephant seals, Año Nuevo State Reserve, California. The seashores, where our terrestrial and marine ecosystems meet, are rich in many forms of life.

Oregon coast. State parks protect much of this northwestern shoreline, and a statewide planning program seeks to limit development in hazardous areas.

Sitka, Alaska. The island archipelago of southeastern Alaska includes magnificent forests, glacier-covered mountains, and fishing towns dependent on the health of the sea.

Glacier Bay, Alaska. This estuary is home to whales, sea lions, salmon, eagles, and other life in a delicate balance that has been upset across many of our shores.

Volcanic mountains and cliffs on the island of Kauai. The Hawaiian Islands are ringed with tropical shores.

Tybee Island, Georgia. The construction of seawalls and jetties creates an endless cycle of beach erosion that requires constant and expensive replenishment of sand.

Gulf Coast near the mouth of the Rio Grande River and the Mexican border, Texas.

spilling out into the ocean—bulges into the central Gulf with its marshes and mudflats. Farther west, around the coastal bight of Texas, the sandy shore of Padre Island stretches southward as the world's longest barrier island and America's longest undeveloped shoreline outside Alaska. Here, the Laguna Madre pools for 125 miles as a backwater behind the barrier islands, historically rich in life but now channeled, silted, and polluted by dredging for the Intercoastal Waterway, a shipping canal that extends from the Northeast to Texas.[17]

Dramatically different, the West Coast runs for 7,863 miles along the edge of California, Oregon, and Washington. With its warm and sunny climate, southern California gives rise to the grandest of all beach cultures. Then, mountains from Santa Monica northward dominate the shoreline. Travelers consider Big Sur's spectacular headlands one of the most scenic coastlines in the world. Farther north, the waters of Monterey Bay hide the largest underwater canyon attached to the contiguous states, 11,800 feet deep, exceeding any canyon on land.

One of few sea-level breaks in the mountain fortress of the West Coast, San Francisco Bay extends inland until it merges with the delta of the Sacramento and San Joaquin Rivers. Waters of the bay flow out to sea through the bottleneck of the Golden Gate, a gap in the coastal mountains spanned by one of America's favorite bridges.

Northern California, Oregon, and much of Washington offer an incomparable world of green mountain slopes covered with oaks, grasses, and evergreens on steep, erodible hillsides pitching down to sea, a landscape shrouded by fog in summer and soaked by rain in winter. Visual treats await around every corner: splendid rock headlands, redwood forests, herds of sea lions. The Oregon Dunes, north of Coos Bay, rise higher than any other coastal dunes in America, and the rest of the state greets the sea with rugged shores and sea stacks of rock that look like bread loaves and pyramids. Farther north, the shore of the Olympic Peninsula in Washington includes the largest tract of wildland along the Pacific coast between the Baja Peninsula and British Columbia.

Puget Sound reaches far inland with its 1,700 miles of shoreline once buried in glacial ice, now a wending complex of bays, islands, and marshes. Development dominates in the Seattle-Olympia corridor on the eastern side, but islands with farmland and scattered homes lie throughout. At the northwestern limits of Washington, 200 conifer-covered islands of the

San Juan Islands chain have been named; another 275 rise as rock piles or tufts of trees above high tides in the Strait of Juan de Fuca.

A forested island archipelago takes over to the north, running for 580 airline miles along the British Columbia coast to the border of Alaska and then continuing northward and westward. Alaska's seashores wind through a maze of inlets for a total of 31,383 miles, making up 35 percent of America's shoreline. In southern Alaska, the collision of continental plates has heaved up mountains and created our newest landscape. The geologic action continues in our day with events such as the 1964 earthquake, 8.75 on the Richter scale, and with steaming eruptions always a possibility on the volcanic Alaska Peninsula. Giant forests of old-growth conifers decorate the shores, which are backed by mountains that rise to glacial heights even on some of the islands. Here, the world's largest bears feed in coastal streams fleshy with salmon—a food source that also attracts bald eagles by the thousands. Whales of the West Coast migrate each summer to these cold, plankton-filled waters.

Alaska's coastal extravaganza continues with the volcanic Aleutian Islands, dotting the Pacific in a 1,600-mile chain ending in Attu, the last American island before Siberia. The Aleutians are a landscape still in process; forty-seven of the chain's eighty volcanoes have erupted with lava or fumes since 1760.[18] Back on the mainland, the combined Yukon-Kuskokwim Delta dominates Alaska's western coast. Then, beyond timberline, the Bering Sea runs northward to the Arctic Ocean. That final American seashore lies icebound for much of the year, still rich with fish, seals, and polar bears but now torn with political debate over the use of land.

On the Front Line of Conflict

Between 1975 and 1995, the coastal population of the United States swelled by 41 million, with long-term growth running 15 percent higher than that of the nation at large. While 3 percent of the American landscape is urbanized, 14 percent of the coast is. And demographers expect the trend to continue; three out of four people might be living within coastal counties by the year 2025.[19]

Nowhere is the seacoast boom so evident as on the barrier islands of the East Coast and Gulf shores, where parks and reserves protect only 45 of 134 major islands.[20] Rapid growth has inflated property values and taxes and forced out longtime residents of coastal towns, including whole communities of African Americans.[21]

With tens of thousands of new buildings going up, hurricanes extract billions of dollars' worth of damage on the barrier islands and lowlands up and down the eastern seaboard, much of it owing to development that has destroyed the islands' ability to absorb the brunt of the storms. According to coastal geologist Orrin Pilkey, buildings were constructed "in the wrong place at the wrong moment in geologic time."[22] With winds of seventy-four miles per hour or more, hurricanes strike the southeastern and Gulf coasts an average of once a year. In 1989, Hurricane Hugo ripped into South Carolina, leveling houses in its path with an impressive show of force, but 90 percent of those who lost their houses rebuilt on the same storm-prone lots.[23] Hurricane Fran in 1996 shattered beachfront homes on Topsail Island, North Carolina, causing $4 billion in damages. It obliterated houses, tossed concrete septic systems as if they were cardboard boxes, and pitched mobile homes a mile from their moorings. The damage of that storm was dwarfed by that of Hurricane Andrew in 1992, which destroyed 90 percent of the mobile homes in Dade County, Florida, and caused an estimated $20 billion in losses. Had the storm hit twenty miles north, at Miami, it might have caused $65 billion in damages and killed hundreds of people.[24]

Orrin Pilkey for many years championed protection of the islands and warned that "the beaches on the ocean side of the barrier islands are probably the most endangered in the United States."[25] Worse than just sanctioning the development of Topsail Island, the state encouraged and subsidized it by building a new road. Oceanfront land where the old road had been was turned over to private developers. Homes and condominiums went up in a hurry and then came down even faster in the storm. Taxpayers shouldered heavy costs of resulting property damage attributed to an "act of God."

Turning a natural event such as a hurricane into a national disaster costing billions of dollars, shoreline development has been encouraged by public infrastructure such as roads, water lines, and sewers and even more by disaster relief that gives people money to rebuild in the same hazardous places. A study by the Department of the Interior reported that the development of an average acre of shoreline costs about \$82,000 in federal subsidies, in 1996 dollars.[26]

Enabling the worst kinds of shoreline development, seawalls of concrete, steel, or stone built along the shore are intended to deflect the explosive force of waves and protect buildings behind them. The walls indeed take the hit of the waves and protect the buildings for a time, but this is only a skirmish in the war against the waves. The walls do nothing to prevent the surf from plucking sand off the beach and dragging it back to sea; in fact, they make the situation far worse. Seawalls prevent the storm waves from depositing new sand, and they target all the waves' energy at the base of the wall rather than allowing the waves to dissipate their force across a gentle slope. Thus, the beach beneath the wall erodes with no ability to rebuild itself. First among the casualties is the public beach, no longer available for people's use. Undercut walls eventually collapse or require costly and continual importation of sand.[27]

Just as troublesome, jetties or groins consist of rocks piled up in the water like levees perpendicular to the shoreline—structures intended to trap sand and retain beaches in place. But jetties prevent the usual migration of sand, which is naturally delivered by the waves. These don't roll straight in from the sea; rather, they come in at an angle with prevailing winds. They transport sand in the same direction in a process known as littoral drift. On an open beach, one wave might move a handful of sand a few feet from left to right, but the next wave brings more sand to take its place. However, when a jetty interrupts the waves' flow, sand collects on its upwind side. On the other side, a corresponding erosion occurs, with no incoming sand for replacement.

Much as a levee on one side of a river pushes the water higher on the opposite bank, jetties worsen beach erosion for people living downwind of them.[28] Scrambling to claim any sand they can, the neighbors construct jetties of their own. Built at great expense, demolishing shoreline and offshore habitat, and with dubious long-term results, the structures now appear in series along the eastern beaches. New Jersey alone has more than 300 of them.[29]

Many of the large jetties and seawalls have been built by the Army Corps of Engineers. Even though those structures are now a major cause of beach erosion, the Corps continues to recommend building more of them, presumably a never-ending task in this era of rising sea level. Eighty percent or more of the U.S. shoreline is eroding, and the seawalls and jetties are only making the situation worse.[30] Taking action against this widespread folly, Maine, North Carolina, and South Carolina have passed laws banning further "hard stabilization" of their shorelines.

The typical response to accelerated beach erosion caused by seawalls and jetties is to import sand by pumping or trucking it, an activity euphemistically known as "beach nourishment." Miami Beach is the ultimate example of a built-out city scrambling to survive after the seashores' defense system—once operating for free—was destroyed. With the dunes all bulldozed, seawalls erected at oceanfront hotels, and artificial jetties fingering out into the surf, the 300-foot-wide expanse of sand in front of posh resorts disappeared. At a cost of $68 million, the Corps pumped 14 million cubic yards of sand from the ocean floor back onto the beachfront, and each following year on average, the Corps has had to import 190,000 more cubic yards just for maintenance.[31] Facing a dwindling supply of sand, county officials for a while considered barging it in from the Bahamas—literally importing foreign soil to shore up the continent of North America.[32] And because the newly applied sand is a soft, calcareous material, waves grind it into mud that quickly smothers the living coral reef offshore.[33]

That's just one example of beach nourishment. At Sea Bright, New Jersey, five and a half miles of beach were replenished for $36 million, not counting substantial ongoing expenses.[34] The beach at Ocean City, New Jersey, has been replenished forty times; in 1982, $5 million was spent to replace the city's sand, a capital improvement that lasted all of two and a half months. Erosion on a renourished beach can occur ten times faster than on a natural beach. Pilkey reported that only 12 percent of the replenished beaches on the Atlantic coast lasted more than five years.[35]

For these ultimately futile programs benefiting only beachfront residents, landowners typically pay 5 percent of the costs; state and county taxpayers, 30 percent; and federal taxpayers, 65 percent.[36] In 1995, President Clinton proposed a budget that would trim the responsibilities of the Corps on the seashore to projects in the "national interest," but representatives from coastal states beat back the proposal. In 1998, the president proposed that the beach nourishment subsidy of $100 million per year be cut to one-quarter that amount.[37]

Aggravating a bad situation in the high-risk hurricane belt, sea level is ominously rising. In the 20th century it's come up about nine vertical inches, which equates to a lot of encroachment on low-gradient shores. Islands in North Carolina are losing three to five horizontal feet of beach per year. Owing to erosion and sea-level rise, the high-water mark on Long Island is about a hundred feet inland from where it was in 1950.[38] And the invasion of the ocean will accelerate. A 1995 United Nations panel predicted a sea-level rise of one and a half feet in the 21st century because of global warming resulting from the burning of fossil fuels.[39] That alone may mean a two-mile landward advance of water in the Southeast, and some scientists estimate a catastrophic rise of up to six vertical feet by 2100.[40]

The only real solutions to the problems of beach erosion are not seawalls, jetties, and caravans of dump trucks importing sand, but adequate setbacks from the water so that beaches and dunes can do their timeless, free work of dissipating the waves' energy and protecting the rest of the land from damage. Coastal experts recommend a "strategic retreat"—not rebuilding damaged homes and requiring substantial setbacks for new construction.[41] They recommend that the Corps quit making coastal erosion worse with its seawalls and jetties and instead use its resources to relocate buildings out of harm's way.[42]

While what is built on the shore determines the fate of the seacoasts, what washes up on the beach can also be troublesome. Too often, the proverbial "gift from the sea" is something wretched. State water quality data reveal that 10 percent of our coastal waters fail safety tests for swimming, and they tend to be the 10 percent closest to cities. Sewage and polluted runoff are the main culprits. In *Testing the Waters,* the Natural Resources Defense Council reported 3,522 beach closings and pollution advisories in 1995—an alarming 50 percent increase over the year before.[43]

Awareness of coastal pollution hit a high in the summer of 1987 when medical wastes including blood-filled syringes washed ashore on beaches teeming with swimmers in New York and New Jersey. After the story hit the front pages, $3 billion in tourism revenues was lost.[44] The once routine ocean dumping of toxins such as radioactive waste has largely been eliminated, but myriad pollution problems remain.

For example, overfertilized runoff from farmland feeds algae that smother the coral of the Florida Keys, which is exceptionally sensitive to light and pollution. Compounding the problem, algae-eating fish can no longer do their cleanup job because pesticides and other effluents kill them off.[45] Climbing global temperatures also pose ominous threats to coral worldwide as water depth increases and warmer water bleaches the delicate reefs. Scarcely less threatened, sea grasses have been reduced by 20 to 100 percent across estuaries of the Gulf of Mexico, with deadly effects on fisheries. Reasons for the decline include pollution, dredging, development, and increased hurricane activity.[46] And the storms may get worse with the higher temperatures of global warming.

Revolting in their effects, oil spills have fouled beaches from Maine to Alaska. Crude oil smothers marine organisms, kills mammals and birds, blankets sand in dark ooze, and destroys marshes and estuaries where animals and plants breed and grow. Leaks from tankers and drilling platforms have devastated fishing and recreation economies and left toxins in sediment for years.[47] Accidents range from ubiquitous seepage and relatively minor spills, such as one on an oil barge off Rhode Island in 1996 that killed 2 million lobsters, to the 11-million-gallon disaster of the *Exxon Valdez,* which tarred 1,500 miles of pristine Alaska shores in 1989. Had the spill occurred off California, it would have oiled the shoreline from San Diego to San Francisco and beyond. Six of the ten largest U.S. oil ports are located on the Gulf of Mexico, and most of that seashore has been tainted with oil at one time or another. Perennial proposals to drill for offshore oil along the coast of northern California incite bloody political battles. Drilling platforms have even been proposed on Georges Bank, off the storm-ripped coast of New England, for many years one of the most productive fisheries of the world.

Facing composite threats, ocean fisheries have become the sites of one of the most alarming crises in the entire environmental agenda at the turn of the 21st century. Experts estimate that 80 percent of American coastal fisheries are in serious trouble.[48] Georges Bank has seen a collapse of its cod, flounder, and haddock fisheries, once believed to be inexhaustible. In Chesapeake Bay, overfishing and parasitic diseases have nearly ended the once great oyster harvest.[49] The catch of Atlantic sturgeon in the bay dropped by 90 percent, and fishing for sturgeon is now banned. Some of the most prolific staples of northeastern life could go the way of the walrus, once seen off Massachusetts, and the great auk, a penguinlike bird once seen in great flocks on the northeastern coast—both driven to extinction. Crashes in fisheries for salmon, lobsters, crabs, oysters, shrimp, tuna, sharks, and a host of other species in coastal areas of the United States result in a loss of $8 billion per year; 300,000 people lost their jobs from 1993 to 1996, with more yet to come.[50]

Overfishing by heavily equipped commercial fleets is one of the problems, as the worldwide harvest of seafood has quadrupled since 1950.[51] Though the increased catch may appear to be evidence of plentiful fish, in reality it indicates a collision course with disaster. The reason more fish were being caught was that they were simply hunted harder. Technology has armed whole navies of commercial trawlers with sonar and satellite tracking ability. Even aircraft aid tuna fishermen in spotting these fast-swimming masters of the sea. Now, with too few fish left to reproduce and with their habitat ruined, the crashes are under way. Pitiless new technology has wiped out the cod fishery that supported Canadian and American families for 400 years. Net-dragging trawlers literally dredge the sea-floor, not only snagging everything that lives there but also ravaging the entire ecosystem—the underwater equivalent of clear-cutting, with no regard for anybody returning to fish again.[52]

Even after the U.S. government expelled foreign fleets to waters 200 miles offshore, American fishermen filled the void with potent equipment that continued the ruthless harvest, and their political power blocked enactment of the needed controls. This phenomenon is known as "the fisherman's problem"—each fisherman believes it is in his best interest to catch all he can and to make as much money as possible while the resource lasts.[53] In this saltwater version of the tragedy of the commons, cutting back means only that somebody else gets the last fish. Each individual opposes regulation, knowing it would mean that he too would have to take less. An illogical degree of optimism prevents some of these people from foreseeing the inevitable. The result has been a total crash of even the most plentiful species, with most fishermen now out of work and many of them collecting government relief checks in the once great ports of the Maritime Provinces, New England, Chesapeake Bay, Florida Bay, California, and the Pacific Northwest.

To reverse this dismal trend, a study by the David Suzuki Foundation recommended that local communities be given authority over their own fisheries—a process the authors found to be historically effective, given one important qualification: the people must also control the outside influences on their fishery.[54] In the United States, most fishery decisions are delegated to eight regional fishery management councils governed by political appointees, including many who represent the commercial seafood industry and fail to heed the advice of government scientists.[55]

Filling the gap when ocean fisheries crash, fish farms now flood the market and mask the decline of natural stocks, much as feedlots on the Great Plains replaced the buffalo and the old-time cattle ranches. Many biologists believe that fish farming offers not the answer but a whirlpool of more enmeshed, unsolvable problems. Raising fish in pens or hatcheries pollutes estuaries, spreads diseases to wild fish, compromises the gene pool of native fish when farmed fish escape, and displaces wild stocks.[56]

The National Audubon Society, the Natural Resources Defense Council, and other groups are working to solve the problems of ocean fisheries, including overstocked fishing fleets, uncontrolled use of trawlers, subsidies for overfishing, chronic bycatch that kills four times as many fish as those intended for market, pollution, and habitat degradation both in the sea and along its productive shores. Without success in all of these areas, the decimation of ocean fisheries will be yet another chapter in the ongoing tragedy of nature's destruction in America.

Mobilizing at Sea Level

Considering that so many people know the seashore as a special place and that generations of Americans have flocked to the coasts for recreation, protection of the ocean's edge has been remarkably late and moderate in coming. But there has been lasting progress.

A few cities long ago set aside swatches of waterfront for intensive recreational use, such as Coney Island in New York and the shorelines at Hermosa Beach and Santa Monica in the Los Angeles area. These serve important purposes but are small and scarcely more natural than parking lots.

Some states with foresight established larger parks at seashores; Oregon was especially effective in conserving a network of public land that links the Northwest's breathtaking beauty in its rocky headlands, seaside forests, and isolated crescents of beach. While 90 percent of Maine's shore is privately owned, 90 percent of Oregon's is open to the public. California also bought a system of oceanfront state parks. Many of these efforts were made simply to gain recreational access to the water and a view of the sunset, yet the larger state parks have also saved scenic and biological gems such as Point Lobos, south of Carmel, and Patrick's Point, on the north coast.

Congress has created only a few national parks along seashores, but these include the showcases of Acadia National Park, protected through the benefaction of the Rockefeller family in Maine; shell-covered beaches of the Everglades on the wetland coast of Florida; and a spectacularly wild reach of the Olympic Peninsula in Washington.

It wasn't until the movement to create national seashores blossomed that a larger view of protection took hold. In 1935, a government study recommended the preservation of twelve beach areas, but a reluctant Congress established only one of them, at Cape Hatteras. Even there, scarcely anything happened because of landowner opposition until 1953, when the government finally bought some property. Taking another crack at the seashore job, planners for the National Park Service issued *Our Vanishing Shoreline* in 1954 and recommended that national seashores be established at fifty-four areas totaling 640 miles.[57]

As do so many successes in land protection, the national seashores owe their life to motivation stemming from personal experience. John F. Kennedy had lived at his family's seaside retreat near Hyannis, Massachusetts, and once in office, the young president pushed bills to protect seashores. With Secretary of the Interior Stewart Udall driving the program and with talented staff members who recognized the importance of waterfronts, a system of seashores took shape—one of the most extraordinary leaps of growth ever for the National Park Service.

Ten national seashores gained protection in the 1960s and early 1970s. The prototype, Cape Hatteras National Seashore Park in North Carolina, adjoins the completely wild Cape Lookout for a total length of 127 miles—two-thirds of the barrier island chain called the Outer Banks. Hatteras residents fought government involvement, so to sweeten the deal, the Park Service for several decades maintained dunes that protected private land in eight villages. Today, anyone who drives through the northern third of the Outer Banks—a clutter of beach houses, condominiums, and strip malls—can see what would have happened to the whole cape without federal protection.

At Cape Cod, Massachusetts, landowners also resisted protection, derisively calling the national seashore proposal "JFK's park." They negotiated life-tenancy agreements allowing them to remain when the Park Service bought the land. Cape residents eventually supported the goals of protection, however; after the federal program had acquired 45,000 acres, local governments continued the effort, spending $18 million on open space in the 1980s with the approval of two-thirds of the voters.[58]

Fire Island National Seashore, within a bus ride of 18 million New Yorkers, extends for thirty-two miles on the southern shore of Long Island. Designated in 1964, this national seashore nailed shut the coffin of a proposed four-lane highway the length of the island. National seashore status likewise rescued Assateague Island in Maryland from a 5,850-lot subdivision. Combined with Chincoteague National Wildlife Refuge, the two areas protect thirty-seven miles of barrier beach. Georgia's largest barrier island, Cumberland Island, remains a haven of untracked sand, marshes, and oak forests. Canaveral National Seashore offers twenty-four miles of dazzling white beach, the longest undeveloped shore on the eastern side of Florida, with Cape Canaveral, the famous rocket launch facility, only at its southern end. The Gulf Islands National Seashore guards the coasts of Florida and Mississippi, providing nature's respite from an otherwise heavily developing middle-America Riviera where even gambling casinos have gained a toehold. In Texas, the Padre Island National Seashore takes in seventy miles of white sand. In California, Point Reyes National Seashore caps this stellar collection with a 72,000-acre reserve of oceanfront cliffs, broad beaches, and seismic mountains. Whales spout just offshore, and San Francisco area residents can picnic, stroll, and explore during an afternoon in the wild.

Unquestionably important in their quality and strategic locations to serve both people and ecosystems, the national seashores have saved meaningful reaches of shore, yet nationwide they cover only 500 miles—about 0.5 percent of the shoreline.

Even in this limited form, the national seashore movement stalled out with opposition from landowners and with budget cuts. But in different ways, more recent efforts to protect coastlines have met with success. In 1997, for example, The Conservation Fund and other groups acquired 9,000 acres along the Maine coast near the town of Cutler. The Nature Conservancy bought fourteen barrier islands and preserved them as the Virginia Coast Reserve, a remarkable collection running southward from

Assateague Island and sometimes called the last great coastal wilderness in the East.[59] After Georgia's Coastal Marshlands Protection Act of 1970 dissuaded the Kerr-McGee Corporation from mining for phosphate on the jewel of Little Tybee Island in Georgia, the corporation planned a second-home city but ended up deeding the island to the Conservancy. Monroe County, Florida, passed a tourist impact tax and raised $1 million in 1994 to buy critical open space on the Florida Keys. Land trusts and governments have secured additional shorelines around America, though soaring property values mean that only developers can afford most of the oceanfront land.

Beyond acquisition, a regulatory approach to address questions of public costs has had limited success in protecting the seashores of some states. As a model for effective action, California established the San Francisco Bay Conservation and Development Commission in 1965 to plan for San Francisco Bay, and in 1969 it began to regulate land use. In 1972, state voters expanded on the idea and enacted a coastal initiative calling for regulation of development along the state's entire 1,200-mile shoreline. The success of this far-reaching proposition, promising at least nominal state involvement in big land-use decisions, marked one of the most important victories ever for coastal conservationists. In 1975, the legislature followed up on that vote of the people by adopting the California Coastal Protection Act, which created a commission responsible for public access and protection of shoreline beauty. The measure directed that development be sharply regulated outside cities and that ocean views be preserved. However, the governor, the Senate Rules Committee, and the speaker of the assembly appoint commission members, so effectiveness of the program comes and goes on the alternating winds of politics. Another pathbreaking state, Oregon, enacted legislation in 1969 recognizing the public's right to use beaches up to the vegetation line, and in 1971 the state created the Oregon Coastal Conservation and Development Commission to draw up a shoreline plan.[60]

With these states proving that progressive action is possible, interest grew at the national level. In 1969, a congressionally created commission issued *Our Nation and the Sea* and recommended that the federal government encourage states to better manage their shorelines.[61] Hoping to come to grips with development that was eating up the waterfronts, Congress passed the Coastal Zone Management Act of 1972 (CZMA). But efforts to enact binding requirements on new condominiums, commercial centers, public facilities, and homes along fragile seashores fell again and again to the ax of compromise, and the final law, administered by the U.S. Department of Commerce's National Oceanic and Atmospheric Administration, required nothing. It merely implored states to regulate their coastal zones and to channel growth into existing urban areas where it could be accommodated. Federal incentives included matching funds for planning and protection of some sanctuaries.[62]

One might regard adoption of the CZMA as the moment when the environmental movement of the 1970s hit the wall of political limitations. Earlier gains for open space, clean air, and water quality had accomplished much, but planning for land use remained the great unfinished agenda. Pro-development congressmen defeated the proposed National Land Use Policy and Planning Act by eleven votes. Like the CZMA, it would only have provided money to states and encouraged precautions with fragile lands, but unlike the CZMA, it would have applied nationwide. Virtually every other industrial democracy in the world has enacted a national land-use policy.[63] The CZMA, weak as it is, is as close as Congress has come to adopting such a land-use program. Among all our landscapes, only the seashore had the well-defined identity and attachment to people that is necessary to launch a national initiative for the land.

Eventually, all coastal states signed up under the law. Meaningful programs were hammered together in Connecticut, Maryland, Massachusetts, Michigan, New Jersey, North Carolina, and Oregon, with California already doing well.[64] Fifteen states established at least some type of setback legislation. Compared with doing nothing, the CZMA has offered some protection to estuarine waters, curbed the riskiest coastal development, and enticed states to plan better.[65] But serious disappointments stem from the facts that the guidelines focus on orderly development rather than resource conservation, that federal standards and funding fall short, and that enforcement of even well-conceived programs is often weak.

After the national seashore strategy ran out of steam and efforts to regulate the most onerous development became snared in an anti-government backlash directed at the CZMA program, President Jimmy Carter saw the need for alternative approaches and issued an executive order in 1977 for agencies to develop a plan specifically to protect the barrier islands. The new tack combined conservation goals with the political tenor of the times: reduce federal intervention. And subsidies amounted to federal intervention. The government had been backing coastal growth by paying for roads, water lines, and sewers; by sharing costs of storm insurance; and by doling out disaster relief so people could rebuild in the same old places. All these drains on the taxpayer worsened the costs of future disasters.

Picking up on the presidential directive and recognizing that 6,000 acres of barrier islands were being developed per year, Congress in 1982 finally enacted the Coastal Barrier Resources Act, eliminating federal money related to new construction on sections of the islands deemed un-developed. The government neither prohibited nor regulated land use; it merely cut subsidies in an attempt to discourage growth. To be considered undeveloped, an area had to have less than one building per five acres. Fitting into the criteria, 186 sections of coast with 670 miles of privately owned shoreline in the Atlantic and Gulf states were enrolled. In 1990, Congress added more areas, including Great Lakes frontage, for a total of 1,200 shoreline miles. Reaction by the states varied. Florida reinforced the program by prohibiting the spending of state money as well; North Carolina undermined the effort by approving state roads to serve construction.[66]

For a while, development nearly stopped in the zero-subsidy zones while proceeding apace in nondesignated areas. But eventually, the stakes got to be so high that the subsidies didn't matter so much. The General Accounting Office in 1992 found that development had occurred in nine of thirty-four areas studied; the long-term effect of this progressive but limited program was questionable.[67] Overall disaster costs continued to soar; federal relief for all types of disasters but principally floods and coastal storms in the 1993–1998 period totaled $15 billion, a fourfold increase from previous years.

To protect shorelines and reduce taxpayer expenses, the act needed to be extended into developed areas. But the so-called conservative Congress in 1997 did just the opposite, undermining the program by retracting eight areas, including a nesting site for rare sea turtles. Politicians whose rhetoric in the 1990s defined the terms *anti-government* and *free enterprise* voted without qualms to unleash renewed federal subsidies for developers. As Beth Millemann of the Coast Alliance explained, "This is nothing but a giveaway of taxpayer money to wealthy people to build second homes on the beach."[68]

More action is needed, and with growing interest in protecting the natural functions of the seashores, people everywhere around the edge of America are becoming involved. With traditional organizing and lobbying, Maine residents labored to stop a bulk cargo port on Sears Island. Citizens on California's northern coast tenaciously fought offshore leases for oil rigs on their magnificent rocky seashore.

Statewide in California, coastal supporters fought the efforts of Governor Pete Wilson and the legislature to undermine the California Coastal Commission by stacking it with developers, and the issue contributed to a Democratic takeover in the elections of 1998. People in Kodiak, Alaska, opposed a senseless proposal for a rocket launch facility that defined the term *pork barrel;* consuming federal dollars by the millions, it will scarcely be used on that remote, rainy, and magnificent wild shore.

In one of the greatest campaigns to restore an estuary, local people and government agencies are working to return to health Chesapeake Bay, an exemplar of the connections between rivers and estuaries, farmlands and commercial fisheries, watersheds and ocean biology. Polluted runoff proved to be the bay's linchpin problem, and reclamation efforts were aimed at reducing contamination by 40 percent. Stepping up to face the challenge, Maryland used state funds to protect river corridors and wetlands and thereby reduce the foul wastes coming from farms and floodplain development. By 1997, government agencies, nonprofit groups, and foundations had protected 24,000 acres of critical watershed property draining into Chesapeake Bay, and some of the programs were just picking up momentum.[69]

Author Anne Simon summarized goals for seashore protection all around the outside edge of America by calling for action "to restore the coast to its optimum natural function and keep it that way. . . . What's in question is an evolutionary leap such as no generation before us has attempted."[70]

Encircling It All

On the beach at Malibu, just north of Los Angeles, I watched Pacific rollers swell until the slanting light of late afternoon shone directly through them in translucent jade. Then the waves broke and tossed spume and a mist of salt air up and down the coast as far as I could see. Surfers, looking in the distance like seals, waited for the wave of their dreams, paddled as it approached, caught the downward slope, stood up on their colorful boards, and streaked ahead on the shining roll of ocean. A hundred people strolled along the popular beach, holding hands, swinging their arms in vigorous exercise, or pointing for their friends to see something of interest out in the sea—a cloud outlined by the sun, a white pelican diving for fish, a ship bound for Asia.

With sky-high metabolisms, a few children pranced in the foam, but November was too late for the tanned bevy of swimmers who pack this beach in summer. Aware of autumn even in southern California, Ann and I walked to the wet line of expired surf and then followed a smooth arc of sand to the mouth of Malibu Creek. It riffled with freshwater flowing into the sea, constantly refilling the ocean and paying back the loan of moisture the clouds had inhaled off the Pacific and sprinkled in a blessing of rainwater over the tops of the mountains.

There at the seashore I could symbolically see everything about America's landscape. The Santa Monica Mountains, rising from my feet, crowned the background with a roughened outline of peaks. They signified high country that could just as well have been the continental divide in the Rocky Mountains. Here, in microcosm, was the whole country, the entire landscape in an eyeful. Oaks and sycamores and especially chaparral softened the peaks, slopes, and valleys in the way of good forests— they blanketed the mountains with a crown of leaves and an anchor of roots. Where fires had burned, grasslands had reinstated themselves. Bone-dry after the six-month aridity of California's summer, great swaths of the watershed above me had burned only a year ago and now seemed like a desert, while a true desert lay just beyond those mountains, in the rain shadow the Santa Monicas cast over the interior hills.

Through all of this, Malibu Creek plunged down as rivers and streams everywhere do, gathering water, gaining force, nourishing the riparian edge. Just a few miles above me, the stream lay trapped by Rindge Dam, except that this dam plugging Malibu Canyon was brimful with soil washed off the land, and the stream drifted not through a reservoir but across a perched plain of dried silt before spilling uselessly over the concrete wall of the dam. Local people want to demolish the dam. If they do, steelhead will fin their way once again from the ocean, past this seashore where I stood, and up Malibu Creek to spawn in streams that drain the Santa Monica Mountains, an island of nature amid the megalopolis. There is hope.

Where I stood, the creek reached sea level and finally flattened out in wetlands and a salt marsh. At the edge of high tide, cordgrasses waved in the sea breeze, red-winged blackbirds roosted and screeched, and mallards dipped their heads to pluck underwater plants. Along with all the other seashores, this one defined the edge of the landscape and encircled all that we know as America.

CHAPTER 8

AMERICA IN THE 21ST CENTURY

Wanting to see it all—I recently spent two months traveling across the country.

The trip began in the tiny town of Westport, on the north coast of California, where I had holed up in a friend's house during the rainy season. There, at low tide, you can explore among sea-battered rocks usually covered by water, and find colonies of mussels, anemones, and starfish that could claim to be the farthest-west inhabitants of the country. At high tide, you can watch the breakers crash against steep cliff faces—the western front of land that's slowly rising up with the tremors of every earthquake. The land there at the edge reminded me that everything changes, even the apparently solid bedrock as it floats and drifts, underlain by the earth's molten core.

Though reluctant to leave behind the sound of the sea and the moist salt air, I had my sights on the far eastern shore of the continent, and as I drove across the Coast Ranges new discoveries enticed me on a journey that would tie together the landscapes of America. I would see samples of them all.

Just when I thought I must be banking into my hundredth tight curve going up a damp mountain road under fog-dripping second-growth redwoods, I topped the ridge and coasted down the other side into a parkland of Douglas-firs and stately blue oaks scattered in meadows. My heart thumped with a primitive pleasure so elemental that it might go back to the early days of humanity when fit ancestors of mine roamed other savannas rich in game.

Digressing to the south, I transected the Central Valley—an outdoor factory of industrial agriculture plumbed by canals, ditches, headgates, pumps, and siphons attached like catheters and intravenous tubes to the Sacramento River, which winds, levee-bound, down the middle of the tabletop plain. In the valley's midst lies the urban throb of Sacramento, with a fine inner city but traffic-jammed suburbs flooding out across the farmland like angry water from a broken dam.

The van's engine and my spirit both warmed as I climbed the next range to the east, the big one, the Sierra Nevada. Its foothills of live oak and manzanita had been grubbed out for new roads and brush-hooked for subdivisions, but blessed relief came when the evergreens of Eldorado National Forest took over, scenting the air with sugar pine, redcedar, and white fir, all of them shading the ground from the searing heat of California's summer sun.

Never will I cross the Sierra without stopping somewhere near the top to pay my respects to John Muir's Range of Light and muse over the intensity of winters I've spent there, deep, deep in snow. So once again I got out, tested the chill air in my thirsty lungs, and stretched my legs on that bracing bedrock of white granite. From a north-facing slope, I packed nine-month-old snow into jars and buried them in my cooler to guard against the blistering hot drive to come when I rolled down off the mountain refuge.

For a few days I crossed the Great Basin Desert, with its sagebrush plains, alkali basins where mile-wide alluvial fans led me up the slopes of mountains peppered with junipers and down the eastern sides to wide-sky vistas welcoming more of the same. The nights closed vacuum silent around me except for coyote howls, as raw in wildness as a grizzly tooth yet as lyrical as the song of a Baltimore oriole. Standing alone on a rock at night, I could almost feel the pinpoints of thousands of stars.

Eventually, my Ford van hummed up the western flank of the Rockies and onto the backbone of that great range, where I wandered for some days among the alpine ridges and quickly crossed ranchland posted "no trespassing" in the valleys between. Then, to the east, the Great Plains rolled out forever in glorious space, the country dry but grassy, the rivers shallow but winding among cottonwoods and swales. All the sandy alluvium making up that terrain—so different from the mountains yet intimately related to them—had washed off the Rockies following their upheaval beginning 70 million years ago.

I crossed the Missouri River, which had been traveled almost two centuries before by Lewis and Clark. Some sections of the river can be reclaimed to health, but the "Big Muddy" I saw was locked up in dams and reservoirs for hundreds of miles at a time. Then I veered northward across the tallgrass zone now called the corn belt. Field after field was deep in stalks and tassels, now and then broken by chocolate-brown rivers of foul farm runoff; the country's richest soil was literally bubbling down to the Mississippi River en route to the sea.

At Minneapolis I crossed that centerpiece river, already spaciously wide 500 miles from its source. Then I curved northward again into the bog-and-lake land of the northern Midwest. For a week I listened to loons, paddled my canoe on amber swamp water, and strolled the windswept shores of Lakes Superior and Michigan. On maps, the western side of Lake Huron still looks lightly settled, like a window to the days when explorers sought the mythic Northwest Passage, but what I found was mile after mile of mowed lawns, lakeshore houses, and Keep Out signs.

Farther south, I navigated the urban maws of Detroit and Chicago, smoky, hustling, and full of siren wails at night. I then entered the tangled, green forests of the East, hazy and humid yet so much more hospitable than the West—far more livable in many ways. You can garden easily. You can drill a well almost anywhere. You don't have to irrigate. You can cut firewood on your own land. Pennsylvania claims the largest rural population in America, and I passed town after small town across the Allegheny

Mountains and Pocono Plateau, entering the early American realm of New England, where centuries-old houses and towns impart a comforting, enriching sense of mature community.

Three more days' travel on splendid winding roads, with lots of stops at scenes of satisfying beauty in fenced fields, steepled villages, and regrown forests, brought me to the seashore of Massachusetts. There, on the beach at Cape Cod, with two months of vivid impressions behind me, at dawn, I stepped out of the van to watch the sun rise on America.

At these shores, nearly four hundred years ago, European colonists began to arrive. They had left many of their belongings behind but brought their cultures with them, including Old Country attitudes about land. Enduring among the immigrants' influence were four groups; the story of their mark on our lives is told by historian David H. Fischer in *Albion's Seed*.[1] Arriving in New England, the Puritans brought a rigid work ethic, a religious fervor that dominated their relationships with nature and everything else, and a self-righteous worldview. In Virginia, English settlers brought a system of plantations, exploitation of workers and soil, and imperious male dominance. The Quakers of Pennsylvania brought an open-minded tolerance of others, a respect for the Indians as fellow human beings, a pious and unwavering belief in peace, and a powerful adherence to personal property values because property had been taken away from them in England. The big influx proved to be Scottish, Irish, and English settlers from the rough-cut war zone of the northern British Isles. These "borderlanders" settled in the Appalachians and brought a scrappy love of fighting and an extraordinary fervor for individual freedom no matter what. The progeny of this final group, with a heritage both genetic and cultural, settled much of the South, Midwest, and western interior regions of the country.

While European settlers started out with these antecedent cultures soaked in self-serving ideas about property, the contentious nature of their relationship with the land was heightened by challenges faced on the frontier. It threw up inhospitable barriers to anyone ill prepared or unwilling to accept on the Creator's terms the dark woods and the dank swamps, the windy plains and the seasons of biting change. The Indians provided a model for such acceptance, but settlers regarded them as part of their problem and the Indians' way of life not something to be emulated.[2]

The Indians had certainly manipulated the land by hunting, by killing off ice-age mammal species, and by burning areas to allow the growth of grasses, shrubs, and berries for wildlife and people. Southwestern Indians even irrigated what they could, but from a wide perspective, it scarcely amounted to a scratch in the desert. None of the changes caused by the Indians seemed significant compared with what even the earliest white settlers imposed.

The Indians' tenure of at least 12,000 years was backed up by their recognition of people's dependence on healthy land.[3] The Haudeno-saunee (Iroquois), for example, believed that for any action, people needed to consider the effects on the seventh generation to follow. In the Cher-okee language, *Eloheh* meant "land." It also meant "history," "culture," and "religion." With this sense of unity still ingrained, Cherokee spokesman Jimmie Durham in 1978 said, "Is there a human being who does not revere his homeland, even though he may not return?" He added:

> We cannot separate our place on earth from our lives on the earth nor from our vision nor our meaning as a people. We are taught from child-hood that the animals and even the trees and plants that we share a place with are our brothers and sisters. So when we speak of land, we are not speaking of property, territory, or even a piece of ground upon which our houses sit and our crops are grown. We are speaking of something truly sacred.[4]

But the newcomers sought to conquer the wilderness while keeping their European ways intact, and they embraced property as the chief currency for status and wealth, even calling it *real* estate.

The industrial revolution in the late 19th century dramatized the Euro-American culture's separation from nature even more than the "con-quest" of the frontier had done, and with ironclad strength and brazen new wealth it bred more control and more consumption. As if hypno-tized by its metronomic qualities, people believed in the power of the machine and in its uncompromising force, and they adopted the notion that the land and the rivers were just big machines as well. Anything required to bend nature to economic gain was justified. Sustainability, cooperation, stewardship—those could all theoretically have been para-digms for our culture, but the chimera of unlimited prosperity flooded out all other goals. To extract wealth from the land, destruction of its natural process was encouraged and rewarded, and the Euro-American culture grew, with few setbacks, into what we see today.

No matter how intrusive the new culture's touch on the land, no matter how virulent the fight against wilderness on the frontier, and no matter how one-sided the industrial economy's parasitism of the natural world, the extent of damage remained limited by low numbers of people for many years. But a population that was once limited has now overflowed.

Starting and Ending with People

Nearly doubling in the last half of the 20th century, the American population was 270 million in 1998 and increasing by about 2.5 million per year. With such growth, one might expect everything human-made also to have doubled, from houses and cars to garbage, asphalt, and streetlights dimming the stars at night. But in fact, it's more than that; the per capita rate of material consumption has doubled as well, increasing our consumptive capacities by 400 percent in only fifty-eight years. Between 1960 and 1987, the acreage considered urbanized multiplied by two. And aside from the increase in new dwellings, the size of the average house jumped by 25 percent during the 1980s, though the size of families did not grow. Each year, highway departments paved 11,200 more miles of road.[5] The number of motor vehicles grew at twice the rate of population growth from 1970 to 1995, and the number of miles driven per vehicle also increased by 20 percent.[6] These trends continue.

For most people, population growth is not a distant problem but one that affects them directly, in their own communities, every day. Crime increases with population. Anybody from a small town or rural area will unhesitatingly confirm this fact after visiting a large city, but statistics bear the trend out as well.[7] Taxes also increase with population. This, too, is obvious to anyone who has paid taxes in a rural community and then moved to an urban or suburban one. In Loudoun County, Virginia, economists found that for every $1.00 in tax revenues collected, $1.28 in services was required for residential land uses, while only $0.11 was required for farmland. And the more a community grows, the more expensive it becomes to maintain basic services. In the early 1990s, roads, water lines, sewers, and parkland needed for each new home in booming Portland,

Oregon, cost $28,500—an expense that will have to come from taxes.[8] According to author William Ashworth in his book on economics, "The biggest creators of new taxes are not the tax-and-spend welfare Democrats in Congress, but the economic development committees of the Chamber of Commerce."[9]

Housing costs likewise increase with population growth, as a comparison of most small versus large communities will show. When Portland grew by 35,000 people per year between 1991 and 1995, housing costs jumped by 32 percent. But median income rose by only 8 percent; many local families found themselves priced out of the market.

In the face of current population growth, open lands all across America are threatened and hard-earned environmental gains of the past are in danger of being wiped out. For example, through vigorous conservation measures, per capita use of energy barely increased from 1970 to 1990, but total energy use still rose by 36 percent, with nine-tenths of the increase from population growth.[10] This affects mountaintop removal for coal in the Appalachians, gas drilling on the eastern front of the Rockies, hydropower dams on salmon streams of the Northwest, and incursions into our last great wilderness on the Arctic Coastal Plain of Alaska. For a time, the perceived quality of life in some communities may go up as population increases, but most of our towns, cities, and states passed that point long ago. With a more crowded landscape, the quality of life goes down and the liberties we enjoy and cherish as a birthright are eroded by the pressures of scarcity, competition, and the regulation that goes with overcrowding.[11]

After looking at what's happening to the American land, I can see that all the current talk of personal freedom—from libertarians claiming sovereignty in Montana to a Republican-dominated Congress voting for deregulation in Washington, D.C.—fails to grapple with the real cause of eroding liberties. The culprit is not a mindless bureaucracy but growing numbers of people whose needs and conflicts require that we have regulations on sewage systems, fees for building permits, restricted entry at the most popular national parks, and even two-hour tow-away zones designed simply to give someone else a chance to park his or her car. We didn't have or need these things when our population was small.

Studies have shown that in North America, at current rates of consumption, each person requires 12.6 acres of land for support.[12] A city of 1 million thus requires 12.6 million acres for its support in living space, food processing, commodity production, and waste disposal. And that assumes "productive" land. With these figures in mind, America is not nearly so spacious as it might seem, even beyond the sprawl of the cities.

A phenomenon I call the "delusion of open space" occurs when one flies over the United States. I think everybody experiences this: one looks out the window and sees a lot of "empty" land. But when I consider the facts that water must be available for people to live, that those 12.6 productive acres are needed by each person, that substantial acreage in areas such as floodplains must be available for the earth's built-in maintenance program to function, that habitat must be shared with other forms of life if natural systems are to survive and we're not to be alone in this world, and that a bottomless deficit is accumulating every day because we consume massive amounts of nonrenewable resources just to sustain the population we already have—when I consider all that, I can only conclude that America is full. Indeed, it's overfull, whether "empty" land is seen out the window or not.

Looking at this question in a far more systematic way back in 1972, the Rockefeller Commission concluded that there was no benefit to further population growth in America. In 1980, the *Global 2000 Report to the President* agreed. But neither study had much effect on national policy.[13] By the time the 1990s era of rapid economic growth and runaway materialism rolled around, it had become more and more evident that we were consuming the resources of the earth and of future generations as if the monetary wealth of today's people was the only thing that mattered.

Our current population subsists to a large degree on nonrenewable resources, principally fossil fuels, which will someday run out. This exhaustion of our capital extends to prime farmland, soil, forest productivity, ocean fisheries, groundwater, and minerals.[14] Once these things are gone, how will people live? Renewable resources such as solar power and well-managed forests offer us an answer to this conundrum and a path to the future, but it's not the path we're on. Economist Robert Costanza reported in 1992 that a U.S. population of 85 million could exist on renewable resources at current per capita consumption levels; with half our current rate of consumption, which is how we lived in 1950, renewable resources could support 170 million people—only 63 percent of our current number.[15] Costanza concluded that a reduced population should be our goal. Otherwise, with unlimited numbers of people vying for limited resources on earth, a drastic lowering of the standard of living emerges as the only future in sight.[16] This scenario is graphically seen in the swarming capital city of our next-door neighbor, Mexico.[17] Scarcity, inflation, poverty, regulation, fatal levels of pollution, and an erosion of freedom are unavoidable consequences of an ever-increasing population.

A stable population would mean little additional loss of open space, from mountains to seashore and all across the landscapes of America. While conventional wisdom holds that we must grow, more and more people now wonder why. The population of Pittsburgh, Pennsylvania, has declined by nearly half since 1950, and in the process the city has been transformed from a deadly exemplar of pollution and urban decay to the "most livable city in America," with an unemployment rate of only 4.3 percent. Meanwhile, high-growth cities such as Los Angeles and Miami only got worse.

A goal of stabilizing population does not mean we cannot grow. Free of the struggle simply to accommodate more and more people and free of the all-absorbing efforts to cope with the challenges of an ever larger population—whether this means building a larger church or finding another landfill—people could turn their energies to growth of other kinds: greater meaning in our work, more time for the family, better education, added opportunities to learn and explore, a strengthening of friendships, a heightened sense of community, more closeness to one another and to the earth. Every person can add to this wish list of what could be growing instead of traffic jams, taxes, and the size of prisons.

Even in today's picture—one that history may regard as a depiction of madness—there could be hope because, driven by new cultural desires, by education, by economic imperatives, and by safe, reliable, and accepted methods of contraception, the birthrate among established Americans is quite low. The fertility rate in 1990 hovered at about 2 children per woman—up from 1.8 in 1976 and higher than in Europe, though still at a level that would result in a plateau of population fairly early in the 21st century.[18] But that's not going to happen.

The birthrate of established Americans is low, but because of immigration, the national growth rate continues to soar. According to data from the Bureau of the Census, 60 percent of the increase from 1998 until the year 2050 will come from immigration, along with high birthrates among new immigrants.[19] The National Research Council predicted that two-thirds of the growth before 2050 will result from immigration.[20] Much of this growth owes directly to Congress, which in 1990 increased the rate of legal immigration by 35 percent, the highest level in history—an immigration rate exceeding that of any other nation.[21]

If immigration continues at a high level, the rapid rate of population growth will not subside. The Census Bureau's high estimate, which may be the most realistic, calls for 519 million Americans by 2050. Even the medium estimate calls for 394 million people.[22] And that's only until 2050. At that point, much of the United States will look more like the crowded island of Japan than the America we know. Choosing to have virtually no immigration, the Japanese population, in fact, is expected to shrink while ours increases with no bounds.[23]

Of course, almost all Americans today are descended from immigrants. But consider as well that most of those people came when there were space and resources for them (native Americans certainly disagree, but still, there was clearly more space for immigrants in the past than there is today). Now the situation has changed. Though space and resources are now scarce, an estimated 1 million legal and illegal immigrants move here each year.[24]

It's not fair that my ancestors made it into America unrestricted but that today people from other countries cannot, but neither is it fair that my parents' generation had to deal with both the Great Depression and World War II. Runaway population growth, quite simply, is the great challenge of our time. And many people are aware of this.

A Roper poll in 1997 found that 54 percent of Americans, including majorities of Latinos, supported a reduction of immigration to 100,000 or fewer people per year—one-tenth the 1997 rate. Seventy percent supported a limit of 300,000 or fewer—a number that could still allow for needs such as unification of nuclear families. And regarding overall population, Americans by a seven-to-one margin thought there were already too many people—a view shared widely across lines of race, income, region, and education.[25] This landslide of public opinion should come as no surprise. It's evident in people's choice of living space: we move to suburbs and spacious neighborhoods for more room. We resettle in less crowded regions such as the Pacific Northwest and the Rocky Mountains, we vacation where there's open space, and we try to avoid rush hour.

We're dismayed when the Saturday night movie is sold out or when we have to wait in line for anything.

While many regard population growth as an issue we can do nothing about—beyond the important personal response of having fewer children—that's not true. As advocated by the organization Negative Population Growth, a single act of legislation could lower the legal immigration rate and set America on the course of population stability. Of all the factors in population growth, legal immigration is the one we should be best able to control. We could address the substantial humanitarian obligations tied up in this issue by helping other countries attain population stability and helping them improve their quality of life. This can be done by educating women, which has dramatic spinoff effects across cultures.[26] We could work toward reducing the "push" for immigration by supporting family planning worldwide, reducing resource depletion, and encouraging respect for human rights.[27]

Some people with humanitarian conscience believe that we cannot solve our own population problem until we solve the population problems of the world. But most countries have eschewed that view and adopted low immigration quotas. More important, considering the magnitude of global population growth, many people believe that worldwide overcrowding cannot be solved in time to preserve anything of much value in America if growth continues as it is. They agree that we must do everything we can to find global solutions. But in the meantime, our first responsibility is not for the islands of Tonga—just one of scores of overcrowded countries whose people want to come to America—but for our own country and for the livability, health, and sustainability of our own communities and our own generations to come. They ask, Without saving ourselves, how can we save anyone else?

Many programs worldwide have effectively lowered birthrates with voluntary participation; sixty-three nations have adopted some kind of policy to lower fertility (America is not among them).[28] For example, a program in the Philippines encouraging "small, happy families" strives to improve education on the issue. Supporting such programs (which do not include the strong-armed model of China) may be a far better investment than trying to accommodate the virtually unlimited numbers of people who want to emigrate to the United States from overpopulated countries. Recently in New York City, I hailed a taxicab driven by a fine and thoughtful immigrant from Bangladesh. I asked, "Do other people in your country want to come to America?" Without hesitation, he responded, "*Everybody* in Bangladesh wants to come to America." Even if his statement was rhetorical, consider that the population of his country of origin is 135 million. Much closer to home, the already overcrowded Central American nations will see a sevenfold population increase in just one lifetime at current rates of growth.[29] Even if we were to open the floodgates of immigration to the United States, we would scarcely put a dent in the demand from Central America alone.

In spite of a global situation in which there is little hope of stabilizing population in time to protect America from enormous levels of immigration and the attendant effects of rapid growth, some environmental groups, such as the Sierra Club and the National Audubon Society, have declined to take a position on the issue. "Immigration is an extremely divisive topic," explained Pat Waak, director of Audubon's population program. "We prefer to work on creating a broad constituency. Half the pregnancies in the U.S. are unintended, and that alone presents a huge mission."[30]

Some people still argue that unlimited population growth will serve us well by offering cheap labor, more consumers, and cultural diversity. But in looking deeply at the land and striving to understand its workings and meanings, I can draw only one conclusion: the earth is finite, and unlimited numbers of people cannot live on a limited earth.

Our population doubled between 1940 and 1998, as it will likely double again in the 21st century, and this process of doubling needs to be understood as the virtually exponential growth that it is. Biologists, who see this kind of thing often in experiments, use this analogy: If duckweed on a pond doubles every week and only one square foot is now covered on a 100-acre pond, when will the whole pond be covered? It will take only twenty-six weeks. That's fast. But the real lesson for our society is this: in the twenty-fifth week, the pond will be only *half* covered. At that point, there will appear to be plenty of open water. Yet in fact, the pond will be completely covered only one week later. If America does not already appear to be full, it certainly seems to be half full, which allows us only one more doubling cycle to bring about change and take responsibility for our numbers.

Otherwise, what will happen? According to demographic analyst Lindsey Grant, at current growth rates it would take only 600 years for the world's human population to reach the absurdity of one person for each square meter of ice-free land.[31] Obviously, that won't happen. A mass die-off from disease, starvation, or warfare over scarce resources will intervene, likely with unparalleled horror and human suffering. So if adjustments are to be made, why not make them now, before the level of suffering escalates? Why not now, while we still have something of value left in America?

If we are to cross over to a path of caring for the land and thereby caring for our children and grandchildren, it must be on three great bridges of change. The first is population stability because everything else we try to do will otherwise be undone by the needs of more and more people. The second bridge is a land ethic powerful enough to touch people in their hearts and to affect choices they make in their daily lives. The third is a political movement that puts the goal of stewardship ahead of big money that is constantly being reinvested in politics to assure continuing exploitation.

The Ethical Alternative

Forester Aldo Leopold forged the pioneering work on an American land ethic, first in an article in 1933 and again in *A Sand County Almanac* in 1949. His words remain timeless:

> All ethics so far evolved rest upon a single premise: that the individual is a member of a community of interdependent parts. . . . The land ethic simply enlarges the boundaries of the community to include soils, waters, plants, and animals, or collectively: the land. . . . In short, a land ethic changes the role of *Homo sapiens* from conqueror of the land-community to plain member and citizen of it. It implies respect for his fellow-members, and also respect for the community as such.[32]

Historian Roderick Nash identified Leopold as the first powerful, well-grounded advocate in Western history to call for an ethical responsibility to the nonhuman natural world.[33] Leopold, however, knew that few people in his day subscribed to this ethic.

Now, fifty years later, I wonder how far we have come. Is the land ethic accepted yet? With plenty of evidence that it's not, author Wallace Stegner in 1985 maintained, "The land ethic is not a widespread public conviction."[34] Hardly more hopeful, author Charles Little wrote, "We search frantically for tiny indications that a land ethic, at least a prelusive one, can really exist in America."[35] Although these discouraging words come from two elders who knew what they were talking about, we have come a long way since 1949. To judge that distance, consider the yardstick of our laws.

At the federal level and in every state, we now have policies, programs, and budgets addressing soil loss, forestry, mining, recreation, wildlife, fish, water, air, historical preservation, and public land. These efforts fall far short, but they do have effect. And even with private land, we've made remarkable strides in recognizing public responsibilities since Leopold's time. Where the least ambitious zoning of floodplains or other regulations amounted to heresy at mid century, local land-use controls are widespread today. Only a handful of municipalities had floodplain zoning in 1949; more than 19,000 now do, and zoning applies to 88 percent of coastal communities.[36] These and other local land-use regulations do not go far enough, they too often shrink in compromise, and the most rural regions have done little, but still, the public role in land use has leaped far ahead of where it was a generation or two ago.

Though a backlash has stalemated what some analysts called a revolution in land-use regulation in the 1970s, the changes have nonetheless been profound.[37] In 1998 Jerry Walls, a professional planner for thirty years in Pennsylvania, said:

> We face the cumulative effects of land-use practices of the past, but we've made real progress. Twenty years ago, zoning for all the townships in our county was a long-range goal. Now we have it. But even better, we're seeing our second and third generations of ordinances. They're getting better as people see the problems. The town officials, the planners, and the developers are all starting from more informed positions, further up the ladder. Many more tools are available, from zoning to environmental laws, from land trusts to the phasing of infrastructure. We're far more effective in planning than we were in 1970.[38]

Walls believes that even when a land ethic seems to have little influence on permits issued for new shopping malls and subdivisions, the effect is nonetheless present. "Here's a big difference between now and thirty years ago: today you can have this discussion about a land ethic with almost anybody, from a home builder to a fisherman, from a county commissioner to a farmer. They know what you're talking about. And most of them agree that a land ethic of some kind is in order."

Reflecting on the changes since Leopold's time, environmental historian Samuel Hays of the University of Pittsburgh also finds evidence of progress. "The visible part of the ethic is in the activities of organizations dedicated to better land use—the 1,100 land trusts, for example. The members of those organizations, the money they raise, the studies that they and government agencies undertake—all these things illustrate that, at some level, a land ethic is alive."[39] The organizations Hays speaks of are evident everywhere: nationwide, more than 10,000 conservation groups had been formed by the early 1990s, and the number was growing by 300 per year.

The very facts that President Ronald Reagan in the 1980s launched an anti-stewardship offensive by fueling the "sagebrush rebellion" to privatize public land and that Congress in the 1990s pushed the agenda further with efforts to rescind environmental laws and redouble the subsidies for even the most shortsighted of development reveals that those politicians had something to push *against*—a newborn land ethic reflected in law. Furthermore, the most determined efforts of Congress in the mid-1990s retracted only a few gains of the previous twenty years. This is a far cry from the lack of support Aldo Leopold lamented in the 1940s when he wrote, "The case for a land ethic would appear hopeless but for the minority which is in obvious revolt against these 'modern' trends.'" In the 1990s, public outrage at cutting environmental protection reflected not merely a minority in revolt but a mainstream consensus of powerful proportions.

Consider another great change since Leopold's time: science now plays a pivotal role and has emerged as an effective tool in promoting a land ethic. While conservationists in 1900 argued only for the sublime beauty of Hetch Hetchy Valley when it was slated for damming, and in 1956 they argued mainly about the integrity of the National Park System when they stopped construction of Echo Park Dam, today they argue about biological diversity and fragmentation of habitat, about nitrate poisoning and carbon in the atmosphere. Science now weighs in on the most arcane specifics, such as how water should be released from a dam, and also on the broadest of worldviews. In 1992, for example, the internationally renowned Union of Concerned Scientists reported on the cumulative effects of environmental problems: "No more than one or a few decades remain before the chance to avert the threats we now confront will be lost." In *The World Scientists' Warning to Humanity,* signed by ninety-nine Nobel Prize winners, the organization warned that if action is not taken, the prospects for humanity will be "immeasurably diminished." Chairman Henry Kendall added, "This kind of consensus is truly unprecedented. . . . Natural systems can no longer absorb the burden of current human practices."[40]

During Aldo Leopold's time, people considered economics to be the chief stumbling block to a land ethic. He wrote, "Land-use ethics are still governed wholly by economic self-interest, just as social ethics were a century ago. . . . The 'key-log' which must be moved to release the evolutionary process for an ethic is simply this: quit thinking about decent land-use as solely an economic problem. Examine each question in terms of what is ethically and esthetically right, as well as what is economically expedient." His words reflect a sharp wisdom, but regarding economics, the tide has turned.

Economic thinking has shifted to recognize that people value the health and welfare of the land and that regional and national economies require these assets as well. In *Economic Well-Being and Environmental Protection in the Pacific Northwest,* thirty economists concluded in 1995 that a good environment underpins a good economy. "The Pacific Northwest does not have to choose between jobs and the environment. Quite the opposite: a healthy environment is a major stimulus for a healthy economy."[41] The arguments for land protection no longer conflict with economic concerns but rather draw on economic arguments about public costs, unnecessary subsidies, and private profitability. In 1995, Undersecretary of State Timothy Wirth repeated what has become an axiom: "The economy is a wholly owned subsidiary of the environment."[42]

Thomas Power, chairman of the Department of Economics at the University of Montana, Missoula, made a fortified case that protecting land increases land values at personal, community, and statewide levels for the simple reason that beautiful places are more desirable than ravaged ones. "This should prompt a fundamental shift in the economic role we envision for our natural landscapes. Increasingly, nature should be viewed not as a warehouse of raw materials but rather as the precious backdrop that makes an area's living environment desirable."[43]

Yet while a healthy environment makes economic sense for a community or society, that does not mean an individual will turn away from profits to be made by damaging the earth. The "key-log"—to use Leopold's term dating from the days of logjams in rivers—is no longer economics per se but rather questions of equity and personal and corporate greed. To address such issues, economic incentives could be established to encourage people to do what is right for the land. For example, rather than depending so heavily on taxes people pay for the work they do and the property they own, we could levy taxes for pollution and for conversion of open land to suburban sprawl. To do so would be logical because we would then be taxing activities that require tax expenditures and that deplete society's bank account of natural wealth.[44]

Looking deeper into our undershooting of the land ethic, Leopold wrote, "The proof that conservation has not yet touched these foundations of conduct lies in the fact that philosophy and religion have not yet heard of it." But today, both fields have. A brilliantly written letter by U.S. Catholic bishops titled "Catholic Social Teaching and the U.S. Economy" in 1984 recognized that in regard to natural resources, "the goods of this earth are common property and that men and women are summoned to faithful stewardship rather than to selfish appropriation or exploitation of what was destined for all."[45] Somehow catching more news coverage than the erudite bishops did, evangelical preachers in the late 1990s launched a veritable crusade for better care of the earth, rallying to support the Endangered Species Act as the modern-day Noah's Ark and working to persuade Congress that it's just not right to kill off what God has created.[46] Though some Christian fundamentalists have lumped the protection of nature in with liberal causes they considered godless, social survey analysts considering the issue concluded that religion overall is "reinforcing and justifying" support for environmental protection.[47]

If science, economics, and religion have supported the adoption of a land ethic, why has the idea failed to reach full fruition? Why do we still await the time when it's socially unacceptable to harm the earth and when peer pressure alone prevents abuse? Beyond the big motivation of greed, people operate in enigmatic ways. It's clear, for example, that we enjoy and cherish natural beauty. Nature's splendor decorates our calendars and postcards; clear-cuts, strip malls, and overgrazed range do not. The scenic places are the ones where we go when we have a choice, during vacations. The beautiful neighborhoods bordering parks and lakes are the ones where people most want to buy homes if they can afford them. A 1995 survey done for some of the nation's largest home builders showed that "natural open space," bike trails, and walking paths topped the list of what Americans most want in communities where they move.[48] So if it's quality landscapes we value, then why do we still allow so much destruction? If we've grown to regard the old forests as cathedrals decked out with ancient life and shafts of godly light, why have we allowed 98 percent of them to be cut down?

Author John Daniel suggests that we appreciate the natural world, but not in a deep enough way. "We tend to value it with a sentimental aestheticism, as something beautiful or peaceful or magnificent."[49] Or it may be that we indeed appreciate the natural world but are unable or unwilling to confront other people who, for personal gain, are willing to chip away at that world. Everyone in town might hate the clear-cut on the hillside above the local water supply reservoir, but people feel powerless to stop it. Or they are fearful of confronting the timber company or the next-door neighbors about what they are doing. Appreciation of good land may be real and widespread, but our laws are ineffective in holding those who disagree to high standards of conduct.

Then, too, progress on a land ethic is perversely dragged down because people simply fear change. Rightly so; virtually every problem outlined in this book is a result of change. But the change inside our heads demanded by adoption of a land ethic is considered by some to be more onerous than the changes otherwise imposed on the land itself. People grow accustomed to those physical changes—some of them happen only one acre at a time or, for that matter, one tree or one fish at a time. Although the cumulative effect promises an entirely different land and a wholly different life, people let the development happen and in the end see their valley erased and suburbia enshrined. Once the old way of life is eradicated, they are left with traffic, urban sprawl, crime, higher housing costs, new taxes levied to cope with all the new problems, a lack of fresh, local produce, and no place to hunt, fish, or go for a walk.

And here is what really counts in the ongoing battles over land: capitalizing on the public's innate resistance to change, people who profit by depleting the natural world carefully style their arguments into one grand dogma, at once opposing both change and big government. They say, "No new regulations." They equate publicly mandated responsibility with bureaucratic meddling. As a result, new attitudes to further a land ethic and thereby protect the real America of mountain majesty and fruited plain are painted as "un-American" and "big government," and on the teeth of this public relations buzz saw, support for responsible use of the earth splinters. Some regulatory processes do need to be overhauled, but blanket vilification of public involvement allows the physical changes to steamroller ahead, obliterating the land and country we have known and loved.

When land-use questions enter the public arena, chief among people's fears is the loss of personal freedom. People came to the New World and fought wars for personal freedom. It is fundamentally a part of American culture, one of few principles of governance that can exceed the expectation of a healthy environment. So those wanting to protect their ability to make money at the expense of a healthy landscape bend their arguments to embrace the topic of personal freedom, and the vested interests working under their own money-first mantra have elevated the rhetoric of personal freedom to an art form. Once people are riled up about private rights and headed down the path of hot-collared debate, they can easily ignore the fact that other people's freedom is impaired when water is polluted or when suburban sprawl crowds out an established way of life.

The ideological resistance to regulation and the knee-jerk response it prompts are supported by catchy slogans, time-tested through several centuries of Americana. An example is "I own my land and can do whatever I want with it." Rather than slogans, we need an understanding of the full picture of America—an awareness of how small actions today will affect the land tomorrow. The changes can be as subtle as paving a dirt road or as seemingly innocent as cattle importing exotic weeds through burs stuck in their hides. Every issue regarding the land, whether it involves a mine in the mountains or a new home on the barrier islands, requires an understanding of that place and of its context in the larger landscape. As this book has shown, it's all quite complicated. But we more easily grasp simplistic solutions that don't require the stretch of assimilating new ideas or the trauma of sacrifice. If you build a taller smokestack, smoke will "go away." But then acid rain results over a much larger area. The real solution is to clean the emissions, replace coal with cleaner alternatives such as solar power, or use less energy, but all these things are harder to do and harder to sell and make less money for the power company. Another example of a simplistic solution is "flood-proofing"— building new houses on piles of fill in flood-prone areas. Unfortunately, that makes floods worse elsewhere. But if homes are built farther back from the river and on higher ground, less damage for everybody results, and the floodplain continues to do its age-old work of accommodating runoff. Embracing a land ethic requires a commitment to understanding problems whose solutions are more difficult than political slogans and more complicated than a television news spot can explain.

In spite of all these stumbling blocks to a land ethic, the message has gotten through to a lot of people. Between 1976 and 1990, the number of people willing to sacrifice economic growth for environmental quality increased from 38 to 64 percent. A public poll in 1993 found that half the respondents regarded environmental problems as "very serious." Eighty-five percent were concerned at least "a fair amount."[50] In 1995, 73 percent of the people considered themselves environmentalists, with support for the environment crossing all socioeconomic lines.[51] Analysts revealed that a substantial change is taking place in the way Americans view the environment. The pollsters concluded, "Americans share a common set of environmental beliefs and values. . . . There is a single cultural consensus. . . . Only one set of culturally agreed upon answers." This contrasts with opinions on issues such as abortion, which elicit two distinct viewpoints. Regarding the environment, marked disagreements were "only among our most extreme groups."[52] However, the analysts cautioned that opinion does not easily translate into action. They blamed a lack of progress on the difficulty of understanding complex issues and on "multiple barriers." For example, a person may want to reduce his use of gasoline but has no bike trail on which to ride to work.

While support for a land ethic has grown on many fronts, vested interests fight with the grip of a tobacco lobbyist to continue what they've been doing. Even when these people represent a minority, they can operate with savvy—vocally, if not belligerently—as demonstrated by the Flathead County case described in chapter 1.

All these problems—greed, superficiality, powerlessness, fear of change—get in the way of putting a land ethic into effect, even when people believe it's important. Confronting the resistance, we see what an enormous stretch Aldo Leopold's idea really is. But the social ethics he referred to also took a long time to develop; slavery was not stopped overnight.

There will be no bloody Civil War over the future of our land. Rather, the reforms needed to pass on a healthy environment to future generations will be made through a new and wider understanding of this place we call home. Writing about Leopold and his ideas, philosopher J. Baird Callicott maintained that education is the fundamental need and the primary way in which our society will truly embrace a land ethic. "When the basic concept of ecology is taught at all levels . . . the land ethic may be transformed from one man's dream to all mankind's reality."[53]

A Political Movement for the Land

The adoption of a land ethic, even by most people, isn't enough. To carry the ethic forward—as our ancestors did with woman suffrage—a powerful political movement is needed. In politics, land is wheeled and dealed, pork-barreled, log-rolled, and swapped for money to buy political ads on television, just like anything else. But it's not just anything else. The land is different. It's the heart of America.

Questions about land seldom drive electoral politics, though the fate of our land is paramount to our communities and homes, to our health, to our future. Without people in elected office who care about the land, the forces of destructive change will roll on until—like the ancient forests of the Appalachians, like the tallgrass prairie of the Great Plains, like the wild salmon of New England—nothing is left. And it's not only a question of regulating the fringe that doesn't believe in having a healthy environment. It's also a question of establishing public policies that reflect a consideration for the future and not just the profits of high-rolling constituents during the next election cycle.

If elected officials really mean what they say about balancing the federal budget in the long term, and they eliminate the subsidies for land destruction, we would go a long way toward rescuing the American landscape. Below-cost timber sales, now associated with most of the logging on federal land, would become an embarrassing chapter of the past. Those who mine on public property would be made accountable to the taxpayers who own the land. Home insurance subsidies to build in hazard zones such as barrier islands and floodplains would stop. The end of water subsidies would trigger efficient use of this precious fluid. On a level playing field of taxation, mass transit might receive the same amount of money that freeways do, and if that were to happen, an entirely different pattern of land use would result. Less dependence on cars would mean less sprawl—a land use that eats up open space at a far greater rate than is required to serve people's needs.[54]

Beyond saving the money now wasted on land-destroying subsidies, important work could be done if people with a land ethic served in Congress. Less than 3 percent of the federal budget is now dedicated to environmental protection. The lowly U.S. Fish and Wildlife Service should be a "Defense Department" of the future with a nationwide priority to accomplish vital jobs of the 21st century. Glenn Eugster, a visionary program director for the Environmental Protection Agency, has called for attention to the green infrastructure of America. "The parks, wetlands, floodplains, and naturally functioning landscapes that give us our quality of life should receive the same kind of support that we give to other infrastructure such as roads and bridges," Eugster said. "Compared with what we spend on just five miles of interstate highway or one overpass, the amount dedicated to open space is chicken feed. Our society stands on three legs—economic, social, and environmental—and we should be taking care of all three."[55]

With a thorough background in conservation work, Ken Olson of Friends of Acadia in Maine reflected on politics and said, "We need a modern Teddy Roosevelt—someone who feels the land in his or her heart, makes natural resources a political priority, leads others to embrace conservation as a national cause, and torques Congress into having to deal with the issues."[56]

The issues involve a lot of land. Biologists Reed Noss and Allen Cooperrider estimated that some degree of protection is needed for half the country if we are to keep natural processes working and maintain viable populations of most native species.[57] Twelve percent of America's land is now reasonably well protected: about 4 percent is in wilderness, 3 percent is in national parks, 3 percent is in national wildlife refuges, and a few percent is in state, local, and private reserves. And land certainly doesn't have to be publicly owned to be protected. Easements and landowner agreements can do much to accomplish important goals.

Safeguarding half of America is a big job, but it's not impossible. The federal government still owns one-third of the country, much of which could be protected. In Florida, where the federal estate is small and the growth rate high, the state has already protected 24 percent of the land, and the figure could go as high as 40 percent under current programs. The popular Hawaiian island of Maui is 40 percent protected. Good possibilities for reserving ecosystem-scale landscapes exist in the Adirondack Mountains, the Everglades, northern Minnesota, the northern Rockies, the Great Basin, the Sierra Nevada, the North Cascades, and Alaska.[58]

If Congress simply reinstated the Land and Water Conservation Fund to its intended purpose—open space protection in return for the sale of offshore oil and gas deposits—we would go a long way toward saving the American landscape (see chapter 1). In fact, this single action of simply restoring the Land and Water funding to its original dedication may be the most important, plausible reform now needed at the federal level.

Through nongovernment acquisition but mostly through easements whereby people keep ownership of their land while agreeing not to develop it, land trusts have safeguarded more than 4 million acres nationwide—an area larger than Connecticut. The trusts set aside 180,000 acres annually in the 1990s, and they grow more effective each year.[59]

Lending some focus and imagination to the nationwide task of protecting land, the nonprofit Wildlands Project proposes a system of protected areas such as existing parks or refuges surrounded by buffer zones of limited development and linked by corridors that allow for migration of wildlife. Grand in its goal of safeguarding America's native wealth, it's a plan that strikes to the core of our needs for habitat maintenance and restoration.[60] Implementation even in a modest form will come only through thousands of choices that confront communities in all parts of the country—choices that once again take us back to the three big issues of population, ethics, and politics.

It is urgent to make the change toward a stable population that believes in a land ethic and also supports that belief politically because once the power of the natural landscape dissolves, the memory of it fades as well. I realized this on a recent trip to Alaska. Canoeing on the Kenai River, I paddled through a rapid and then turned into a ponded eddy below, where I found myself suddenly immersed in a forgotten abundance of life. Sockeye salmon, brilliant with red backs and green heads, quivered just under the surface of the blue-green pool, hundreds of them beneath me, all around me. I had known that my own watershed—the Columbia River in the Northwest—once supported the richest chinook salmon runs in the world, but only when I saw those fish in the Kenai did I really feel the power of that life force—the magic of nature in a relatively unspoiled land. The sight illustrated a sad truth: we don't know what we've lost once it's gone. And not missing it, we simply live, unknowingly, without it.

Taking the First Step

How do we get from where we are now to a stronger and more politically effective land ethic? The distance is daunting unless we keep our eye on the next step in the journey.

Everyone can adopt and care for an acre of backyard, public park, or national forest. One can start by picking up trash and pulling out exotic weeds. The effects would be felt not only on the adopted acre but also in the accumulation of acres and in the stewardship that becomes contagious among neighbors. This phenomenon is seen in urban neighborhoods where one family spruces up their house, followed by another, until the whole block and then the whole neighborhood is upgraded. An organizer of riverfront cleanups, Karen Hodgson of Vancouver, British Columbia, said, "People who are not environmentalists get involved in a cleanup, and then they begin to take ownership of a riverfront. From that time on, they get more and more involved."

The care of an acre can grow to include whole communities. Going beyond personal space, make a map of your homeland and identify what landscape architect Randy Hester calls the "sacred places"—the sites of community importance. "Making an actual, physical map of something you feel in your heart can be quite a powerful experience," he says of this process that he has guided people through in many areas of the country. The mapping exercise can lead to what Charles Little calls "vernacular planning"—action by citizens, on their own, "to preserve and enhance true community, and therefore a sense of place."[61]

To advance the land ethic and stewardship of native places, involve students in studying their neighborhood or their watershed. Once they find out what's wrong, help them interview people and learn how to fix the land. Approach political leaders to see what they've done or what they're willing to do. Support them or campaign for others who will do what is needed.

Convince others that change is essential if the land and its life are to survive. People are influenced by emotions, money, fundamental values, popular support, people they know, personal involvement, and hard information, so use all of these tools.

Work with others and talk to those who disagree about the use of land because a common language is essential to reach common decisions. We need to know one another in order to understand one another, and we need to understand one another in order to live together on earth.

If people lack interest in the health of the land, it may be that they lack the kinds of experiences needed for motivation. Perhaps they've been living under the myth of abundance, or watching television too long, or playing computer games all day. To reinstate the motivation to care for the earth, we need to return to the real thing. We need to go there and take other people with us, especially children, so they can see firsthand the glory of sunrise on the open prairie, the power of a mountain storm, the freshness of a misty waterfall, the hopeful brilliance of new life in wildflowers and wild animals.

This kind of experience is important because of a fundamental fact of human existence: people will continue to live the way they do until they see a better way. There *is* a better way of living on the land—a way that can bypass the problems that have plagued our country. By example, people can show others the new path. It involves driving less, having fewer children, curbing overconsumption, clustering new development, reinvigorating our cities, preventing construction in hazardous areas where floods and mudslides strike, and embracing the simplicity of a life well lived rather than a life that's oversupplied. It involves reserving more open space and wilderness, investing in clean water and functioning farms, setting sustainable limits on logging, and reducing the burning of fossil fuels in order to halt global warming. All of these practices point to a future that's more desirable than the one we now have, with the added bonus of passing on a livable planet to the next generation.

Just as important as any of this, we need to base our future on a new story of the past because any group of people lives under the guidance of its history—its own culturally based story of creation. A true and complete story does not ignore the damage wrought in our push for progress; rather, we should be learning from that damage. The new story might define progress as Aldo Leopold did, based on health and stability of the land, a story with hope stemming from the intrinsic values of mountains, forests, prairies, deserts, rivers, lakes, wetlands, and seashores.

Taking hope from the changes occurring in a movement that's evolving among people of all races and backgrounds, American Indian activist Winona LaDuke wrote:

> Across the continent, on the shores of small tributaries, in the shadows of sacred mountains, on the vast expanse of the prairies, or in the safety of the woods, prayers are being repeated, as they have been for thousands of years, and common people with uncommon courage and the whispers of their ancestors in their ears continue their struggles to protect the land and water and trees on which their very existence is based. And like small tributaries joining together to form a mighty river, their force and power grows. This river will not be dammed.[62]

While destructive change might surround us, part of America remains as it was when the country nourished LaDuke's ancestors and our own, and it can still inspire us to do great things. People like Bob McCullough, working to protect the rivers of Pennsylvania, Christi Norman, saving the wetlands of Puget Sound, and thousands of others working for the good of their land provide proof that there is a better way.

When enough people have known what they needed to know, they've forged ahead to do what was right. Slavery was abolished; women gained the right to vote. The key is combining the intelligence of an informed society with a powerful political movement.

The land ethic of Aldo Leopold took root in the second half of the 20th century. Perhaps, in the first years of a new millennium, those roots will grow and flourish into a great tree of many branches and durable strength.

The Cycle of the Centuries

While I walked on the beach at Cape Cod, the morning sun not only rose on America but climbed above the eastern horizon and then arced halfway across the sky. The time flew. Before I knew it, noon had arrived and I had wandered five miles down the beach to its outermost, easternmost curve. At the foot of a dune there, with the wide Atlantic in front of me, I had reached the end of land, and I considered my current tour of the United States complete.

No less than that, I felt I had completed a cycle of time, one that had started long before my writing ever began. My ancestors, who landed near here looking for a new and better home 350 years ago, were among those who started white settlement in America. With all the other immigrants and their descendants, they brought us, for better and for worse, to where we are today. We've spread out and populated the continent. In the process, much of the natural endowment that the earlier people once knew has been used up. Yet many of the land's qualities remain.

In the course of these earlier chapters, we've seen those qualities and we've seen what has been done to the land. But the past is behind us, the future ahead. What now?

There on the beach, with a fresh wind in my face, I imagined that my next question was similar to one that my blood-line predecessors on this same Atlantic shore so long ago might have asked: Can we shape a new and better life for ourselves on this continent? In wooden boats under the power of wind, they had fled a country that had become crowded and squalid and was ruled oppressively with a lack of foresight and religious freedom. They escaped but learned little about really solving those problems of the British Isles and other countries of origin, and their descendants in America in turn fled from wherever they were and went to some "new" place on this continent. They kept moving, and even I ended up for a short while on the beach at Westport, California, where we emphatically run out of land at the edge of the other ocean. Today, there is no place left to go, and even if there were, we would run a high risk of repeating the same mistakes we've made everywhere we've been.

Now, at the beginning of a new century, it's time to adopt our earth and homeland as if we were going to stay, as if its health and ability to nurture the coming generations really mattered. Surely we've done enough to change the land into something it was not. Surely it is time for the heart of America to thrive again and for all of us to renew the vital beat of life in the land we love.

NOTES

Introduction: The Heart That Gives Life to It All

1. Paul R. Ehrlich and Anne H. Ehrlich, *Betrayal of Science and Reason* (Washington, D.C.: Island Press, 1996), citing D. Myers and E. Diener, "Who Is Happy?" *Psychological Science* 6, no. 1 (1995).

2. Curt Suplee, "One in Eight Plants in Global Study Threatened," *Washington Post,* April 8, 1998, citing a report of the World Conservation Union.

3. William Stolzenburg, "Habitat Is Where It's At," *Nature Conservancy,* November 1997.

4. Oren Lyons, personal communication, 1998.

5. U.S. Department of Commerce, Bureau of the Census, *Statistical Abstract of the United States* (Washington, D.C.: Government Printing Office, 1992), table 30.

6. Lee Clark Mitchell, *Witnesses to a Vanishing America* (Princeton, N.J.: Princeton University Press, 1981).

7. John C. Van Dyke, *Nature for Its Own Sake* (New York: Scribner, 1898).

Chapter 1: An Uplift of Mountains

1. Derek Denniston, *High Priorities: Conserving Mountain Ecosystems and Cultures* (Washington, D.C.: Worldwatch Institute, 1995), 5.

2. U.S. Department of Agriculture, Forest Service, *Report of the Chief: Forests and the Nation's Water Resources* (Washington, D.C.: U.S. Department of Agriculture, Forest Service, 1947).

3. John Muir, *John of the Mountains: The Unpublished Journals of John Muir,* ed. Linnie Marsh Wolfe (Madison: University of Wisconsin Press, 1970), 334 (originally published in 1938).

4. Denniston, *High Priorities,* 39.

5. Jim Howe, Ed McMahon, and Luther Propst, *Balancing Nature and Commerce in Gateway Communities* (Washington, D.C.: Island Press, 1997), 19.

6. Frederick Turner, *Beyond Geography: The Western Spirit against the Wilderness* (New Brunswick, N.J.: Rutgers University Press, 1983), 7.

7. Scott Weidensaul, *Mountains of the Heart: A Natural History of the Appalachians* (Golden, Colo.: Fulcrum, 1994), xii.

8. Peter Farb, *Face of North America* (New York: Harper Colophon, 1963), 135.

9. Lauren Brown, *Grasslands* (New York: Knopf, 1985), 75.

10. Tim Palmer, *The Sierra Nevada: A Mountain Journey* (Washington, D.C.: Island Press, 1988), 215, 297.

11. Palmer, *Sierra Nevada,* 278.

12. Robert McCracken Peck, *Land of the Eagle* (New York: Summit Books, 1990), 226.

13. Frank Graham Jr., "Unnatural Predation," *Audubon,* November–December 1995, 88.

14. Tim Palmer, *The Snake River: Window to the West* (Washington, D.C.: Island Press, 1991), 240.

15. Jeff Gersh, "Subdivide and Conquer," *Amicus Journal,* fall 1996, 16.

16. Urban Land Institute, *The Costs of Alternative Development Patterns* (Washington, D.C.: Urban Land Institute, 1992).

17. Kenneth T. Jackson, *Crabgrass Frontier: The Suburbanization of the United States* (New York: Oxford University Press, 1985); John Turner and Jason Rylander, "Land Use: The Forgotten Agenda," in *Thinking Ecologically,* ed. Marian R. Chertow and Daniel C. Esty (New Haven, Conn.: Yale University Press, 1997), 65.

18. Douglas R. Porter, *Managing Growth in America's Communities* (Washington, D.C.: Island Press, 1997), 105; William H. Romme, "Creating Pseudo-Rural Landscapes in the Mountain West," in *Placing Nature,* ed. Joan Iverson Nassauer (Washington, D.C.: Island Press, 1997), 157.

19. Howe, McMahon, and Propst, *Balancing Nature and Commerce,* 56.

20. Charles Little, *The New Oregon Trail: An Account of the Development and Passage of the State Land-Use Legislation in Oregon* (Washington, D.C.: Conservation Foundation, 1974); Porter, *Managing Growth,* 17.

21. Porter, *Managing Growth,* 19.

22. Florence Williams, "Land-Use Plan Is Disemboweled," *High Country News,* December 26, 1994.

23. Ibid.

24. Ibid.

25. Jamie Williams, interview, 1998.

26. Florence Williams, "Planning for Space," *Chronicle of Community* (published by the Northern Lights Institute), winter 1998.

27. Environmental Protection Agency, *Community-Based Environmental Protection* (Washington, D.C.: Environmental Protection Agency, 1997), 1-1.

28. Howe, McMahon, and Propst, *Balancing Nature and Commerce,* 19.

29. Mike Medberry, "Good Deeds Left Undone," *Wilderness,* annual 1998, 33–36.

30. Jim Robbins, *Last Refuge* (New York: HarperCollins, 1994), 57.

31. Heather Abel, "Montana on the Edge," *High Country News,* December 22, 1997.

32. Peter Chilson, "Coal Miner's Story," *Audubon,* March–April 1994.

33. Harry Caudill, *Night Comes to the Cumberlands* (Boston: Little, Brown, 1963).

34. Louise C. Dunlap and James S. Lyon, "Effectiveness of the Surface Mining Control and Reclamation Act," *West Virginia Law Review,* 88, no. 3 (1986): 547–559.

35. Wyona Coleman, "Environmental Justice in the Coal Fields," *Citizens Coal Council Reporter* (Denver), winter 1998, 9.

36. Ken Ward Jr., "Strip-Mining Battle Resurfaces in State," *Charleston (West Virginia) Gazette-Mail,* March 22, 1998; "Law to Rebuild Mountains Falls by Wayside," *Charleston (West Virginia) Gazette-Mail,* April 3, 1998.

37. Penny Loeb, "Shear Madness," *U.S. News and World Report,* special report, October 13, 1997, 3.

38. Loeb, "Shear Madness," 1; Ward, "Law to Rebuild Mountains," 5A.

39. Loeb, "Shear Madness," 7; Ward, "Law to Rebuild Mountains," 1.

40. Loeb, "Shear Madness," 2.

41. Ward, "Law to Rebuild Mountains."

42. Ibid., 5A.

43. Loeb, "Shear Madness."

44. Tim Palmer, *Youghiogheny: Appalachian River* (Pittsburgh: University of Pittsburgh Press, 1984), 271.

45. Carl J. Mayer and George A. Riley, *Public Domain, Private Domain* (San Francisco: Sierra Club Books, 1985).

46. Ray Ring, "All the King's Horses and All the King's Men," *High Country News,* January 19, 1998.

47. "The Price of Beauty," *Sierra,* January–February 1998.

48. Philip Hocker, telephone interview, 1998.

49. Jon Margolis, "An 1872 Law Still Calls the Shots," *High Country News,* December 27, 1997.

50. George Laycock, "Going for the Gold," *Audubon,* July 1989, 75.

51. Thomas Michael Power, *Lost Landscapes and Failed Economies* (Washington, D.C.: Island Press, 1996), 129.

52. Power, *Lost Landscapes,* 102.

53. George F. Leaming, *Everything Begins with Mining* (Washington, D.C.: National Mining Association, 1997), 3.

54.   National Mining Association, *What Mining Means to Americans* (Washington, D.C.: National Mining Association, 1998), 7.

55.   National Mining Association, *Mining Law Reform* (Washington, D.C.: National Mining Association, n.d.).

56.   Environmental Working Group, telephone interview.

57.   Philip Hocker, telephone interview, 1998.

58.   Joel Bourne, "The End of the Road?" *Audubon,* May–June 1998.

59.   Sally W. Smith, "Wildlife and Endangered Species: In Precipitous Decline," in *California's Threatened Environment,* ed. Tim Palmer (Washington, D.C.: Island Press, 1993), 231.

60.   Fen Montaigne, "All Quiet on the Rocky Mountain Front," *Audubon,* January–February 1998.

61.   Heather Abel, "The Wayward West," *High Country News,* November 24, 1997.

Chapter 2: The Forest Fabric of Life

1.   R. W. Haynes, *An Analysis of the Timber Situation in the United States: 1989–2040* (Fort Collins, Colo.: U.S. Department of Agriculture, Forest Service, Rocky Mountain Forest and Range Experiment Station, 1990).

2.   Jake Page, *Forest* (Alexandria, Va.: Time-Life Books, 1983).

3.   Rutherford Platt, *The Great American Forest* (Englewood Cliffs, N.J.: Prentice-Hall, 1965).

4.   Simon Schama, *Landscape and Memory* (New York: Knopf, 1997).

5.   John J. Berger, *Understanding Forests* (San Francisco: Sierra Club Books, 1998), 3.

6.   Audrey DeLella Benedict, *The Southern Rockies* (San Francisco: Sierra Club Books, 1991), 298.

7.   George Constantz, *Hollows, Peepers, and Highlanders* (Missoula, Mont.: Mountain Press, 1995), 21.

8.   J. R. Sedell, "What We Know about Large Trees That Fall into Streams and Rivers," in *From the Forest to the Sea,* ed. Chris Maser (Portland, Oreg.: U.S. Department of Agriculture, Forest Service, Pacific Northwest Research Station, 1988).

9.   Reed Noss and Allen Cooperrider, *Saving Nature's Legacy* (Washington, D.C.: Island Press, 1994), 269.

10.   Don Gasper, "The Forest Canopy and Flooding," *Highlands Voice* (published by the West Virginia Highlands Conservancy), February 1998.

11.   John Cronin and Robert F. Kennedy Jr., *The Riverkeepers* (New York: Scribner, 1997).

12.   Paul Hirt, *A Conspiracy of Optimism* (Lincoln: University of Nebraska Press, 1994), 102.

13. Patrick Mazza, "An Act of God?" *Cascadia Times,* March 1995. Reports on runoff studies by Gordon Grant, Julia Jones, and Dennis Harris.

14. Intergovernmental Panel on Climate Change, *Climate Change 1995* (Cambridge, England: Cambridge University Press, 1996).

15. Eric T. Sundquist, "Long-Term Aspects of Future Atmospheric CO_2 and Sea-Level Change," in *Sea-Level Change,* ed. Roger R. Revelle et al. (Washington, D.C.: National Academy Press, 1990), 193–207.

16. U.S. Department of the Interior, National Biological Service, *Our Living Resources,* ed. Edward T. LaRoe et al. (Washington, D.C.: U.S. Department of the Interior, National Biological Service, 1995), 385; Thomas R. Karl, Neville Nicholls, and Jonathan Gregory, "The Coming Climate," *Scientific American,* May 1997.

17. Jon R. Luoma, "Warming the Wild," *Audubon,* July–August 1996.

18. Paul Ehrlich and Anne Ehrlich, *Betrayal of Science and Reason* (Washington, D.C.: Island Press, 1996).

19. Bill McKibben, "Warming Up to Kyoto," *Audubon,* March–April 1998, 58.

20. Gerald Jonas, *North American Trees* (Pleasantville, N.Y.: Reader's Digest, 1993), 161; Charles Little, *The Dying of the Trees* (New York: Penguin, 1995), 205.

21. U.S. Department of Energy, *The Potential of Renewable Energy* (Washington, D.C.: U.S. Department of Energy, March 1990).

22. Frank C. Brockman, ed., *Trees of North America* (New York: Golden Press, 1968), 3.

23. Maurice Brooks, *The Appalachians* (Grantsville, W.Va.: Seneca Books, 1965).

24. Robert Leverett, "Will Blozen and the Big Trees of the Great Smokies," *Wild Earth,* summer 1995.

25. Peter Farb, *Face of North America* (New York: Harper Colophon, 1963).

26. Little, *Dying of the Trees,* 147.

27. Lynn S. Kutner and Larry E. Morse, "Where Have All the Flowers Gone?" *Nature Conservancy,* May–June 1996, 7.

28. Noss and Cooperrider, *Saving Nature's Legacy,* 63.

29. Jonas, *North American Trees.*

30. Platt, *Great American Forest.*

31. Francis H. Elmore, *Shrubs and Trees of the Southwest Uplands* (Tucson, Ariz.: Southwest Parks and Monuments Association, 1976), 4.

32. Elliott A. Norse, *Ancient Forests of the Pacific Northwest* (Washington, D.C.: Island Press, 1994), 69.

33. Ruth Kirk, ed., *Enduring Forests* (Seattle: The Mountaineers, 1996), 35.

34. Norse, *Ancient Forests,* 212.

35. Michael Williams, *Americans and Their Forests: A Historical Geography* (Cambridge, England: Cambridge University Press, 1989), 3.

36. William Preston, *Vanishing Landscapes* (Berkeley: University of California Press, 1981), citing Stephen Barton, "Early History of Tulare," *Visalia Weekly Delta.*

37. U.S. Department of the Interior, *Our Living Resources,* 214.

38. Williams, *Americans and Their Forests,* 48.

39. Keith Ervin, *Fragile Majesty* (Seattle: The Mountaineers, 1989), 246; Berger, *Understanding Forests,* 24.

40. Mary Bird Davis, ed., *Eastern Old-Growth Forests* (Washington, D.C.: Island Press, 1996).

41. Gregory H. Aplet et al., eds., *Defining Sustainable Forestry* (Washington, D.C.: Island Press, 1993), 63; Berger, *Understanding Forests,* 24.

42. Bruce A. Stein, "Putting Nature on the Map," *Nature Conservancy,* January–February 1996.

43. U.S. Department of the Interior, *Our Living Resources,* 87.

44. Noss and Cooperrider, *Saving Nature's Legacy,* 196.

45. Ibid., 197.

46. Kirk, *Enduring Forests,* 49.

47. Norse, *Ancient Forests,* 125.

48. Aplet et al., *Defining Sustainable Forestry,* 51.

49. Kathryn A. Kohm and Jerry F. Franklin, eds., *Creating a Forestry for the Twenty-First Century* (Washington, D.C.: Island Press, 1997).

50. Ray Raphael, *More Tree Talk* (Washington, D.C.: Island Press, 1994).

51. Jon R. Luoma, "Whittling Dixie," *Audubon,* November–December 1997.

52. U.S. Department of the Interior, *Our Living Resources,* 215.

53. Southwest Forest Alliance, *Forests Forever!* (Flagstaff, Ariz.: Southwest Forest Alliance, 1966).

54. Nancy Langston, *Forest Dreams, Forest Nightmares* (Seattle: University of Washington Press, 1995); James R. Karr and Ellen W. Chu, eds., *Interim Protection for Late-Successional Forests, Fisheries, and Watersheds* (Bethesda, Md.: The Wildlife Society, 1994).

55. David Yeadon, "California's North Face," *National Geographic,* July 1993.

56. David Harris, *The Last Stand* (San Francisco: Sierra Club Books, 1996).

57. Tim Palmer, "The Native California Landscape," in *California's Threatened Environment,* ed. Tim Palmer (Washington, D.C.: Island Press, 1993), 248.

58. Berger, *Understanding Forests,* 34.

59. George Laycock, "Trashing the Tongass," *Audubon,* November 1987.

60. Norse, *Ancient Forests,* 257.

61. Steven Lewis Yaffee, *The Wisdom of the Spotted Owl* (Washington, D.C.: Island Press, 1994).

62. Kathie Durbin, *Tree Huggers* (Seattle: The Mountaineers, 1996).

63. Paul Koberstein, "A Doomed Species?" *High Country News,* June 13, 1994.

64. Tim Palmer, *The Columbia* (Seattle: The Mountaineers, 1997), 96.

65. Forest Water Alliance, *Our Forests and Our Future* (Everett, Wash.: Forest Water Alliance, 1998), 2.

66. David Dobbs and Richard Ober, *The Northern Forest* (White River Junction, Vt.: Chelsea Green, 1995), xvi.

67. Ibid., 119.

68. Mitch Lantsky, *Beyond the Beauty Strip: Saving What's Left of Our Forests* (Gardiner, Maine: Tilbury House, 1992).

69. Dobbs and Ober, *Northern Forest,* 42.

70. Scott Weidensaul, *Mountains of the Heart: A Natural History of the Appalachians* (Golden, Colo.: Fulcrum, 1994), 218.

71. Jonathan Carter, "Ballot Measures as a 'Political Spike,'" *Wild Earth,* spring 1998, 80.

72. Dobbs and Ober, *Northern Forest,* xx.

73. Ibid., 312.

74. Ibid., 83, 92.

75. Kathie Durbin and Paul Koberstein, "Forests in Distress," *Oregonian,* special report, October 15, 1995.

76. Dan Glick, "Disturbing the Peace," *Wilderness,* annual 1998, 23; John G. Mitchell, "Our National Forests," *National Geographic,* March 1997.

77. Paul Roberts, "The Federal Chain-Saw Massacre," *Harper's,* June 1997, 47; Richard E. Rice, *National Forests: Policies for the Future,* vol. 5, *The Uncounted Costs of Logging* (Washington, D.C.: The Wilderness Society, 1989).

78. Southwest Forest Alliance, *Forests Forever!* 26.

79. Charles F. Wilkinson and H. Michael Anderson, *Land Use and Resource Planning in the National Forests* (Washington, D.C.: Island Press, 1987), 9.

80. Patrick Mazza, "The Mud Next Time," *Sierra,* May–June 1997.

81. Hirt, *Conspiracy of Optimism,* 280.

82. Thomas Michael Power, *Lost Landscapes and Failed Economies* (Washington, D.C.: Island Press, 1996), 146, 158.

83. Palmer, *Columbia,* 82–84.

84. Roberts, "Federal Chain-Saw Massacre," 46.

85. Paul Rauber, "Timber's Errand Boy," *Sierra,* May–June 1997.

86. Lester R. Brown, Hal Kane, and Ed Ayres, "Air Pollution Damaging Forests," in Lester R. Brown, Hal Kane, and Ed Ayres, *Vital Signs* (New York: Norton, 1993).

87. Gary Paul Nabhan, *Enduring Seeds* (San Francisco: North Point Press, 1989), 91.

88. Richard M. Klein and Timothy D. Perkins, "Long-Term Fates of Declin-

ing Forests," in *The Science of Global Change,* ed. David A. Dunnette and Robert J. O'Brien (Washington, D.C.: American Chemical Society, 1992).

89. John Dillon, "Fading Colors," *Audubon,* September–October 1998.

90. Paul Miller, "Concept of Forest Decline in Relation to Western U.S. Forests," in *Air Pollution's Toll on Forests and Crops,* ed. James J. Mackenzie and Mohamed T. El-Ashry (New Haven, Conn.: Yale University Press, 1989).

91. Little, *Dying of the Trees,* 84; Christine L. Shaver et al., "Clearing the Air at Great Smoky Mountains National Park," *Ecological Applications* 4, no. 4 (1994).

92. Douglas Powell, *Forest Resources of the United States* (Fort Collins, Colo.: U.S. Department of Agriculture, Forest Service, Rocky Mountain Forest and Range Experiment Station, 1993).

93. Lucy Braun Association, *Patterns of Forest Health* (Washington, D.C.: Lucy Braun Association, 1998).

94. Harvard Ayers, Jenny Hager, and Charles E. Little, ed., *An Appalachian Tragedy: Air Pollution and Tree Death in the Eastern Forests of North America* (San Francisco: Sierra Club Books, 1998), 77, 113.

95. Constantz, *Hollows, Peepers, and Highlanders,* 202.

96. Ehrlich and Ehrlich, *Betrayal of Science and Reason,* citing C. Federer et al., "Long-Term Depletion of Calcium and Other Nutrients in Eastern U.S. Forests," *Environmental Management* 13:593–601.

97. Jane Hall, "The Atmosphere We Breathe," in *California's Threatened Environment,* ed. Tim Palmer (Washington, D.C.: Island Press, 1993), 36, 41.

98. Jim Caplan, interview, 1998.

99. Raphael, *More Tree Talk.*

100. Ibid.

101. University of Washington, Northwest Policy Center, *Building Forest Wealth* (Seattle: University of Washington, Northwest Policy Center, 1995).

102. Aplet et al., *Defining Sustainable Forestry,* 309.

103. Kathie Durbin, "Has the Forest Service Seen the Light?" *Cascadia Times,* November 1997.

104. Robert E. Lynn, acting director, forest management, USDA Forest Service, correspondence, 1998.

105. U.S. Department of Agriculture, Forest Service, *Cut and Sold Reports* (Washington, D.C.: U.S. Department of Agriculture, Forest Service, 1997), graph titled "Historic National Forest Timber Sale Levels."

106. Dan Glickman, Remarks of the Secretary of Agriculture to the National Audubon Society, Washington, D.C., June 9, 1996, 4, included in correspondence, 1997.

107. Todd Wilkinson, "Forest Service Seeks a New (Roadless) Road to the Future," *High Country News,* April 27, 1998, 8.

108. Mike Dombeck, speech given at annual convention of the National Audubon Society, Estes Park, Colo., July 1998.

109. Christina Bolgiano, "The Great Forest," *Wilderness,* September 1994.

110. Stephen C. Trombulak, "The Restoration of Old Growth: Why and How," in *Eastern Old-Growth Forests,* ed. Mary Byrd Davis (Washington, D.C.: Island Press, 1996), 310.

111. Robert Zahner, "How Much Old Growth Is Enough?" in *Eastern Old-Growth Forests,* ed. Mary Byrd Davis (Washington, D.C.: Island Press, 1996), 357.

112. Aplet et al., *Defining Sustainable Forestry,* 11.

113. Natural Resources Defense Council, "Forever Forests," *Amicus Journal,* September 1997.

114. Sandra Postel and John C. Ryan, "Reforming Forestry," in *State of the World 1991,* ed. Lester R. Brown et al. (New York: Norton, 1991).

115. Marie Dolcini, "Beating the Heat," *The Planet* (published by the Sierra Club), July–August 1997.

116. Hirt, *Conspiracy of Optimism,* 82.

Chapter 3: The World of Grasslands

1. Ann Bleed and Charles Flowerday, eds., *An Atlas of the Sand Hills* (Lincoln: University of Nebraska Press, 1990).

2. Cary Fowler and Pat Mooney, *Shattering: Food, Politics, and the Loss of Genetic Diversity* (Tucson: University of Arizona Press, 1990), 32.

3. Paul B. Sears, *Lands Beyond the Forest* (Englewood Cliffs, N.J.: Prentice-Hall, 1963), 43.

4. Paul G. Risser, "A New Framework for Prairie Conservation," in *Prairie Conservation,* ed. Fred B. Samson and Fritz L. Knopf (Washington, D.C.: Island Press, 1996), 262.

5. Douglas H. Chadwick, "What Good Is a Prairie?" *Audubon,* November–December 1995, 115.

6. Richard Manning, *Grassland* (New York: Viking, 1995), 19.

7. Bernard DeVoto, *Journals of Lewis and Clark* (Boston: Houghton Mifflin, 1953).

8. Russell A. Benedict, Patricia W. Freeman, and Hugh H. Genoways, "Prairie Legacies—Mammals," in Samson and Knopf, *Prairie Conservation.*

9. Otto T. Solbrig and Dorothy J. Solbrig, *So Shall You Reap* (Washington, D.C.: Island Press, 1994), 218.

10. John Madson, *Where the Sky Began: Land of the Tallgrass Prairie* (San Francisco: Sierra Club Books, 1982), 32.

11. Daniel J. Hillel, *Out of the Earth: Civilization and Life of the Soil* (New York: Macmillan, 1991), 160.

12. Lauren Brown, *Grasslands* (New York: Knopf, 1985); Fritz L. Knopf, "Prairie Legacies—Birds," in Samson and Knopf, *Prairie Conservation*, 135.

13. Madson, *Where the Sky Began*, 139.

14. U.S. Department of the Interior, National Biological Service, *Our Living Resources*, ed. Edward T. LaRoe et al. (Washington, D.C.: U.S. Department of the Interior, National Biological Service, 1995), 295; Ivan T. Sanderson, *The Continent We Live On* (New York: Random House, 1961).

15. Peter Farb, *Face of North America* (New York: Harper Colophon, 1963), 195.

16. Anne Matthews, *Where the Buffalo Roam* (New York: Grove Press, 1992).

17. Erla Zwingle, "Ogallala Aquifer," *National Geographic*, March 1993.

18. Ernest M. Steinauer and Scott L. Collins, "Prairie Ecology—The Tallgrass Prairie," in Samson and Knopf, *Prairie Conservation*, 41; Risser, "New Framework," 264.

19. Thomas B. Bragg and Allen Steuter, "Prairie Ecology—The Mixed Prairie," in Samson and Knopf, *Prairie Conservation*, 61.

20. T. Weaver, Elizabeth M. Payson, and Daniel L. Gustafson, "Prairie Ecology—The Shortgrass Prairie," in Samson and Knopf, *Prairie Conservation*, 73.

21. Kathie Durbin, "Conserving Oregon's Biodiversity," *Defenders*, winter 1995, 32.

22. Reed Noss and Allen Cooperrider, *Saving Nature's Legacy* (Washington, D.C.: Island Press, 1991).

23. Thomas Michael Power, *Lost Landscapes and Failed Economies* (Washington, D.C.: Island Press, 1996), 209.

24. Douglas H. Chadwick, "Roots of the Sky," *National Geographic*, October 1993.

25. Catherine Dold, "Making Room for Prairie Dogs," *Smithsonian*, March 1998.

26. Knopf, "Prairie Legacies—Birds," 140.

27. Michael E. Long, "The Vanishing Prairie Dog," *National Geographic*, April 1998, 122.

28. Stephen L. Buchmann and Gary Paul Nabhan, *The Forgotten Pollinators* (Washington, D.C.: Island Press, 1996), 24, 192.

29. Associated Press, "Loss of Habitat Reducing Songbird Populations," *Idaho Falls Post Register*, June 11, 1996.

30. Don Stap, "Dissonant Data," *Audubon*, January–February 1998.

31. Knopf, "Prairie Legacies—Birds," 147; Jon Terborgh, "Why American Songbirds Are Vanishing," *Scientific American*, May 1992.

32. Dan L. Flores, "A Long Love Affair with an Uncommon Country: Environmental History and the Great Plains," in Samson and Knopf, *Prairie Conservation*, 14.

33. Lee Clark Mitchell, *Witnesses to a Vanishing America* (Princeton, N.J.: Princeton University Press, 1981), 55.

34. Todd Wilkinson, "How Real Is the Brucellosis Threat?" *Audubon*, May–June 1997.

35. John L. Eliot, "Disease Makes Pariahs of Yellowstone Bison," *National Geographic*, January 1998.

36. William D. Newmark, "Legal and Biotic Boundaries of Western North American National Parks," *Biological Conservation* 33 (1988): 197–208.

37. Reed Noss, "Cows and Conservation Biology," *Conservation Biology*, September 1994.

38. Manning, *Grassland*, 111.

39. Denzel Ferguson and Nancy Ferguson, *Sacred Cows at the Public Trough* (Bend, Oreg.: Maverick, 1983).

40. Ed Chaney, Wayne Elmore, and William S. Platts, *Livestock Grazing on Western Riparian Areas* (Washington, D.C.: Environmental Protection Agency, 1990).

41. William Stolzenburg, "Habitat Is Where It's At," *Nature Conservancy*, November–December 1997.

42. Donna Davis, "Babbitt Plans Nationwide Battle against Invasive, Noxious Weeds," *Idaho Statesman*, April 10, 1998.

43. Stephanie Flack, "America's Least Wanted," *Nature Conservancy*, November–December 1996.

44. Ted Williams, "Killer Weeds," *Audubon*, March–April 1997, 25.

45. Brown, *Grasslands*, 88.

46. Robert Devine, "The Cheatgrass Problem," *Atlantic Monthly*, May 1994.

47. Davis, "Babbitt Plans Nationwide Battle."

48. Williams, "Killer Weeds," 28.

49. Bruce Berger, *The Telling Distance* (New York: Doubleday, 1990), 153.

50. Jamie Murray, "A Cheatgrass Antidote—Maybe," *High Country News*, August 4, 1997.

51. Williams, "Killer Weeds," 31.

52. Davis, "Babbitt Plans Nationwide Battle."

53. Council for Agricultural Science and Technology, *Grazing on Public Lands* (Ames, Iowa: Council for Agricultural Science and Technology, 1996), 3.

54. Richard Conniff, "Treasuring 'the Lands No One Wanted,'" *Smithsonian*, September 1990, 34.

55. Manning, *Grassland*, 134.

56. Council for Agricultural Science and Technology, *Grazing on Public Lands,* 4.

57. Noss, "Cows and Conservation Biology"; Noss and Cooperrider, *Saving Nature's Legacy,* 64, 221, 250.

58. Jon Luoma, "Discouraging Words," *Audubon,* September 1986, 94.

59. National Cattlemen's Beef Association, *Public Lands Grazing Issue Briefs* (Washington, D.C.: National Cattlemen's Beef Association, 1996), 4.

60. General Accounting Office, *Rangeland Management* (Washington, D.C.: General Accounting Office, June 1988).

61. Matthews, *Where the Buffalo Roam,* 94.

62. Luoma, "Discouraging Words," 194.

63. Richard Conniff, "Federal Lands," *National Geographic,* February 1994.

64. Manning, *Grassland,* 134.

65. Conniff, "Treasuring," 34.

66. Hugh Harper, interview, 1998.

67. Power, *Lost Landscapes,* 183.

68. Noss and Cooperrider, *Saving Nature's Legacy,* 258.

69. Peter Chilson, "An Era Ends: Old Industries Face Reality," *High Country News,* April 27, 1998, 13.

70. Mark Muro, "The Last Roundup," *Arizona Daily Star,* December 13, 1998, 2F.

71. Montana Department of Natural Resources and Conservation, *Riparian Grazing Successes* (Helena: Montana Department of Natural Resources and Conservation, 1995).

72. Stephen Stuebner, "Leave It to the Beaver," *High Country News,* August 24, 1992.

73. L. K. Lee, "Land Use and Soil Loss," *Journal of Soil and Water Conservation* 39 (1984).

74. Rutherford H. Platt, *Land Use and Society* (Washington, D.C.: Island Press, 1996), 13.

75. David L. Carter, *Furrow Erosion Reduces Crop Yields* (Kimberly, Idaho: U.S. Department of Agriculture, Agricultural Research Service, Northwest Irrigation and Soils Research Service, 1988.

76. Gretchen C. Daily, ed., *Nature's Services* (Washington, D.C.: Island Press, 1997), 248, citing D. Pimentel, C. Harvey, and R. Blair, "Environmental and Economic Costs of Soil Erosion and Conservation Benefits," *Science* 267, no. 5201 (1995): 1117.

77. W. C. Lowdermilk, *Conquest of the Land through Seven Thousand Years,* Soil Conservation Service Information Bulletin No. 99 (Washington, D.C: U.S. Department of Agriculture, Soil Conservation Service, August 1953).

78. Tom Daniels and Deborah Bowers, *Holding Our Ground: Protecting America's*

Farms (Washington, D.C.: Island Press, 1997); U.S. Department of Agriculture, Economic Research Service, *Our Land and Water Resources* (Washington, D.C.: Government Printing Office, 1974).

79. Platt, *Land Use and Society,* 24.

80. Jon Narr and Alex J. Narr, *This Land Is Your Land* (New York: Harper-Perennial, 1993), 163.

81. U.S. Department of the Interior, National Biological Service, *Our Living Resources,* 296.

82. Matthews, *Where the Buffalo Roam,* 76.

83. Ernest Callenbach, *Bring Back the Buffalo!* (Washington, D.C.: Island Press, 1996), 118; Bryan Hodgson, "Buffalo: Back Home on the Range," *National Geographic,* November 1994.

84. Power, *Lost Landscapes,* 203.

85. Callenbach, *Bring Back the Buffalo!* 60.

86. Benedict, Freeman, and Genoways, "Prairie Legacies—Mammals," 163.

87. Callenbach, *Bring Back the Buffalo!* 69.

88. Manning, *Grassland,* U.S. Department of Agriculture, *Census of Agriculture* (Washington, D.C.: U.S. Department of Agriculture, 1987).

89. Long, "Vanishing Prairie Dog," 130.

90. Matthews, *Where the Buffalo Roam,* 76.

91. Platt, *Land Use and Society,* 10; Dan Goodgame, "Reigning In the Rich," *Time,* December 19, 1994.

92. Gilbert C. Fite, "The Great Plains: Promises, Problems, and Prospects," in *The Great Plains: Environment and Culture,* ed. Brian W. Blouet and Frederick C. Luebke (Lincoln: University of Nebraska Press, 1979).

93. Lynn Jacobs, *Waste of the West: Public Lands Ranching* (Tucson, Ariz.: Our Public Lands, 1991).

94. Matthews, *Where the Buffalo Roam.*

95. Stanley E. Senner and Brian D. Ladd, "Ecosystem Management and the National Grasslands," in Samson and Knopf, *Prairie Conservation,* 231.

96. Daniel S. Licht, "The Great Plains: America's Best Chance for Ecosystem Restoration," *Wild Earth,* summer 1994.

97. George Catlin, *Letters and Notes on the Manners, Customs, and Conditions of the North American Indians* (New York: Dover, 1973).

98. Brett Hulsey, "Splendor in the Tallgrass," *Sierra,* July–August 1988.

99. Stephen J. Chaplin et al., "A Multiple-Scale Approach to Conservation Planning in the Great Plains," in Samson and Knopf, *Prairie Conservation,* 188.

100. Jo S. Clark, "The Great Plains Partnership," in Samson and Knopf, *Prairie Conservation,* 170.

101. Steinauer and Collins, "Prairie Ecology—The Tallgrass Prairie."

102.   William K. Stevens, *Miracle under the Oaks* (New York: Pocket Books, 1995).

103.   Gene Logsdon, "Fields of Plenty," *Sierra,* November–December 1994, 31.

Chapter 4: The Great, Silent Desert

1.   John Jerome, *On Mountains* (New York: McGraw-Hill, 1978).

2.   James A. McMahon, *Deserts* (New York: Knopf, 1985).

3.   Peggy Larson, *The Deserts of the Southwest* (San Francisco: Sierra Club Books, 1977), 27; William G. McGinnies, *Discovering the Desert* (Tucson: University of Arizona Press, 1981).

4.   Tony Allan and Andrew Warren, eds., *Deserts* (New York: Oxford University Press, 1993).

5.   Larson, *Deserts of the Southwest,* 27, 32.

6.   McGinnies, *Discovering the Desert,* 28.

7.   Larson, *Deserts of the Southwest,* 71.

8.   Ibid., 92.

9.   Priit J. Vesilind, "The Sonoran Desert," *National Geographic,* September 1994.

10.   Doug Peacock, "Desert Solitary," *Audubon,* March–April 1998, 93.

11.   Larson, *Deserts of the Southwest,* 115.

12.   James R. Udall, "The Slickrock Crusade," *Sierra,* March–April 1988.

13.   Ronald J. Taylor, *Sagebrush Country* (Missoula, Mont.: Mountain Press, 1992).

14.   The Nature Conservancy, "Gateway to Canyonlands," *Nature Conservancy,* November–December 1996.

15.   Alex Shoumatoff, *Legends of the American Desert* (New York: Knopf, 1997), 88.

16.   Western Water Policy Review Advisory Commission, *Water in the West: The Challenges for the Next Century* (Denver: Western Water Policy Review Advisory Commission, 1998).

17.   Bruce Seleraig, "Albuquerque Learns It Really Is a Desert Town," *High Country News,* December 26, 1994.

18.   Verne Huser, ed., *Voices from a Sacred Place: In Defense of Petroglyph National Monument* (Albuquerque, N.M.: Verne Huser, 1998), 4.

19.   Donovan Webster, "Where the West Ends," *Outside,* March 1993, 66.

20.   Wayne Merchant, assistant secretary for water and science, U.S. Department of the Interior, Bureau of Reclamation, letter to Congressman George Miller, February 1988; Tim Palmer, *The Snake River: Window to the West* (Washington, D.C.: Island Press, 1991), 63–66.

21.   Mark Obmascik, "Water Policy: Some Farmers Paid Twice," *Denver Post,* July 21, 1992.

22.   Allan and Warren, *Deserts,* 39.

23. Kathie Durbin, "Restoring a Refuge," *High Country News,* November 24, 1997.

24. Steve Johnson, "The Tortoise and the Herd," *Sierra,* December 1985.

25. Reed Noss and Allen Cooperrider, *Saving Nature's Legacy* (Washington, D.C.: Island Press, 1994), 221.

26. Jon R. Luoma, "Discouraging Words," *Audubon,* September 1986.

27. U.S. Department of the Interior, National Biological Service, *Our Living Resources,* ed. Edward T. LaRoe et al. (Washington D.C.: U.S. Department of the Interior, National Biological Service, 1995), 136.

28. Garrett Hardin, "The Tragedy of the Commons," *Science* 162 (1968): 1243–1248.

29. Wayne Elmore and Robert L. Beschta, "Restoring Riparian Areas in Eastern Oregon," *Free Flow* (published by the Pacific Rivers Council), fall 1990.

30. Durbin, "Restoring a Refuge."

31. Dwight Holing, "Lizard and the Links," *Audubon,* January 1988.

32. U.S. Department of the Interior, National Biological Service, *Our Living Resources,* 138.

33. T. H. Watkins, "Staking a Claim," *Wilderness,* summer 1986.

34. Kim Heacox, "A Poet, a Painter, and the Lonesome Triangle," *Audubon,* May 1990.

35. Eliot Porter, Wallace Stegner, and Page Stegner, *American Places* (New York: Greenwich House, 1983).

36. Grand Canyon Trust, "A Working Map of the Colorado Plateau" (brochure) (Flagstaff, Ariz.: Grand Canyon Trust, 1996).

37. Paul Larmer, "Beauty and the Beast," *High Country News,* April 14, 1997.

38. Jon Margolis, "Let's Make a Deal," *Audubon,* March–April 1997, 71.

39. Gary Marsh, Bureau of Land Management, Washington, D.C., telephone interview, April 1998.

40. Gary Paul Nabhan, *Gathering the Desert* (Tucson: University of Arizona Press, 1985).

Chapter 5: Lifelines of Rivers

1. Tim Palmer, *America by Rivers* (Washington, D.C.: Island Press, 1996), 7.

2. University of Colorado at Boulder, Natural Hazards Research and Applications Information Center, *Floodplain Management in the United States: An Assessment Report: Prepared for the Federal Interagency Floodplain Management Task Force* (Washington, D.C.: Federal Emergency Management Agency, 1992).

3. Jon R. Luoma, "Discouraging Words," *Audubon,* September 1996, 92.

4. Lawrence M. Page and Brooks M. Burr, *Freshwater Fishes* (Boston: Houghton Mifflin, 1991), 1.

5.   Lawrence L. Master, Stephanie R. Flack, and Bruce Stein, eds., *Rivers of Life* (Arlington, Va.: The Nature Conservancy, 1998), 4.

6.   Peter Farb, *Face of North America* (New York: Harper Colophon, 1963), 76.

7.   Sandra Postel and Stephen Carpenter, "Freshwater Ecosystem Services," in *Nature's Services,* ed. Gretchen C. Daily (Washington, D.C.: Island Press, 1997), 195.

8.   A. J. Felder and D. M. Nickum, *1991 Economic Impact of Sport Fishing in the United States* (Alexandria, Va.: American Sportfishing Association, 1992).

9.   Judy Meyer, "A Blackwater Perspective on Riverine Ecosystems," *BioScience,* October 1990.

10.   Environmental Protection Agency, *The Quality of the Nation's Water* (Washington, D.C.: Environmental Protection Agency, 1994).

11.   James R. Karr, "Biological Integrity: A Long-Neglected Aspect of Water Resource Management," *Ecological Applications* 1 (1994): 66–84.

12.   Barry Commoner, "The Environment," in *Crossroads,* ed. Peter Borrelli (Washington, D.C.: Island Press, 1988); Richard A. Smith, Richard B. Alexander, and M. Gordon Wolman, "Water-Quality Trends in the Nation's Rivers," *Science,* March 27, 1987.

13.   Environmental Protection Agency, *Quality of the Nation's Water.*

14.   Environmental Protection Agency, *Nonpoint Sources* (Washington, D.C.: Environmental Protection Agency, 1989).

15.   Robert Boyle, "Phantom," *Natural History Journal,* March 1996.

16.   Margaret James and Pamela Moe-Merritt, "Paying the Hidden Price for Poultry," *Headwaters* (published by the West Virginia Rivers Coalition), spring 1997.

17.   Daniel J. Grant, "Jo Daviess Pork Producers Fire Back," *Illinois Agri News,* April 24, 1998.

18.   Ted Williams, "Assembly Line Swine," *Audubon,* March–April 1998.

19.   American Rivers, "Keep Animal Waste Out of Our Water," *American Rivers* (newsletter), fall 1998.

20.   J. Curtis and T. Profeta, eds., *After Silent Spring* (New York: Natural Resources Defense Council, 1993).

21.   John Cronin and Robert F. Kennedy Jr., *The Riverkeepers* (New York: Scribner, 1997), 175.

22.   Environmental Working Group, *Dishonorable Discharge* (Washington, D.C.: Environmental Working Group, October 1996).

23.   Karen Dorn Stelle, "Radioactive Waste from Hanford Is Seeping toward the Columbia," *High Country News,* September 1, 1997.

24.   Christopher Freeburn, "The Hudson Still Hurts," *Audubon,* May–June 1997, 19.

25. Cronin and Kennedy, *Riverkeepers,* 139.

26. John H. Cushman Jr., "States Neglecting Pollution Rules, White House Says," *New York Times,* December 15, 1996, 1.

27. Jenny Coyle, "Right-to-Know-Nothing Laws Boon to Polluters," *Planet* (published by the Sierra Club), November 1997.

28. Greg Karras, *Hidden Polluters of California's Coast* (San Francisco: Citizens for a Better Environment, 1990).

29. Cronin and Kennedy, *Riverkeepers,* 183, 185.

30. National Wildlife Federation, *Pollution Paralysis: State Inaction Puts Waters at Risk* (Vienna, Va.: National Wildlife Federation, 1998).

31. Clean Water Network, *Clean Water Act Reauthorization* (briefing paper) (Washington, D.C.: Clean Water Network, 1995).

32. Natural Resources Defense Council, "Palatable Results on Drinking Water," *Amicus Journal,* winter 1997.

33. National Research Council, *Restoration of Aquatic Ecosystems* (Washington, D.C.: National Academy Press, 1992).

34. U.S. Department of the Interior, National Park Service, *Nationwide Rivers Inventory* (Washington, D.C.: U.S. Department of the Interior, National Park Service), 1982.

35. Master, Flack, and Stein, *Rivers of Life,* 13.

36. Palmer, *America by Rivers,* 303–310.

37. Michael Collier, Robert H. Webb, and John C. Schmidt, *Dams and Rivers: A Primer on the Downstream Effects of Dams* (Denver: U.S. Geological Survey, 1996).

38. David M. Gillilan and Thomas C. Brown, *Instream Flow Protection* (Washington, D.C.: Island Press, 1997); Tim Palmer, *The Snake River: Window to the West* (Washington, D.C.: Island Press, 1991), 97.

39. James R. Karr, J. David Allan, and Arthur C. Benke, "River Conservation in North America: Science, Policy, and Practice," forthcoming.

40. B. L. Swift, "Status of Riparian Ecosystems in the United States," *Water Resources Bulletin,* April 1984.

41. University of Colorado at Boulder, *Floodplain Management.*

42. Jon Christensen, "A Flood of Lessons," *Nature Conservancy,* July–August 1997.

43. Tom Knudson and Nancy Vogel, "The Gathering Storm," *Sacramento Bee,* special report, November 27, 1997.

44. Scott Faber, *The Real Choices Report: The Failure of America's Flood Control Policies* (Washington, D.C.: American Rivers, 1995).

45. Elliot Diringer and Ramon G. McLoed, "Floods Warn Valley of Worse to Come," *San Francisco Chronicle,* March 3, 1996.

46. Knudson and Vogel, "Gathering Storm," 8.

47.   Tim Palmer, *Endangered Rivers and the Conservation Movement* (Berkeley: University of California Press, 1986), 230.

48.   J. Hector St. John de Crèvecoeur, *Letters from an American Farmer* (New York: Dutton, 1957).

49.   Tim Palmer, *Lifelines: The Case for River Conservation* (Washington, D.C.: Island Press, 1994), 127.

50.   Tim Palmer, *The Columbia* (Seattle: The Mountaineers, 1997), 50.

51.   Larry Master, "The Imperiled Status of North American Aquatic Animals," *Biodiversity Network News* 3, no. 3 (1990).

52.   Master, Flack, and Stein, *Rivers of Life,* 18.

53.   William Stolzenburg, "Sweet Home Alabama," *Nature Conservancy,* September–October 1997.

54.   Palmer, *America by Rivers,* 41.

55.   Caroline Larsson, "Fashioning a Flood Relief Policy," *EnviroAction* (published by the National Wildlife Federation), May 1998.

56.   Knudson and Vogel, "Gathering Storm," 2.

57.   Jon Kusler and Larry Larson, "Beyond the Arc," *Environment,* June 1993.

58.   Palmer, *Endangered Rivers,* 179.

59.   Lass Peterson, "Cut Rate Water, Surplus Crops," *Washington Post,* March 8, 1988.

60.   Philip Lansing, *An Economic Analysis of Four Federal Dams on the Lower Snake River* (Boise: Idaho Rivers United, 1995).

61.   Palmer, *Columbia,* 61.

62.   Robert S. Devine, "The Trouble with Dams," *Atlantic Monthly,* August 1995.

63.   Paul Schneider, "Clear Progress," *Audubon,* September–October 1997, 39, 40.

64.   Sierra Club, *Take the Money and Run* (booklet) (San Francisco: Sierra Club, 1996).

65.   Schneider, "Clear Progress," 107.

66.   Robert W. Adler, Jessica C. Landman, and Diane M. Cameron, *The Clean Water Act Twenty Years Later* (Washington, D.C.: Island Press, 1993).

67.   Lisa Henry, "Raccoon River Watershed Project," *River Voices* (published by River Network), February 1996.

68.   Association of State Floodplain Managers, *Using Multi-Objective Management to Reduce Flood Losses in Your Watershed* (Washington, D.C.: Environmental Protection Agency, 1996).

69.   Interagency Floodplain Management Review Committee, *Sharing the Challenge: Floodplain Management into the Twenty-First Century* (Washington, D.C.: Interagency Floodplain Management Review Committee, 1994).

70.   Gilbert White, *Strategies of American Water Management* (Ann Arbor: University of Michigan Press, 1971).

71.   Scott Faber, "Flood Policy and Management," *River Voices* (published by River Network), summer 1997.

72.   Charley Casey and Rita Haberman, "Responding to the 1997 California Flood," *River Voices* (published by River Network), summer 1997.

73.   John D. Echeverria, Pope Barrow, and Richard Roos-Collins, *Rivers at Risk* (Washington, D.C.: Island Press, 1989).

74.   National Wildlife Federation, "Maine Dam Removal Could Establish Historic Precedent," *National Wildlife,* January 1998.

75.   University of Colorado School of Law, Natural Resources Law Center, *Restoring the Waters* (Boulder, Colo.: University of Colorado School of Law, Natural Resources Law Center, 1997).

76.   Tim Palmer, *The Wild and Scenic Rivers of America* (Washington, D.C.: Island Press, 1994), 28.

77.   James P. Barr, *Bringing It Back to Life: The Reclamation of Babb Creek* (Williamsport, Pa.: Pennsylvania Environmental Defense Foundation, 1997).

Chapter 6: Immersed in Lakes and Wetlands

1.   Army Corps of Engineers, *Corps of Engineers Wetlands Delineation Manual* (Washington, D.C.: Army Corps of Engineers, 1987).

2.   William J. Mitsch and James G. Gosselink, *Wetlands* (New York: Van Nostrand Reinhold, 1986), 4.

3.   Katherine C. Ewel, "Water Quality Improvement by Wetlands," in *Nature's Services,* ed. Gretchen C. Daily (Washington, D.C.: Island Press, 1997), 336.

4.   Environmental Protection Agency, *Wetland Fact Sheets* (Washington, D.C.: Environmental Protection Agency, 1995).

5.   Tim Palmer, *America by Rivers* (Washington, D.C.: Island Press, 1996), 129.

6.   Ibid., 130.

7.   Environmental Protection Agency, *Wetland Fact Sheets.*

8.   Army Corps of Engineers, *Water Resources Development Plan, Charles River* (Waltham, Mass.: Army Corps of Engineers, 1976).

9.   Ted Williams, "What Good Is a Wetland?" *Audubon,* November–December 1996, 48.

10.   Ivan T. Sanderson, *The Continent We Live On* (New York: Random House, 1961).

11.   Laurence Pringle, *Rivers and Lakes* (Alexandria, Va.: Time-Life Books, 1984).

12.   Environmental Protection Agency, *Wetland Fact Sheets.*

13.   University of Colorado at Boulder, Natural Hazards Research and Appli-

cations Information Center, *Floodplain Management in the United States: An Assessment Report: Prepared for the Federal Interagency Floodplain Management Task Force* (Washington, D.C.: Federal Emergency Management Agency, 1992).

14. Environmental Protection Agency, *Wetland Fact Sheets.*

15. Stephen D'Esposito, "Okefenokee at Risk," *Clementine* (published by the Mineral Policy Center), autumn 1997, 3.

16. U.S. Department of the Interior, U.S. Fish and Wildlife Service, *The 1991 National Survey of Fishing, Hunting, and Wildlife-Associated Recreation* (Washington, D.C.: U.S. Department of the Interior, U.S. Fish and Wildlife Service, 1991).

17. Williams, "What Good Is a Wetland?" 45.

18. Charles H. Peterson and Jane Lubchenco, "Marine Ecosystem Services," in Daily, *Nature's Services,* 186.

19. Environment Canada et al., *The Great Lakes: An Environmental Atlas and Resource Book* (Chicago: Environmental Protection Agency, Region 5 1987).

20. Pringle, *Rivers and Lakes,* 147.

21. Peter B. Moyle, *Fish: An Enthusiast's Guide* (Berkeley: University of California Press, 1993), 153.

22. Ewel, "Water Quality Improvement by Wetlands," 330.

23. T. E. Dahl, *Wetlands Losses in the United States* (Washington, D.C.: U.S. Department of the Interior, U.S. Fish and Wildlife Service, 1990).

24. Charles Fergus, *Swamp Screamer* (New York: North Point Press; Farrar, Straus, and Giroux, 1996).

25. Kevin Proescholdt, "Boundary Waters Wilderness Attacked in Congress," *Wild Earth,* spring 1998, 54.

26. Bruce D. J. Batt, "Prairie Ecology—Prairie Wetlands," in *Prairie Conservation,* ed. Fred B. Samson and Fritz L. Knopf (Washington, D.C.: Island Press, 1996), 77.

27. University of Colorado School of Law, Natural Resources Law Center, *Restoring the Waters* (Boulder: University of Colorado School of Law, Natural Resources Law Center, 1997), 15.

28. Tim Palmer, *The Sierra Nevada: A Mountain Journey* (Washington, D.C.: Island Press, 1988), 54.

29. Clyde McDonald, "Water Supply: A New Era for a Scarce Resource," in *California's Threatened Environment,* ed. Tim Palmer (Washington, D.C.: Island Press, 1993), 82.

30. Mark Matthews and Paul Larmer, "Pollution in Paradise," *High Country News,* November 25, 1996, 10.

31. Ibid.

32. Moyle, *Fish,* 225.

33. Jon R. Luoma, "Biography of a Lake," *Audubon,* September–October 1996.

34. William Ashworth, *The Late, Great Lakes* (New York: Knopf, 1986).

35. Theo Colborn, Diane Dumanoski, and John Peterson Myers, *Our Stolen Future* (New York: Dutton, 1996).

36. Ashworth, *Late, Great Lakes,* 61.

37. Paul Rauber, "Deep-Sixing Two-Strokes: Putting an End to the Recreational Oil Spill," *Sierra,* January–February 1998, 22.

38. Alexander J. Horne and Charles R. Goldman, *Limnology* (New York: McGraw-Hill, 1994), 318; Pringle, *Rivers and Lakes,* 154.

39. Anthony Ricciardi, "The Exotic Species Problem and Freshwater Conservation," *Wild Earth,* spring 1998, 44.

40. U.S. Department of the Interior, National Biological Service, *Our Living Resources,* ed. Edward T. LaRoe et al. (Washington, D.C.: U.S. Department of the Interior, National Biological Service, 1995), 447.

41. Luoma, "Biography of a Lake."

42. Stephanie Flack and Elaine Furlow, "America's Least Wanted," *Nature Conservancy,* November–December 1996, 18.

43. Dahl, *Wetlands Losses.*

44. Peter Steinhart, "Empty the Skies," *Audubon,* November 1987; Sally W. Smith, "Wildlife and Endangered Species: In Precipitous Decline," in Palmer, *California's Threatened Environment,* 227.

45. Barry Nelson, "Troubled Shores: The Ocean, Bays, and Estuaries," in Palmer, *California's Threatened Environment,* 111.

46. Lisa Viani-Owens, "Poison Ponds," *Terrain,* October 1996, 21.

47. George Laycock, "What Water for Stillwater?" *Audubon,* November 1988, 25.

48. Tom Harris, *Death in the Marsh* (Washington, D.C.: Island Press, 1991).

49. Alan Mairson, "The Everglades Are Dying for Help," *National Geographic,* April 1994.

50. Ann Vileisis, *Discovering the Unknown Landscape: A History of America's Wetlands* (Washington, D.C.: Island Press, 1997), 302.

51. John G. Mitchell, "Our Disappearing Wetlands," *National Geographic,* October 1992.

52. Michael Berryhill, "Birdie in the Bottomlands," *Audubon,* July–August 1996, 96.

53. "Permit Twenty-Six Is All Wet," *Amicus Journal,* spring 1997, 7.

54. Vileisis, *Discovering the Unknown Landscape,* 319.

55. Environmental Working Group, *Swamped with Cash* (Washington, D.C.: Environmental Working Group, 1996).

56. U.S. Environmental Protection Agency, citing the National Environmental Forum Survey, conducted by Times Mirror Magazines, Inc., 1994.

57. Williams, "What Good Is a Wetland?" 52.

58. National Wildlife Federation, "Natural Wetlands Win," *National Wildlife,* January 1998, 10.

59. Vileisis, *Discovering the Unknown Landscape,* 325.

60. Ashworth, *Late, Great Lakes,* 47.

61. Paul Schneider, "Clear Progress," *Audubon,* September–October 1997, 40.

62. Vileisis, *Discovering the Unknown Landscape,* 7.

63. Ibid., 300.

64. Jon Kusler, "Regulating Sensitive Lands," in *Land Use Issues of the 1980s,* ed. James H. Carr and Edward E. Duensing (New Brunswick, N.J.: Rutgers University Press, 1983).

65. Douglas H. Chadwick, "Sanctuary: U.S. National Wildlife Refuges," *National Geographic,* October 1996.

66. Paul G. Risser, "A New Framework for Prairie Conservation," in Samson and Knopf, *Prairie Conservation,* 269.

67. Joseph W. Koebel Jr., "An Historical Perspective on the Kissimmee River Restoration Project," *Restoration Ecology,* September 1995.

68. Environmental Protection Agency, *Quality of the Nation's Water.*

69. Bruce Lambert, "Restoring Shores of Original Occupants," *New York Times,* May 11, 1997.

70. David Helvarg, "Restoring the Everglades," *National Parks,* March–April 1998, 26.

71. Christi Norman, interview, 1998

Chapter 7: At the Edge of the Land

1. Wesley Marx, *The Frail Ocean* (New York: Ballantine, 1967), 100.

2. Don Hinrichsen, "Pushing the Limits," *Amicus Journal,* winter 1997.

3. John Clark, *Coastal Ecosystem Management* (Malabar, Fla.: Krieger, 1983), 267.

4. Anne Simon, *The Thin Edge* (New York: Harper & Row, 1978), 44.

5. Environmental Protection Agency, *Wetland Fact Sheets* (Washington, D.C.: Environmental Protection Agency, 1995).

6. David F. Costello, *The Seashore World* (New York: Crowell, 1980).

7. John R. Stilgoe, *Alongshore* (New Haven, Conn.: Yale University Press, 1994), 337, citing John Hooker Packard, *Sea-Air and Sea-Bathing* (Philadelphia: P. Blakiston, 1800).

8. *Simon,* The Thin Edge.

9. Bob Hansen, National Oceanic and Atmospheric Administration, telephone interview, 1998.

10. Costello, *Seashore World,* 117.

11. Timothy Beatley, David J. Brower, and Anna K. Schwab, *Coastal Zone Management* (Washington, D.C.: Island Press, 1994).

12. Theodore Steinberg, "Do-It-Yourself Deathscape: The Unnatural History of Natural Disaster in South Florida," *Environmental History,* October 1997.

13. John N. Cole, "Off Key, Out of Reach," *Audubon,* July–August 1996.

14. John F. Ross, "The Miracle of the Reef," *Smithsonian,* February 1998, 90.

15. Don Stap, "Hammocks Get a Rest," *Audubon,* March–April 1998, 18.

16. Douglas Bennett Lee, "America's Third Coast," *National Geographic,* July 1992.

17. Tom Horton, "Spoil of the Laguna Madre," *Audubon,* March–April 1998.

18. Don Greame Kelly, *Edge of a Continent* (Palo Alto, Calif.: American West, 1971).

19. Hinrichsen, "Pushing the Limits."

20. Peter Holmes, "Threading the Thin Edge," *NRDC Newsletter* (published by the Natural Resources Defense Council), December–January 1978–1979.

21. Beatley, Brower, and Schwab, *Coastal Zone Management,* 52.

22. Orrin H. Pilkey and Katharine L. Dixon, *The Corps and the Shore* (Washington, D.C.: Island Press, 1996), 20.

23. Dashka Slater, "Taken by Storm," *Sierra,* May–June 1995.

24. Roger A Pielke, *Hurricane Andrew in South Florida* (Boulder, Colo.: National Center for Atmospheric Research, 1995).

25. Pilkey and Dixon, *Corps and the Shore,* 15.

26. Jon Luoma, "Oceanfront Battlefront," *Audubon,* July–August 1998, 56.

27. Pilkey and Dixon, *Corps and the Shore,* 40.

28. Beatley, Brower, and Schwab, *Coastal Zone Management,* 24.

29. Marx, *Frail Ocean,* 33.

30. Pilkey and Dixon, *Corps and the Shore,* 31.

31. Holmes, "Threading the Thin Edge."

32. Steinberg, "Do-It-Yourself Deathscape," 430.

33. Pilkey and Dixon, *Corps and the Shore,* 85.

34. Jennifer Ackerman, "Island at the Edge," *National Geographic,* September 1997.

35. Pilkey and Dixon, *Corps and the Shore,* 78, 87.

36. Ackerman, "Island at the Edge."

37. Luoma, "Oceanfront Battlefront," 53.

38. Susan Gilbert, "America Wasting Away," *Science Digest,* August 1986, 32.

39. Ackerman, "Island at the Edge."

40. Beatley, Brower, and Schwab, *Coastal Zone Management,* 29.

41. Ibid.

42. Pilkey and Dixon, *Corps and the Shore,* 225.

43. Sarah Chasis and Dare Fuller, *Testing the Waters VI: Who Knows What You're Getting* (New York: Natural Resources Defense Council, 1996).

44. Ted Williams, "Now the Blackstone Runs Blue," *Audubon,* November–December 1995, 30.

45. Fred Ward, "Florida's Coral Reefs Are Imperiled," *National Geographic,* July 1990.

46. U.S. Department of the Interior, National Biological Service, *Our Living Resources,* ed. Edward T. LaRoe et al. (Washington, D.C.: U.S. Department of the Interior, National Biological Service, 1995), 275.

47. Beth Millemann, *And Two if by Sea* (Washington, D.C.: Coast Alliance, 1986), 45.

48. Natural Resources Defense Council, *Hook, Line, and Sinking* (New York: Natural Resources Defense Council, 1997).

49. Tom Horton, "Chesapeake Bay," *National Geographic,* June 1993, 78.

50. Carl Safina, *Song for the Blue Ocean* (New York: Henry Holt, 1997), 43.

51. Michael Parfit, "Diminishing Returns," *National Geographic,* November 1995.

52. Carl Safina, "Scorched-Earth Fishing," *Issues in Science and Technology* (published by the University of Texas at Dallas), spring 1998, 33.

53. Arthur F. McEvoy, *The Fisherman's Problem* (Cambridge, England: Cambridge University Press, 1990).

54. Evelyn Pinkerton and Martin Weinstein, *Fisheries That Work: Sustainability through Community-Based Management* (Vancouver, B.C., Canada: David Suzuki Foundation, 1995).

55. Safina, *Song for the Blue Ocean,* 43.

56. Jon Fleischman, "Muddying the Waters," *Audubon,* March–April 1997, 66.

57. U.S. Department of the Interior, Bureau of Outdoor Recreation, "Planning for Coastal Zone Recreation," *Outdoor Recreation Action,* fall 1975, 10.

58. Jim Howe, Ed McMahon, and Luther Propst, *Balancing Nature and Commerce in Gateway Communities* (Washington, D.C.: Island Press, 1997), 95.

59. Curtis Badger, "Of Ancestors and Islands," *Nature Conservancy,* November–December 1997.

60. U.S. Department of the Interior, Bureau of Outdoor Recreation, "Planning for Coastal Zone Recreation," 14.

61. Commission on Marine Science, Engineering and Resources, *Our Nation and the Sea* (Washington, D.C.: Government Printing Office, 1969).

62. Nathaniel P. Reed, "Recreation and Public Access in the Coastal Zone," *Outdoor Recreation Action* (published by U.S. Department of the Interior, Bureau of Outdoor Recreation), fall 1975.

63. Charles Little, *Hope for the Land* (New Brunswick, N.J.: Rutgers University Press, 1992).

64. Beatley, Brower, and Schwab, *Coastal Zone Management,* 61.

65. Ibid., 104.

66. Don Salvesen, "Sand Castles," *Amicus Journal,* winter 1997, 29.

67. General Accounting Office, *Coastal Barriers* (Washington, D.C.: General Accounting Office, 1992).

68. Salvesen, "Sand Castles," 31.

69. The Conservation Fund, *1996 Year in Review* (Arlington, Va.: The Conservation Fund, 1997), 4.

70. Simon, *The Thin Edge,* 165, 170.

Chapter 8: America in the 21st Century

1. David Hackett Fischer, *Albion's Seed: Four British Folkways in America* (New York: Oxford University Press, 1989).

2. Lee Clark Mitchell, *Witnesses to a Vanishing Frontier* (Princeton, N.J.: Princeton University Press, 1981), 11.

3. J. Baird Callicott, *In Defense of the Land Ethic* (Albany: State University of New York Press, 1989), 177.

4. Peter Matthiessen, *Indian Country* (New York: Penguin Books, 1979), 119.

5. U.S. Department of the Interior, U.S. Fish and Wildlife Service, *Restoring America's Wildlife, 1937–1987,* ed. Harmon Kallman (Washington, D.C.: U.S. Department of the Interior, U.S. Fish and Wildlife Service, 1987).

6. *The American Almanac: Statistical Abstract of the United States, 1993–1994* (Austin, Tex.: Reference Press, 1993).

7. Claude Fischer, *The Urban Experience* (New York: Harcourt Brace Jovanovich, 1980).

8. Gregory R. Nokes and Gail Kinsey Hill, "The Faster the Growth, the Faster the Tab Mounts," *Portland Oregonian,* October 24, 1995.

9. William Ashworth, *The Economy of Nature* (Boston: Houghton Mifflin, 1995), 169.

10. Mark W. Nowak, *Immigration and U.S. Population Growth* (Washington, D.C.: Negative Population Growth, 1997), 7.

11. Lindsey Grant, ed., *Elephants in the Volkswagen: Facing the Tough Questions about Our Overcrowded Country* (New York: W. H. Freeman, 1992); Leon F. Bouvier, *Americans Have Spoken: No Further Population Growth* (Washington, D.C.: Negative Population Growth, 1997), 2.

12. Mathis Wackernagel and William Rees, *Our Ecological Footprint* (Philadelphia: New Society Publishers, 1996).

13. Grant, *Elephants in the Volkswagen,* 237.

14. Paul R. Ehrlich and Anne H. Ehrlich, "The Most Overpopulated Nation," in Grant, *Elephants in the Volkswagen.*

15.   Robert Costanza, "Balancing Humans in the Biosphere," in Grant, *Elephants in the Volkswagen.*

16.   David Pimentel and Marcia Pimentel, "Land, Energy and Water," in Grant, *Elephants in the Volkswagen,* 30.

17.   Alan Riding, *Distant Neighbors: A Portrait of the Mexicans* (New York: Vintage Books, 1984), 254.

18.   Grant, *Elephants in the Volkswagen,* 225.

19.   Leon Bouvier and Roy Beck, "Immigration Number One in U.S. Growth," *The Social Contract,* winter 1991–1992.

20.   National Research Council, *The New Americans: Economic, Demographic, and Fiscal Effects of Immigration* (Washington, D.C.: National Academy Press, 1997).

21.   Vernon M. Briggs Jr., "Political Confrontation with Economic Reality," in Grant, *Elephants in the Volkswagen;* Nowak, *Immigration and U.S. Population Growth.*

22.   Jennifer Cheesman Day, *Population Projections of the United States by Age, Sex, Race, and Hispanic Origin, 1995 to 2050* (Washington, D.C.: U.S. Department of Commerce, Bureau of the Census, 1996).

23.   Meredith Burke, *Uncoupling Growth from Prosperity: The U.S. versus Japan* (Washington, D.C.: Negative Population Growth, 1997).

24.   Leon F. Bouvier, *Peaceful Invasions: Immigration and Changing America* (Washington, D.C.: Center for Immigration Studies, 1991).

25.   Bouvier, *Americans Have Spoken;* Tim Palmer, *California's Threatened Environment* (Washington, D.C.: Island Press, 1993), 31.

26.   Al Gore, *Earth in the Balance* (Boston: Houghton Mifflin, 1992), 311.

27.   Frank Sharry, "Immigration and Population in the United States," in *Beyond the Numbers,* ed. Laurie Ann Mazue (Washington, D.C.: Island Press, 1994), 387.

28.   John R. Weeks, "How to Influence Fertility," in Grant, *Elephants in the Volkswagen,* 188.

29.   Robert W. Fox, "Neighbors' Problems, Our Problems," in Grant, *Elephants in the Volkswagen.*

30.   Pat Waak, interview, 1998.

31.   Grant, *Elephants in the Volkswagen,* 143.

32.   Aldo Leopold, *A Sand County Almanac* (New York: Oxford University Press, 1949).

33.   Roderick Nash, *Wilderness and the American Mind* (New Haven, Conn.: Yale University Press, 1973).

34.   Wallace Stegner, "Living on Our Principal," *Wilderness,* spring 1985.

35.   Charles Little, "In a Landscape of Hope," *Wilderness,* spring 1985, 27.

36.   Timothy Beatley, David J. Brower, and Anna K. Schwab, *Coastal Zone Management* (Washington, D.C.: Island Press, 1994).

37.   Fred P. Bosselman and David Collins, "The Quiet Revolution in Land Use Controls," in *Land in America,* ed. Richard N. L. Andrews (Lexington, Mass.: Lexington Books, 1979).

38.   Jerry Walls, interview, 1998.

39.   Samuel Hays, interview, 1998.

40.   Union of Concerned Scientists, *World Scientists' Warning to Humanity* (Cambridge, Mass.: Union of Concerned Scientists, 1992).

41.   Thomas M. Power, ed., *Economic Well-Being and Environmental Protection in the Pacific Northwest* (Missoula: University of Montana, Department of Economics, 1995).

42.   Timothy Wirth, "The Human Factor," *Sierra,* September–October 1995).

43.   Thomas M. Power, *Lost Landscapes and Failed Economies* (Washington, D.C.: Island Press, 1996), 4.

44.   Robert Stavins and Bradley Whitehead, "Market-Based Environmental Policies," in *Thinking Ecologically,* ed. Marian R. Chertow and Daniel C. Esty (New Haven, Conn.: Yale University Press, 1997), 105.

45.   Charles Little, *Hope for the Land* (New Brunswick, N.J.: Rutgers University Press, 1992), 211.

46.   Jeffrey Smith, "Evangelical Christians Preach a Green Gospel," *High Country News,* April 28, 1997.

47.   Willett Kempton, James S. Boster, and Jennifer A. Hartley, *Environmental Values in American Culture* (Cambridge, Mass.: MIT Press, 1995), 94.

48.   Henry L. Diamond and Patrick F. Noonan, *Land Use in America* (Washington, D.C.: Island Press, 1996), 96.

49.   John Daniel, *The Trail Home* (New York: Pantheon Books, 1992).

50.   R. E. Dunlap, G. H. Gallup, and A. M. Gallup, "Of Global Concern: Results of the 1993 Health of the Planet Survey," *Environment* 35, no. 9 (1993).

51.   Kempton, Boster, and Hartley, *Environmental Values,* 4, 7; Brent S. Steel, Peter List, and Bruce Shindler, "Conflicting Values about Federal Forests," *Society and Natural Resources* 7 (1994): 158.

52.   Kempton, Boster, and Hartley, *Environmental Values,* 7, 211.

53.   Callicott, *In Defense of the Land Ethic,* 237.

54.   Leif Eric Lange, "Transportation and the Environmental Costs of Auto Dependency," in Palmer, *California's Threatened Environment,* 65, 75.

55.   Glenn Eugster, interview, 1998.

56.   Ken Olson, interview, 1998.

57.   Reed F. Noss and Allen Y. Cooperrider, *Saving Nature's Legacy* (Washington, D.C.: Island Press, 1994), 171.

58.   Rocky Barker, *Saving All the Parts* (Washington, D.C.: Island Press, 1993), 245.

59.   Land Trust Alliance, *Land Trusts: The Front Line of Land Protection* (Washington, D.C.: Land Trust Alliance, 1997).

60.   Reed F. Noss, "The Wildlands Project Land Conservation Strategy," *Wild Earth,* special annual issue, 1992.

61.   Little, *Hope for the Land,* 28.

62.   Winona LaDuke, "Like Tributaries to a River," *Sierra,* November–December 1996, 45.

FURTHER READING

For more information, detail, and depth of insight, I encourage readers to pursue the sources cited in the text. Narrowing down a bibliography is difficult, but I've made an effort in the following short list. These are books I regard as exceptionally important, powerful, engaging, or timely in their coverage of the American landscape today.

Introduction and General Interest

Saving Nature's Legacy by biologists Reed Noss and Allen Cooperrider is a fine sourcebook and primer on conservation biology and the need to care for the land's life-support systems. *The Work of Nature,* by Yvonne Baskin, is outstanding in its message that human systems depend on natural systems. Popular for many years, *Face of North America* by Peter Farb is a geography of the continent written for the general reader. Jerry Mander's book *In the Absence of the Sacred* addresses technology and many underlying causes of landscape distress today. *Moment in the Sun* by Robert Rienow and Leona Train Rienow was published in 1967, but I regard this classic as the most important book of all in launching the modern environmental movement. Along with Henry David Thoreau's *Walden,* it may have been the most influential book of my life, and it is still an important, shocking, informative read.

Chapter 1: An Uplift of Mountains

Mountains and Man by Larry Price is a thorough and useful sourcebook. *On Mountains* by John Jerome entertains and informs and is a fine introduction to this rugged geography. Though I mostly avoid guidebooks and regional profiles in this list, Scott Weidensaul's *Mountains of the Heart: A Natural History of the Appalachians* covers the East quite well, and I can't help recommending my own *Sierra Nevada: A Mountain Journey* as a book full of western mountain experience, lore, and information.

Chapter 2: The Forest Fabric of Life

More books have been written about forests and the issues of forest management than about any other landscape, but Charles Little's *The Dying of the Trees* is in my opinion the most important one ever published. I found Elliott Norse's *Ancient Forests of the Pacific Northwest* especially useful, as it outlines the region's ecology and the threats to it. A scientist with a good writing style, George Constantz takes us to the Appalachians in *Hollows, Peepers, and Highlanders*. John Berger offers a fine introduction to forest issues in *Understanding Forests*. Though more up-to-date information is now available, the problem of global warming is expertly portrayed in Bill McKibben's *The End of Nature* and with an even broader, mind-expanding perspective in Jeremy Rifkin's *Entropy: Into the Greenhouse World*.

Chapter 3: The World of Grasslands

Richard Manning has produced a fine work in *Grassland,* indispensable for anyone who wants to know more about this sweeping mass of America today. *Bring Back the Buffalo!* by Ernest Callenbach of *Ecotopia* fame is a superb testimonial to that idea. Though it's a collection of articles, *Prairie Conservation,* edited by Fred Samson and Fritz Knopf, covers the scientific territory well and will prove a fine reference for anyone in the field of grassland study and management.

Chapter 4: The Great, Silent Desert

While forests corner the market for books on issues of the landscape, the stark simplicity and silent mystery of deserts have put the landscape essayists to work more than has any other place. The king of popularity here is the irreverent Edward Abbey, whose reputation is built on *Desert Solitaire,* though my favorite collection of this master is *The Journey Home.* Of compelling substance, *Empires in the Sun* by Peter Wiley and Robert Gottlieb tells the often seamy story of growth in the desert region, and Marc Reisner's *Cadillac Desert* is the engrossing tale of water development and the people who made it happen.

Chapter 5: Lifelines of Rivers

Since 1980, I have been writing mostly about rivers. I recommend my *Lifelines: The Case for River Conservation* for its overview of river problems and what people are doing about them; *America by Rivers* is a popularized river geography. *The Riverkeepers* by John Cronin and Robert F. Kennedy Jr. is a lively account of battling pollution and immense, hostile forces.

Chapter 6: Immersed in Lakes and Wetlands

Ann Vileisis's *Discovering the Unknown Landscape: A History of America's Wetlands* is a superb account of the wetland landscape and our regard for it and also an award-winning model of environmental history. For lakes, I had to depend largely on magazine and journal articles. William Ashworth presents a dated but vivid account in *The Late, Great Lakes*.

Chapter 7: At the Edge of the Land

The Thin Edge by Anne Simon is the criterion book here, an accessible overview that suffers little with the passing of time. Orrin Pilkey's *The Corps and the Shore* offers an important indictment of coastal management. *The Frail Ocean* by Wesley Marx is the oceanic classic written in 1967, now joined by the extraordinary work of Carl Safina in *Song for the Blue Ocean,* a must-read for anyone who has ever looked out to sea.

Chapter 8: America in the 21st Century

For the supremely important issue of population, I recommend a collection by demographers and others called *Elephants in the Volkswagen,* edited by Lindsey Grant. A far more serious book than it sounds, it includes much about the conundrum of immigration. Paul Ehrlich and Anne Ehrlich's *The Population Explosion* should be required reading for the literate world today. Central to the theme of this chapter is Aldo Leopold's essay "The Land Ethic" in *A Sand County Almanac.* Crucial aspects of the economy can be understood through Thomas Power's *Lost Landscapes and Failed Economies.* Issues of ethics are presented with rare eloquence by Thomas Berry in *Dream of the Earth,* and Al Gore has given us a fast-paced overview of the environment from the political side in *Earth in the Balance.*

ACKNOWLEDGMENTS

My most heartfelt thanks go to my wife, Ann Vileisis. This book benefited from her enthusiasm, insight, and gifted editing skill. As an author, historian, partner, and friend, she participated in the evolution of this book from the first faint glimmer to cover-bound reality. Editor Barbara Dean likewise believed in this effort and offered fine guidance. Pat Harris copyedited the manuscript with her expert abilities. All the dedicated members of the Island Press staff were a pleasure to work with.

Yvon Chouinard of Patagonia, Inc., played a vital role by providing me with a grant to cover some of my time while I wrote the book; thanks to Jill Zilligen for her help. The Richard King Mellon Foundation also generously provided me with a grant; my sincere thanks for the interest of all the trustees of that foundation, which has done so much for landscape protection all over America.

Julie Holding in Patagonia, Arizona, opened her home to Ann and me in the fall of 1998, as did Margot and Alan Hunt in Kelly, Wyoming, while they lived elsewhere in the winter and spring of 1998. John McCarthy shared his Boise, Idaho, home with us in the fall of 1996 when I was starting the book.

I offer special recognition to geographer John Harper of Humboldt State University not only for reviewing material in this book but also for a lifetime of excellent work in his profession. Ever since his graduate studies in the Sierra Nevada and his book on the Mineral King controversy there, he has been a force for the good of the American landscape and an inspiration to untold numbers of students.

Sections and chapters of the manuscript were reviewed by an experienced team of professionals, including Chris Brown, Mason Brown, Ernest Callenbach, Jim Caplan, Don Elder, Glenn Eugster, Samuel Hays, Julie Holding, Steve Hollenhorst, John Kuzloski, Pam Lichtman, Ed Lytwak, Brian Martin, Mike Medberry, Barry Nelson, Christi Norman, Ken Olson, Mike Prather, Florence

Williams, Jamie Williams, and Rebecca Wodder. Their great knowledge and dedication of time are much appreciated.

Additional scores of informed professionals and citizens contributed by providing me with information and interviews. I especially want to thank Jerry Walls and Jim McClure for reflections in the final chapter. Mark Anderman of Terry Wild Studios printed my black-and-white photographs. Finally, to write a book of this scale and scope, and to do it on a modest budget and in less than a lifetime, I could not possibly rely on primary research. While I did use primary sources and interviews, my success in reporting on America's wide-ranging landscapes depended on the work of hundreds of other writers. I drew on vast amounts of published work, much of it gratefully cited as sources for each chapter.

INDEX